THE SOCIAL USES
OF SOCIAL SCIENCE

THE SOCIAL USES

OF

SOCIAL SCIENCE

The Papers of Robert Redfield

VOLUME II

EDITED BY MARGARET PARK REDFIELD

 THE UNIVERSITY OF CHICAGO PRESS

Library of Congress Catalog Card Number: 62-10995

THE UNIVERSITY OF CHICAGO PRESS, CHICAGO & LONDON
The University of Toronto Press, Toronto 5, Canada

To R. M. H., gratefully

CONTENTS

INTRODUCTION

The social uses of social science are not exhausted when we have said that social science can improve the efficiency of industrial production or test the aptitude of young people for one kind of occupation or another. Social science is one of the ways to form our convictions as to the good life. This it does not as preaching does it, by telling us what the good is and what our duty is. It does not do it as ethics does it, by examining central questions as to the nature of conduct and by criticizing and formulating systematic rules of conduct. It does it by remaining science. It does it by making clear to us where our choices lead us and what means must be employed to reach what ends. It does it by extending our understanding of where our ideals are in conflict with each other. And it does this through those intensive studies of particular societies and particular men which are not ordinarily carried on in ethics and which are outside the power and responsibilities of the preacher. . . . Social science is not only a box of tools. It is also a light.[1]

The social scientist who subscribes to "the common morality of the scientific mind," and is devoted to "objectivity, honesty, accuracy, and humility before the facts," will not necessarily feel any further professional obligation to the world. Robert Redfield thought that the scientist—in particular the social scientist—has a special responsibility to his society, a responsibility derived from the moral understanding which belongs to his science. His feeling did not originate in religious training—as the child of non-churchgoing parents he felt himself detached from any religion, Christian or otherwise—nor from science as it was presented to him. Of his professional training he wrote:

Like many another at the time when I was young, I was told by my teachers that the business of the social scientist, like that of other scientists, is to describe, not evaluate. I was persuaded to believe in the moral antisepsis of science. I wonder if I really did believe in it. I wonder if, as a young anthropologist, I imagined myself a student of the early Iroquois, studying methods of torturing prisoners. Did I conceive of the cool purity of my notebook, myself dispassionately reporting?

As a young man, Redfield was hardly troubled by such questions but was rather concerned to discover his place in the world. He felt himself not ambitious, disinclined to an aggressively competitive society. Santayana's philosophical account of the life of reason suggested the possibility of a life lived on one's own terms, but it was not clear what those terms were to

---

[1] Robert Redfield, "The Social Uses of Social Science," address delivered at the Honors Convocation, University of Colorado, 1947.

be. Biology, his first choice, did not seem to provide the answer, and he took up law only for want of something better.

Redfield never underestimated the worth of his training in law. He wrote, "It gave me my first real discipline." But having been admitted to the bar, he did not find gathering data in his father's law office on special assessments for sewers very inspiring. Restlessness and rumor of a renascent Mexico brought by a Mexican friend led to a visit there. He found this country, which was just beginning to rediscover its Indian heritage, even more interesting than he had hoped and, on returning to Chicago, decided to leave the law and take up the study of anthropology under Fay Cooper-Cole and his sociologically oriented father-in-law, Robert E. Park. Though none of Redfield's studies were carried out under Park's direction, the influence of the latter was important, and the two men remained close through the years.

Redfield was fortunate in entering anthropology while it was still a new, vigorously growing discipline; here he could freely exercise his capacities, both for rigorous work and for human understanding. His intimate participation, usually with his family, in the life of peasant communities in Mexico and Guatemala not only educated him in different and simpler ways of life but also gave him a deeper understanding of his own culture. Later contact with the highly developed civilizations of the East, particularly those of India and China, further encouraged him to see life with the differently colored glasses of other people and developed his interest in the "world-wide conversation."

In the Department of Anthropology at the University of Chicago (with which he was associated during all but his first year of teaching) he found able and congenial colleagues. He began teaching while the university was being reorganized by Robert Maynard Hutchins. A view of education which saw it principally concerned with "finding the good life and the good state" by inquiring into "the nature of man and the ends of life"[2] appealed to Redfield as to many others. Redfield, in his "Genius of the University," writes of that time in faculty meetings when there was sometimes talk about education rather than mere "housekeeping." "I can still recall the exhilaration of such unusual moments. There was aroused a joyful urge in the breast; one felt something grow within, something essential and true." For this reason, though his friends predicted that it would injure his career in research, he accepted, in 1924, the post of Dean of the recently established Division of the Social Sciences.

The deanship, which lasted for twelve years, does not seem to have limited his scientific production; and it deepened a commitment to a broadly conceived social science. In spite of the pressure of day-to-day affairs, he

[2] Robert M. Hutchins, "Aims of Education," *Education for Freedom* (Baton Rouge: Louisiana State University Press, 1943), p. 24.

remained more concerned with the common ground of the various disciplines than with their formal relationships. Soon after becoming Dean he wrote:

I appear to be talking about the methods and logic of the social sciences rather than about university training in those fields. But it is the organization of a group of men who are re-examining these matters in the light of teaching and the guidance of research that helps make a university. . . . The formation of a Division of the Social Sciences does not, of course, bring a general social science into existence . . . but it has certainly exposed these problems to an unusual airing.[3]

Communication with his students was more important to Redfield even than the company of his colleagues and far more important than administrative chores. Dealing with advanced students in a seminar or younger people in a discussion group of the College, he never conceived of teaching as simple instruction. On the discussion of problems of the Division he wrote, for example, "The students, many of them, find all this exciting and interesting . . . the alert student is aroused and participates in talk and thinking."[4] So, too, he welcomed the inclusion of a "reading period" in the University quarter, not only because it gave more time to the professor for research, but especially because it encouraged independent thinking among students. His insight into the nature of education grew—and not only education in formal institutions of learning. Whether concerned with professors and students in universities, children in grade schools or in peasant villages, or adults continuing to educate themselves, he was interested in the variety of ways in which education may be, and often is, actually carried on.

The training of an anthropologist is held to give special competence in biological questions of race. As a scientist Redfield concerned himself less with biological race than with its social definition—"Race Is What We Make It."[5] As citizen as well as scientist he worked for a just relation between the races. After Pearl Harbor he took up the cause of the Japanese-Americans evacuated from the West Coast, visited a number of War Relocation camps, and talked with evacuees and staff.[6] In one statement on the race problem he expressed his attitude toward social action in general:

If one wants to accomplish a reform against long-standing opposition the only strategy is to keep at it, keep at it, and to keep at it. I think one must take

---

[3] Robert Redfield, "Training in the Social Sciences under a Divisional Organization," *Association of American Universities, Journal of Proceedings and Addresses,* 1934, pp. 107–16.

[4] *Ibid.*

[5] Unpublished paper, 1942.

[6] *See* Robert Redfield, "The Japanese-Americans," in W. F. Ogburn (ed.), *American Society in Wartime, Charles R. Walgreen Foundation Lectures* (Chicago: University of Chicago Press, 1943).

every measure that is reasonable, and just, and dispassionate. . . . I think there
is one limitation on the steps that might be taken . . . accomplish no good end by
a bad means.[7]

He was sympathetic to the work of the NAACP and was happy to be able
to contribute to its efforts against racial discrimination, utilizing his training in law as well as in anthropology. Also, for three years (1947–50) he
acted as director of the American Council on Race Relations, making it a
center for intelligent advice on dealing with racial problems.

Though actively committed, he thought it important to preserve a critical and detached judgment. In a letter to a friend he wrote:

What you write about the tendency to protect minorities because one is sorry
for them, from criticism, even from the publication of unfavorable facts about
them, hits right at an important and growing weakness. If we do not stop the
tendency, the Negroes and Jews too will get themselves into a position dangerous to them and corrupting to us all. The point is: Every man must take the
consequences of his acts, as a man, no matter what his privilege or lack of
privilege. The complementary point of course is: The privileged have the obligation to provide the underprivileged with the means to become underprivileged
no longer. . . .[8]

Redfield's activities in this period of his life may be traced in many
places: records of court testimony on the question of equality of opportunity for the Negro student, transcripts of University of Chicago Round
Table discussions (which, under the direction of George Probst through
the years 1938–55 dealt with the problems of the day in a weekly radio
broadcast), papers and notes unpublished, and published papers in a wide
range of journals including *Common Cause* (now defunct) and the *Bulletin of the Atomic Scientists*. From 1943 on he found stimulus and support in
discussions sponsored by Hutchins between men drawn from a variety of
professions. These took place under the auspices of the Commission on
the Freedom of the Press, the Committee To Frame a World Constitution,
and the Fund for the Republic with its more recently established Center
for the Study of Democratic Institutions—all of which worked toward that
intelligent participation in the world's affairs in which he believed.

Redfield's personal philosophy is best expressed in informal talks, many
of them given as convocation or graduation addresses. Some of these are
included in this volume. His "sermons," as he called them, were not in-
tended so much to preach to others as to express his own faith in the possibility of a good life which the individual could, and must, choose for himself.

[7] Letter to Lisa Redfield Peattie, Winter, 1942.

[8] Letter to Everett Hughes, April 20, 1949.

What makes a life worth living, and a man worth having, are principles to live by and, if necessary, die by. I am one who thinks there is no universal and absolute standard of the right, but that each man may work out for himself the principles which guide his being. What is important is that we know what we will to do, because that for us is the right, and so are free to do it.[9]

I thank Milton Singer and Sol Tax for their interest in this volume. To Malcolm Collier I am especially grateful for her thoughtful concern and advice given on the section about education. James Redfield made helpful criticisms of the Introduction.

Margaret Park Redfield

[9] Robert Redfield, "The Education of the Will," convocation address delivered at Elmhurst College, Elmhurst, Illinois, May, 1943.

PART I

THE EDUCATIONAL EXPERIENCE

THE READING PERIOD AT THE UNIVERSITY OF CHICAGO

It has long been assumed, in teaching the higher learning in this country, that education takes place only while the professors are talking. A course of study begins, it is customarily understood, with the first lecture and ends with the last. In between the professor talks. Discussion period and laboratory work vary the form of the talk, but instruction in some form goes on throughout the term or quarter. When the lectures come to an end, then too does learning, and the fall of professorial silence on the campus is a signal that work is over and vacation has begun. Perhaps our students have now become conditioned, in the manner of Pavlov's well-known dogs, so that the young brain begins to cerebrate only when there strikes upon the ear the sound of multitudinous lectures. Or is the effect of this long treatment to lull rather than to stimulate?

In the Division of the Social Sciences of the University of Chicago we have been trying a little experiment to discover if education can go on even when the professor is not talking. We have suspended classes and asked learning to continue. We have explored the possibility, furthermore, that a reduction in the amount of lecturing might not only save time but also improve education. This paper is a first report of that experiment.

For the past seven years, beginning in the autumn of 1934, instruction has been offered in the Division according to the following plan. Formal instruction is limited to six weeks at the beginning of each quarter. At the end of the quarter there is a period of two weeks for discussion and examination. During the three or four weeks (depending on the length of the quarter) between the six-week period of formal instruction and the two-week terminal period, the instructor does not meet with his classes. There are no course lectures, and an effort is made to avoid the scheduling of extracurricular talks during the period. The student is told to use the period for reading and reflection. The plan thus calls for the reduction of formal lecturing by almost one-half and the substitution for the formal lectures omitted of a fortnight of discussion and of a three- or four-week period when there is no instruction at all.

The original suggestion of a reading period came to us probably from the intervals without lectures at certain English institutions of higher learning. A student who goes to Oxford University for an education makes

Abridged and reproduced with permission from an article in John Dale Russell (ed.), *New Frontiers in Collegiate Instruction* (Chicago: University of Chicago Press, 1941), pp. 171–79.

use of certain periods of the year to read and to think without the immediate guidance and without the immediate distraction of lectures. At Harvard University there is also in operation a plan of instruction by which classes are concluded several weeks before the end of the semester. The course continues, however, in the form of independent study by the student, until it is brought to a close by the final examinations at the end of the semester.

There is evidence that opinion, both among the students and among the faculty, is preponderantly favorable to the plan and to its continuance. So far as evidence goes, support for the plan has grown, not diminished. At the end of the first year of operation of the plan the (then) seven Departments making up the Division were asked to canvass opinion in their faculties. These opinions were presented severally by the men consulted and collectively from each Department. Furthermore, some of the instructors invited their students to express their views of the plan. The expressions of opinion that resulted from this canvass represented nearly every instructor and a sampling of those students who happened to be invited to express their opinions and who took the trouble to do so. The instructors expressed a strong majority opinion in favor of continuance of the plan, although many who so voted were critical of the plan in its details or regarded the experiment as yet inconclusive. In expressing this markedly favorable judgment, the professors were in considerable part reflecting the benefit which they themselves took from the plan. Many of them emphasized the gain to them of ten or eleven weeks a year for research or other work. A smaller majority was sure that on the whole the students benefited from the reading period. The students who responded to requests for their opinions divided almost equally as to continuance of the plan. It was noted both by supporters of the plan and by its critics that there were proportionately more good students than poor students in the group that favored the plan. The opinion has since been expressed more than once that the plan helps along the education of the superior student more effectively than it does that of the inferior student.

More important than what students and faculty think of the plan is the effect it is having on education at the University. But of course it is much more difficult to find out about this. The fact that most of those who have had experience with the plan support it, and for the reasons which motivated its originators, at least is no evidence that it is working badly.

At this stage of the experiment the impressions of those who have observed its operation, since its inception, in the classrooms, in the offices of administration, and in the office of the Dean of Students, may be as trustworthy evidence on its value as any evidence available. The first thing I would say is that the introduction of a reading period is a step forward in higher education. The second thing I would say is that the step would be a longer one if all instructors took the trouble to make the reading period work effectively.

It is a step forward for two reasons. It transfers a reasonable share of the responsibility for education to the student himself. This is where it must rest, if the individual is to be truly educated. In so far as the student, given momentum by the professor, continues to educate himself now without the professor's voice in his ears, he carries on that self-education which is the mark and reward of education, and which can last throughout life.

It is, or could be, a step forward in higher education for the second reason that it calls for an improvement in the lectures given by the professor. One of the striking differences between higher education in English universities and higher education at American universities is that in the latter there are so many more lectures and so many more bad ones. At its worst, a lecture says badly what could be easily read in a poor book. A better lecture says well what can be read in a good book, and an occasional lecture says well what is available in no book at all. The introduction of the reading period in the Division of the Social Sciences required the professor to give fewer lectures and so gave him the chance to give better ones. The professor had a choice. He could simply leave off some of the lectures he had given under the old plan of eleven or twelve weeks of lectures. If he made no other change in his course, then the introduction of the reading period left the student worse off than he had been before—unless the professor's lectures were so bad that it was better simply to have fewer of them. As I cannot imagine such a condition at the University of Chicago, I must conclude that in a case where the professor merely decapitated his course, education suffered.

In other cases, however, the professor took the opportunity to compose new and better lectures. He reflected on the material he had been presenting in the light of recent developments in his field and in relation to the books which his students might read. He then developed new lectures which either presented the fundamental aspects of the field of knowledge of the course, leaving the student to carry out an intensive special study in the remaining weeks of the course, or set forth such a pattern of investigation as the student might then follow in the reading period. Some of the professors who did this found themselves preparing careful syllabi by which to relate the student's independent work quite explicitly to the lectures and to the library. Some of the professors who really revised their courses to take advantage of the reading period planned carefully the discussion to be held in the last two weeks of the course. Several have arranged panel discussions carried on by students, each of whom prepared his contribution.

My general conclusion is that the introduction of the reading period has worked a benefit to education where the instructor has labored to take advantage of the reform and has seen it as an educational device. It has worked best in the case of the better professors, just as it has worked best in the case of the better students. Where students have resented it as a breach of contract or where instructors have resented it as a break in routine, it has not improved education and may have worsened it. The reading period is, therefore, like many other things, a way to improve education for those who have the will to use it properly.

CAN RULES OR TUTORS EDUCATE?

The question to which my remarks this evening are addressed was put by Emerson in the words that appear in the printed announcement of this meeting. In full form his question was

> Can rules or tutors educate
> The semigod whom we await?

It is apparent that Emerson was thinking of an educational product more remote than the children that are graduated from the Laboratory Schools of the University of Chicago. Being the parents of those children, you and I know that—excellent as they are—they are not semigods, and we do not expect them to be. We ask of education only that it make of our children better men and women than we have been.

It may be asked whether even that modest improvement can be accomplished by the schools we have in the society we have. As an educator myself, I venture to put the question in unfriendly terms: Is it possible for educators to educate? The question is not as absurd as it sounds. An affirmative answer is not self-evident. In view of the long history of mankind, it is only recently that education has been attempted by professional educators. Most of the children that have lived on earth became adults without the benefits of schools. In the primitive societies, in which I am interested, children acquire their education simply through increasing participation in adult life; their parents and other kinsmen give them such instruction as they get; and their development takes place within customs and institutions that are consistent and coherent. In such societies professional educators are not needed. Children become rounded and complete adults because the culture in which they live is rounded and complete. This was the nature of education for hundreds of thousands of years. In medieval society, where religion provided such integration as there was, education was chiefly by the church. Secular professional edu-

An address to the Parents Association of the University of Chicago Laboratory Schools, March 16, 1943.

cation appeared in modern times, in secular society with disintegrated culture. It has not been many generations since education was moved out of the home into the school, and the move occurred because something was happening to both the home and the community. Education used to be accomplished by principles and parents; now it is attempted by rules and tutors. The question therefore is: in such society as we have today, can educators educate?

The answer is easy if all that we ask of education is that it teach our children how to do things. There is no doubt that educators can do that. Educators can and do teach our children how to read, to add and to subtract, to operate orange-crate grocery stores, and to put on their overshoes themselves. The success educators achieve in these directions is extended into higher learning, where young people are taught to build bridges or to try legal cases and are instructed in photography, automobile driving, and how to be airline hostesses. Educators are also notably successful, it seems to me, in helping the child to feel at home among his peers and in getting him used to working and playing with others to the mutual convenience and pleasure of all. Among the habits and techniques which education can give the child are the habits and techniques of social intercourse. In the small families and the small apartments of the modern city there is little chance for the child to learn these habits, and the school must do what the age-grade and the play group once did.

Moreover, the educator does fairly well, it seems to me—although not as well as he might—in developing the general intellectual capacities. The school can, and sometimes does, establish habits of regular and persistent work. I have myself seen a miracle of accomplishment in this quarter: my small son now does a page of subtraction facts with reasonable promptness; three months ago an attempt to do so produced an agony of procrastination. Furthermore, the schools do something not inconsiderable in developing critical judgment, in establishing respect for evidence, and in creating those many and related general skills which fall under the head of intellectual competence. My impression is that here the way is less clearly lighted by pedagogic understanding and that the gifts of the particular teacher are at least as important in determining success as are instructional devices; nevertheless, I suppose the achievements of the educator here to be significant.

Have I, perhaps, now admitted in effect, that educators can make an educated person? Do the achievements of the teachers that I have just recognized add up to an education? I have said that the educator can give our children the necessary techniques of modern living. I have admitted that in schools the child can acquire many practical and vocational accomplishments from arithmetic to court practice and that he can there learn how to work, much of how to get along with his fellows, and something of how to think. Is not such a person educated? I am describing a very paragon of accomplishments. Would not a child with such an education become the kind of adult we want? What more do we want of the men and the women who are to take our places?

It seems to me that we want much more. It seems to me that I have left out the most important part of a really educated man. I have left out all the content. I have given only the form. The being that I have conjured up is educated only in the sense that he knows how to do this and that, but he is not, as I have described him, a human being at all. He is a machine. Any machine can do things. But a man *is* something. A. N. Whitehead, characterizing religion, put it so: "You use arithmetic, but you *are* religious." You are, more generally, all your intimate convictions. An educated man has intimate convictions, and those convictions are in harmony with one another and with the life that man chooses to lead. To educate a man it is not enough to teach him how to read printed words, to use logarithms, to get on amiably with his fellows, and to check off examples of straight versus crooked thinking. These are goods, but they are only instrumental goods. I recognize that the teaching of these capacities is an important part of education; if I seem not to do justice to it in the rest of what I say it is because I am immediately interested in another part. An educated man has not only instrumental knowledge but also substantial knowledge. He knows something; moreover, he cares about what he knows. He has first things to put first. There are ends from which he will not be diverted and for which he will give up much. He knows what is for him the good life.

In a primitive society there is no problem about determining the good life. It is something given and taken pretty much for granted. In a primitive society the intimate convictions of one person are much the same as another and are developed in the course of living without formal education. Of course, in any one such society only one set of intimate convictions is possible, and this is not exposed to much criticism. From the point of view of modern man this is a serious objection to the primitive solution of the problem. But the point is that under modern conditions we cannot find intimate convictions that are ready-made and durable; those we do take over in early years are soon challenged; and we have, on the whole, come to distrust ready-made convictions anyway. We are committed to a society of free minds. We are free to work out, each man for himself, our intimate convictions, and if we don't work them out we aren't likely to have any. If we don't work them out we are likely to get along with mere habits and the shreds of old dogmas. The uneducated man, I suggest, does just this. The educated man, in the full sense of education which I am here adopting, has developed—through critical thinking—his own consistent and convinced understanding of the good life.

Emerson's question is to be understood in the light of this understanding of education. Can the schools develop intimate convictions? Can they make our children into men and women who know what is for them the good life?

I hasten to declare that I have not brought with me this evening the answer to this question. I am aware that it has been provided with many answers. Indeed in one form this question has become the sixty-four-dollar question for educators of the twentieth century. This has happened, I think, largely because there is no common conviction as to what the good life is; or because in so far as we know what it is, we are afraid we aren't going to have it. So we ask the schools to do something about it. The confidence the people of America have in their schools is notorious. The schools are expected to teach every vaguely defined value which the American people think they cherish or are, somehow, seeking to recognize. If the American people are unclear about what they believe in and want to become clear, they generally ask the schools to teach it. The schools are to teach democracy, Americanism, and character. I am told that two states in the Union have passed laws requiring teachers to train their pupils in "honesty, kindness, justice, and moral courage." If our people are troubled by crime or isolationism or internationalism or communism or just plain general disorder, the schools are told to go and teach the opposite.

It is no wonder that educators come to believe in their powers, not only to make children over, but even to make society over. One educator asks, "Dare the Schools Make a New Social Order?" and is inclined to take the dare. Another, more moderate, proposes that the schools make themselves the ally of progressive changes taking place in the social order and carry on the work of education within the frame of reference provided by the democratic ideal. Still another advocates direct study of political and ethical ideals for the good life of the whole free society.

I do not know whether the schools can make society reorganize itself. I doubt if the schools can create a coherent vision of a desirable social life in a society that lacks such a vision. It seems to me that the schools will continue to include people with many different visions of the desirable society and with different kinds of convictions and lack of convictions. I doubt that the schools will become a social movement, or, short of totalitarianism here, an organ for the propagation of a dogma. So long as the winds of doctrine blow around our land they will blow through the schools. The problem of the moral order is, of course, not exclusively that of the schools but involves all our institutions. Even the home has still something to do with it, although the home is certainly not in the favorable position in which it once was. The average length of residence of the farm family on any one farm is about six years; half of the rural children go to the city;

and in the city they meet with employment turnover and the annual moving day. Father and mother are home with the children once in a while, but also present are Aunt Jemima, Captain Midnight, and Jack Armstrong, the All-American boy. The fact must be recognized that neither the family nor the school nor any other group holds the average child long enough to justify the assumption by that group of the principal responsibility for giving an education, understanding that word in the large sense. Moreover, the school and the home are competitors of each other, in that the time the child spends in one represents time taken from the other.

It does not seem to me to follow, however, that the schools have no influence upon the development of intimate convictions in young people. It is not a matter of indifference what the schools do. While I am not sure just how much the schools, as distinguished from the other parts of our society, can do in building a good society, I think the schools do much to make good men and women. It seems to me that it is possible to distinguish between better education and worse without waiting to define the New Society or the role of the school in bringing it about. It seems to me that educators occasionally do help the young person in the difficult task of forming his intimate convictions and that occasionally the schools, while trying to do this, fail. On this matter I have some crude, offhand, third-rate notions which I now proceed to inflict upon you.

I doubt that either character or social values can be taught directly. I doubt that intimate convictions can be created by telling children that intimate convictions are important. I doubt that a philosophy of living is achieved by talking about how a philosophy of living is a good thing. I have the idea that by some educators more reliance is placed on formal teaching devices than is justified. I sometimes suppose, probably mistakenly, that the effort to develop values is attended with some confusion. The emphasis appears in some cases to be a verbal emphasis. The problem of teaching social values appears especially in that branch of learning known as the social studies, and as I spend some time in that branch myself I venture to extend these unfriendly remarks. At its worst the instruction in the social studies confuses intelligence with a vague sort of goodness. The pupil is told he ought to have a pattern of values, and he then tells himself that he has one. The pupil may be required to make a list of the ten requirements of a good home or to appraise his progress in facing the facts. I do not suppose the worst of such examples to be in our own schools, but in the worst of them the teacher seems to me to be trying to create coherent values by means of exercises directed to that end. The social studies developed out of the need felt to give young people some understanding of the society in which they live. They have become confused with the need felt to establish a moral order in this country. In trying to accomplish both, some teachers may fail to accomplish either. Understanding is clouded with moralization. The teacher feels that he is called upon not only to develop the intelligence but to teach the right. In some of these enterprises it is doubtful if the right is being learned, and it is difficult to discover just what the right is. Perhaps the right is whatever is in this week's *Nation.*

This is perhaps the worst that the schools do. But there is also a best that they do. I think that teachers help young people to develop intimate convictions when they cause them to read and consider good books and when they work with them on subject matter that is felt to be important. I think that it is not enough for the teacher to know how to read the words of the book or how to teach the subject matter. I think, to help in forming intimate convictions, it is also necessary that the teacher feel that, for him, the book is good, and that, for him, the subject matter is important. It seems to me more desirable that the teacher's enthusiasm attach to the book and to the study of something—music, pond-life, or housing problems—than that it attach to teaching methods or the value of values.

Good books are the public records of the intimate convictions of good men; they provide the suggestions and the guides for the new attempts that each man must make for himelf. They are to be met with at every level of difficulty, from *The Tailor of Gloucester* to *David Copperfield* to *King Lear* to Aristotle's *Ethics.* There is a view in some quarters that the appropriateness of a given book is confined to a certain bracket of years in the human life, but it seems to me simpler and wiser to hold that on the whole a book is suitable for any child that shows a disposition to try to understand it and for any older person who still enjoys it.

The reading of good books seems to me a necessary part, or the substantial part, of getting a good education. But it is only a part. I do not believe that it is alone sufficient. There is a world to be lived in, to be understood, and to be controlled. The good books help in the understanding and controlling of that world. But I think it is also needful to deal with what happens more immediately about us and to learn, through orderly study of it, how it can be made more meaningful. We do not have to choose between the book and the laboratory; we must have both. The contemporary event and the classical utterance are not rivals; they complement each other. We must read and study the world around us as we read. Our immediate experience, and that which comes to us one degree less directly in descriptive account, historical document, newspaper and statistical report, we must transmute into ordered understanding.

It seems to me that values that the school can develop in the child are values that come with working with subject matter and in coming to enjoy and to respect the understanding and appreciation that come from working with it. The artist or the scientist or the scholar is not neutral about what he does. He cares about it. I do not think that the best teachers

I have known were the teachers who were most concerned with teaching methods. They were concerned with how to learn. They were the ones who cared about something—books or pictures or people or algebra—and communicated to me, not only how to study it, but their own feeling of its importance. My daughter writes me that W. H. Auden declares that there can be no real education without passion. I think this statement says what I am trying to say. In the primary school and the high school and the college I remember teachers who wanted themselves to understand or to appreciate whatever subject they were concerned with and so communicated to me something of that passion for understanding or appreciation. They are the teachers I remember. If I had had more of them I should have obtained an education.

I do not think of education as handing down accumulated fact. I do not think of education as drawing out of the child something rolled up within him that needs only to be unrolled. I certainly do not think of education as pedagogic devices. I think of education as sharing the habits of learning, of appreciating, and of critically thinking. I suppose these habits to be shared and developed when children or adults work together.

We began this evening by looking at the outside of a really educated man and then came to consider his inside. Outside we find the tools of learning and living. Inside we hope to find a moral order. Is it possible to ask the schools to put a moral order into a child who lives in a society characterized, more or less, by moral disorder? We have a free society. It is so free that the individual is free to stand for almost anything or for nothing. The schools *can* help the individual to make his own moral order. I believe they do it best when they don't try to do it directly. You can't legislate goodness or inculcate liberalism. You can, I believe, study this disordered world and, by opportunity and example, get young people to study it, too, and to appreciate it. You can communicate critical thinking about books and critical analysis of events. The teacher who studies something other than teaching may be the best teacher if he gets young people to study it with him. It is in these ways that rules and tutors educate.

CULTURE AND EDUCATION IN THE MIDWESTERN HIGHLANDS OF GUATEMALA

When education is considered as it occurs in a modern society, we think first of the school. In a primitive society there are neither schools nor pedagogues; yet we speak of the "education" of the primitive child.

Reproduced with permission from *American Journal of Sociology,* XLVIII (May, 1943), 640–48.

In so doing we are, of course, recognizing a conception of education much wider than the domain of the school; we are thinking of it as "the process of cultural transmission and renewal"—a process present in all societies and, indeed, indistinguishable from that process by which societies persist and change.

When we describe education in such school-less and bookless societies, we are likely to fix attention upon other institutions which obviously and formally express and communicate the local tradition. Such are ceremony, myth, tribal and familial symbols and stories, initiation ceremonies, and men's houses. In these we recognize a certain fixity and emphasis of major elements of culture, and we see that in their perpetuation and repetition these elements receive restatement and are communicated to the young. Indeed, we have come to think of primitive societies as providing a well-organized and self-consistent system of institutions by which children are brought up to think and act as did their fathers. In such societies we connect education with traditional forms expressive of a rich content. In comparison with the educational effect of a katchina dance upon a Hopi child, a chapter in a civics textbook seems pretty thin, educationally speaking.

To the invitation to give an account of the educational process, I respond from a point of view of certain rural communities in the midwestern highlands of Guatemala which are neither modern nor primitive but in many respects intermediate between a simple tribe and a modern city. Educational institutions among these rural mountain-dwellers do not quite conform to either the primitive or civilized type. These people have schools, but the schools are of small importance. They have ceremonies and legends, but these forms do not have so much content as one might suppose. In these Guatemalan societies schooling is far from accomplishing what our educational experts claim generally for schools. On the other hand, ceremony and myth do not come up to the standard set by many primitive societies. In this part of the world there are no central and powerful educational institutions around which an essay can conveniently be written.

The situation is not without value, however, for students of the cultural process. In recognizing in this part of Guatemala the limited educational influence of schools, on the one hand, and of traditional forms, on the other, one is brought to see aspects of education which underlie all formal institutions. People in Guatemala do get educated (in the sense that the heritage is transmitted) with adjustments to meet changing circumstances, even though many of them never go to school and even though there are no great puberty ceremonies, with revelations of the sacred *alcheringa* and narrations of totemic myths, such as occur among Australian aborigines. In this paper I shall make some observations on certain features of these highlands societies in so far as the educational process is concerned; and I shall, in particular, call attention to aspects of that process which are probably to be encountered in every society. I call attention to them because education is ordinarily studied without much reference to them.

As I look at the school in the little village where I once was resident, it appears to me to play a greater part in changing the culture of the people than in handing it on from one generation to the next, although its influence in the direction of change is indirect. Nearly all the time in the school is given to learning to read and to write and to calculate. Some children acquire a fair command of these arts; others do not. The arts of literacy have many practical uses, and their possession carries some prestige. They improve the opportunities for gainful employment, and their possession disposes the individual to seek his fortune in the town or in the city. In some cases success in school leads to higher education in the city and so to participation in urban civilization.

The majority of people of this community are Indians; a minority are a Spanish-speaking people of mixed ancestry known as Ladinos. The cultures of the two groups are identical in many areas of experience; in others they are still notably different. Where both kinds of people live in the same settlement, both attend the same school. The school makes more change for the Indian than for the Ladino, because through association with the Ladinos in the school he learns Spanish and in not a few cases is disposed to put off Indian dress, to live in the manner of the Ladinos, and so to become a Ladino. There is here no obstacle of prejudice or law to prevent this not infrequent occurrence. The school is one important institution, therefore, through which the Indian societies tend to lose members to the Ladino society and so ultimately to disappear.

As such an instrument of acculturation and culture change, the school is only one among a number of effective institutions. The penitentiary deserves mention, for, although its liberalizing influence is less widely distributed than in the case of the school, not a few individuals profit by this form of widened experience and return to the village with a new song, a new trade, and a less parochial view of life. The common custom of bringing up other people's children is also effective, as when the child is an Indian brought up in a Ladino household. Of such individuals it may later be said that "that Ladino is really an Indian," but the ethnic origin of the individual carries little or no social disadvantage and is quickly forgotten.

Considered as an institution helping to preserve the local culture, the role of the school is small. I venture the assertion that the abolition of schools in these highlands would leave the culture much as it is. Except for the texts of prayers recited on many occasions, little of the rural

Ladino heritage depends on literacy. And, furthermore, it is only necessary that a few individuals in each society be literate so as to preserve
access to written or printed sources. Indeed, for generations the Indian
cultures in the more isolated societies have got along with a semiprofes-
sionalization of literacy. A few individuals in each village or group of
villages were trained to read the Mass; the central government sent from
the city a literate person to deal with the written communications of
formal government. The more pagan religious ritual was, and still is,
stored, unwritten, in the memories of a small number of professionals.
Their knowledge is highly specialized and is little understood by the
layman.

The village school in this area devotes little time to instruction other
than the purely technical; and the little "cultural" instruction which it
gives has small support in other branches of the village life. Some instruction is given in Guatemalan history and geography. What is taught is not
reinforced by books in the homes, because there are almost no books in
the homes. Nor is the instruction closely related to the content of oral
tradition. The knowledge that Columbus discovered America is perpetuated in the school and is possessed by most Ladinos as an item of information, but few people whom I interrogated were able to tell me that
that discovery was the event commemorated by the little celebration
which the government orders to occur each year in the village municipal
building on October 12. (Of course the more sophisticated townsman
understands the meaning of the occasion.) At any rate, Columbus is no
tribal or village legendary hero.

As not a great deal is accomplished by formal instruction in the school,
one might suppose the lack to be made up by a great deal of deliberate
inculcation and discipline in the home. At least with regard to the rural
Ladino society, I am sure that this is not the case. Children are taught to
do what they are expected to do chiefly as an aspect of coming to perform
the tasks of adults. Moments of instruction are not segregated from moments of action. Boys are taught to farm and girls to cook as they help
their elders do these things. Along with instruction in the practical arts,
parents comment on conduct, saying what is "good" and what is "bad."
The word *pecado* is applied to innumerable interdicted acts, from those
which are regarded as mildly unlucky to those to which some real moral
opprobrium attaches. Some parents will select a serious and special moment in which to convey sex instruction, and sometimes other subjects
will be somewhat formally inculcated; but on the whole I should say that
instruction in the home is casual and unsystematized.

Certainly it is not characteristic of this Ladino culture that the young
gather around the knees of the old to listen reverently to a solemn exposition of the holy traditions and sacred memories of the people. Indeed,

in this society, as in our own, it is hard to find the holy traditions, let alone to get anyone to listen while they are expounded. Most instruction that occurs in the home or outside it is connected with the practical arts of life.

It seems to me interesting that, while few of these Ladinos are today teaching their children the prayers of their Catholic tradition, they do take pains to teach them the traditional forms of address and salutation, which in these cultures are complicated and elaborate. It is characteristic of this people that requests and other communications are not abruptly and directly presented but are wrapped in highly conventional preliminary and terminal utterances; also, in general, among them polite language is regarded as seemly conduct.

It also seems to me that this formal language is a way in which people preserve their personal lives from too easy invasion and that it is therefore a useful art. It is, moreover, one which every man must practice for himself. The case is different with the prayers. Apparently it is not thought sufficiently important that every child have formal language in which to talk with God. It is, however, thought important that the prayers be recited by someone on the occasions of novenas for the saints and following a death. But all that is necessary is that one or a few persons be available to recite the prayers. It would not greatly surprise me if in these villages the reciting of Catholic prayers became a paid profession, as are now the reciting of a Mass by priest or layman, the teaching of the spoken text of a dance-drama, or the playing of the little flageolet which accompanies processions bearing images of the saints.

This observation about the teaching of prayers and of mannerly speech may be generalized into two wider characterizations of these Guatemalan cultures. The point of view on life is practical and secular rather than religious or mystical; and formal activity is more than usually large, it seems to me, in proportion to the content of symbolic meaning which underlies it. This statement I am disposed to make about both the Indian and the Ladino cultures, although there are differences of degree or kind in these respects between the two.

For the rural Ladinos it may be safely asserted that religious pageantry and mythology do not play a large part in the education of the individual. The Christian epic is known very incompletely; it exists in the form of many unco-ordinated fragments of lore, and it is not vividly presented in any coherent or impressive way. These country people read very little sacred literature; they very rarely hear sermons; and there is no important traditional ceremony or drama in which it might be expressed. An exception in part must be made for the ninefold repetition at Christmas time of the journey of Mary and Joseph and for the little enactment of the birth of the child. The effigies of and stories about Christ, and in less degree and importance of and about the saints, do constitute a body of lore in which significant traditional conceptions are perpetuated. But these ceremonials occupy a very small part of the time and interests of the Ladinos, and the element of mere entertainment in them is very large.

For the Indian, more is to be said as to the contribution of ceremony and myth to the educational and cultural process. The cult of the saints is more elaborate, and ritual observances are more extensive. Justification for the statement that the culture of the Ladinos is more shallow or less integrated than that of the Indians is in part to be found, it seems to me, in the fact that most stories told among Ladinos—and they like to tell and to hear stories—deal chiefly with fairies, witches, talking animals, and the adventures of picaresque personages and that these stories are not regarded as true and are not thought of as describing the world in which the individual lives. They are recognized as fanciful creations that serve to entertain. The Indian, on the other hand, is disposed to regard the stories which he tells as true. Taken as a whole, the Indian's stories deal with men and animals and supernatural beings that he believes to exist about him, and their telling helps to define and redefine the conventional world in which the Indian lives.

A story well known in the Indian village of San Antonio tells how St. Anthony was once a man who dwelt in that village as other men, and how, counseled by his friend, Christ, whom he sought to rescue when our Lord's enemies were after him, he took the form of a saint so as to help the village where he lived and worked. The story offers an explanation for the origin of every significant element of costume and accouterment in the effigy of St. Anthony as customarily fashioned and as it exists in the village church; and it explains and justifies by reference to the saint's divine will many of the elements in the cult now customary: the marimba, the masked dancers, the fireworks, incense, and candles. Indeed, except that the content of the story is of Old World origin, the story in feeling and form is quite like many origin or hero myths that are told among non-Europeanized Indians.

A study of the educational process among these Indians would certainly have to take into account the existence of these stories and the circumstances under which they are told. It is plain that their telling helps to communicate and perpetuate the tradition of the group. It is significant that in the Indian villages every man passes through a series of public services; that in the course of many of these employments he spends long hours sitting in company with his age-mates and his elders, and that the elders at such times tell stories and relate episodes. The Ladino society is almost entirely without such an institution.

The existence of such a story as the one about St. Anthony is another evidence of the power within a culture to make itself, if such an expression may be employed. We may be sure that no priest set out to teach just this story to the Indians of the village. The story has grown in the course of generations of speculation upon an effigy and a ritual already sanctified and mysterious. Indeed, we catch glimpses of this process to-day when we hear of Indians who have found new explanations for some element of decorative design in church, or when an ethnologist's inform-ant begins to offer speculations of his own.

Yet I am struck with the fact that even in the case of the Indian cul-tures there is more form than content in their collective life. In this same village of San Antonio there is performed every year in Holy Week a se-ries of ceremonies occupying several days. It is generally understood that these ceremonies are a representation of the Passion of our Lord, and a general air of gravity attends them. But in my notes is a list of elements of the ritual for which none of my informants has been able to offer any explanation at all. Structures are erected and taken down, and effigies are used to which no meaning is assigned other than mere custom. One could fill many hundreds of pages with a detailed account of the goings and comings, the processions, the handing-over of effigies, the ritual drinking and bowing and the like, which custom provides must be car-ried on each year in one of these Indian villages among the groups of men in whose custody rest the images of the saints. On the other hand, even making liberal allowance for the relative difficulty of getting trust-worthy information on the meanings of these acts, I feel sure that little could be said about the symbolic connections these acts have with the content of tradition. Yet, even in so far as these rituals have no symbolic meaning, they do maintain traditional ways within which behavior is regulated, and, therefore, they have their place in a broad investigation of the educational process in these communities.

The relatively formal or external aspect of much of the Guatemalan cultures is conspicuously illustrated in the dance-dramas. These are per-formed by Indians at most Indian festivals and very infrequently are performed by Ladinos at Ladino festivals. The observer sees a score of men dressed in brilliant and fantastic costumes, carrying highly special-ized objects in their hands, and dancing, gesturing, and reciting long lines of set speech. The performance might be an enactment of some centrally important holy myth. It is, as a matter of fact, nothing of the sort. There are about a dozen dance-dramas known in Guatemala. Most of these have spoken text. Specialists possess these texts and at festival time are hired to teach groups of Indians to speak them and to perform the accompany-ing dances. The texts are in oratorical Spanish, and it is rare that an In-dian understands well what he is saying. The general theme of the drama is known: if the dance called "The Conquest" is danced, the combat be-tween Alvarado, the Spanish invader, and the pagan Indians is understood. But the tradition means little to the dancers; they will just as well enact Cortes' triumph over Montezuma, if that dance is cheaper to put on or provides a better show. The dance is performed, indeed, because a group of men is willing to put money and time into doing something lively for the festival. It may be compared to putting on a minstrel show in another culture or hiring a merry-go-round. The comparison is not quite fair, but it suggests the truth.

In these societies of which I write, then, the educational process is not greatly dependent upon institutions organized for pedagogical purposes or upon organized and deliberate instruction within the family or other primary group. The ceremonial and other expressive customs which we find in every society are significant educationally here in Guatemala, too; but at least this one observer finds that, compared with some other societies, there is a great amount of formal machinery for the regulation of activities without corresponding symbolic content. To a marked extent the transmission of culture takes place within a complex of regulations: the traditional machinery of government and of ritual observances, the superimposed police control of the Guatemalan national government, the general traditional emphasis upon forms of utterance and conduct.

Nevertheless, an investigation of the educational process in these communities would be far from complete if it were to consider only institutions, pedagogic or ceremonial, as elements in that process. Here, as elsewhere, the heritage of the group is communicated and modified in situations much less clearly defined than any of which mention has so far been made in this paper. I refer to that multitude of daily situations in which, by word and gesture, some part of the tradition is communicated from one individual to another without the presence of any formal institution and without any deliberate inculcation. This class of situations corresponds in a general way with what Spencer called the "primary forms of social control."

Let us imagine that we are standing unseen outside a house in the village where I am living. Within the house some Ladino women are praying a novena, and outside it six men and two boys stand around a little fire and talk. Someone compares the heaping-up of pine cones made ready for this fire to the heaping-up of twigs by Indians at certain places on hilltops where, by Indian custom, the traveler strokes away the fatigue from his legs with a twig and then adds the twig to a growing pile. As soon as the comparison has been made, one man of those beside the fire expresses derision at this Indian belief, which is well known to all present. Others briefly indicate similar disbelief in the custom. Another man then makes a remark to the effect that what does in fact serve to relieve tired legs is to rub rum on the ankle-bones. A younger man—apparently unfamiliar with this remedy—asks how this can be effective, and the older man explains that the rum heats the nerves that run near the ankle-bone and that the heat passes up the body along the nerves and so restores strength. The explanation is accepted; the apparent physiological mechanism provides a warrant for accepting the worth of rum as a remedy.

After a short period of silence, conversation begins about snakes, one man having recently killed a large snake. A young boy, apparently wishing to make an effective contribution to a conversation in which he has as yet played no part, remarks that the coral snake joins itself together when cut apart. The man who laughed at the Indian belief about tired legs scornfully denies the truth of the statement about coral snakes. Another older man in the group comes to the support of the boy and in a tentative way supports the truth of the belief as to coral snakes. A younger man says that it is not true, because he cut apart such a snake without unusual result. The skeptical man appeals to the company; another witness offers testimony unfavorable to the belief. The boy has not spoken again; the other man who ventured to support him withdraws from the argument. But this man wishes, it seems, to restore his damaged prestige. With more confidence he offers the statement that some animals *can* do unusual things: the monkey, when shot by a gun, takes a leaf from the tree in which he is sitting and with it plugs the wound. The smaller of the two boys, who has not yet spoken, adds that the jaguar can do this also. Discussion breaks out, several persons speaking at once; the trend of the remarks is to the effect that, although undoubtedly the monkey can do as described, the jaguar is unable to do so. The quick statements of opinion break out almost simultaneously, and very quickly thereafter the matter is dropped. The bystander recognizes that there is substantial consensus on the points raised; the boy is apparently convinced.

We may safely assume that in such a situation as this the states of mind of the participants in the conversation with reference to the points at issue differ from one another less at the conclusion of the conversation than they did at the beginning. The matter is not ended for any one of them, of course; subsequent experiences and conversations about fatigue, snakes, and monkeys will again modify their conceptions, or at least redeclare them. We may suppose also that the outcome of this particular conversation—an apparent consensus in favor of rum and against twigs, supporting the belief about monkeys and unfavorable to the beliefs about coral snakes and jaguars—will not be duplicated exactly in the next conversation that occurs among similar men on these subjects. We are not so simple as to suppose that by attending to this little talk we have discovered "the belief" of the Ladinos on these points. The personalities of the influential men, the accidents of recent experiences had with monkeys or snakes, and, indeed, probably also the general tone of the moment, which may or may not have been favorable to the serious reception of a marvelous story, are among the factors that have entered into the situation. They have brought about, not a conclusive conviction, but a sort of temporary resting-place of more or less common understanding. We may think of the outcome of such little exchanges of viewpoint as the component of many forces. Because each man's state of mind at the time of the conversation is itself the component of many such forces, most of which have been exerted within the same community of long-intercommunicating men and women, it is likely to be not greatly different from that of his neighbors. Still, there are always individual differences; and it is largely in such little happenings as that which took place around the pine-cone fire that these differences are made influential and that they come to be adjusted one to another.

The episode may be recognized as one of that multitude by which the heritage is transmitted. It was a tiny event in the education of the people. Some part of the heritage with reference to the treatment of fatigue and with reference to the behavior of certain animals passed from older people to younger people—and, indeed, it passed also from younger people to older people, for oral education is a stream that flows through all contemporaries, whatever their ages.

At the same time it was a small event in which the culture of the group underwent a change. Some old people in the community tell me that when they were young they heard about the ability of the coral snake to join itself together and did not doubt its truth.

Perhaps the boy who advanced the belief received his first knowledge of it from such a grandfather. After this evening around the pine-cone fire he will treat grandfather's remarks with a new grain of skepticism. Some of the men who took part in this conversation have traveled and have lived in the city among men whose tradition disposed them more readily to laugh at the story of the coral snake, and the effects of such experiences were also registered in the outcome of the evening's conversation. The result of these various influences was to shift, though ever so slightly, the center of gravity of the community beliefs on these points.

Furthermore, the trifling occurrence was also an event in the transmission of tradition from one group to another. No Indian took part in the conversation, but one man, who was born an Indian but had lived long among Ladinos, stood silent in the dark edges of the group. As an ethnologist who has talked with Indians, I know that the belief about getting rid of fatigue by brushing the legs with twigs is by them generally accepted, and great credence is given to beliefs as to the ability of injured animals to treat themselves. Now there has impinged upon that silent Indian a set of forces tending to shift the center of his belief; and now, when he takes part in a similar discussion among Indians, he is more likely to be on the skeptical side of the center of consensus than if he had not been here this evening. It is largely by the accumulating effect of innumerable such occurrences that the culture of the Indians and that of the Ladinos are becoming more and more alike.

We are not to suppose that it is always the Indian who is disposed to change his mind so that it becomes more like that of the Ladino. For certain reasons the predominating trend tends to substitute Ladino tradition for that of the Indians. But the Ladino has in four hundred years taken on a great deal from the Indians—the techniques of maize-farming and the use of the sweat bath, to mention just two elements—and he still learns from the Indian. The episode around the pine-cone fire could be matched by an episode in which Indians, showing Ladinos the nicked ears of wild animals, by this evidence tended to persuade the Ladinos that these animals were indeed under the domestication of a supernatural protector inhabiting the woods.

It is a fair guess that in any society the process of education depends more on such events as represented in the conversation I have reported than it does upon all the formal pedagogical devices which exist in the society. In the speech and gestures which take place in the home, in the play and work groups, and wherever people talk naturally about matters that are interesting to them, the tradition is reasserted and redefined. In these situations the culture is not merely spoken about; it is acted out; it happens before the eyes and even through the persons of children, who by this means, in large degree, are educated. This basic part of the educational process takes place in every society and probably to such an extent that societies are greatly alike in this respect. Upon the flow of such experience are erected those more clearly defined institutions of the folk traditions, as well as the deliberate enterprise of pedagogy and propaganda. As to these, societies will be found greatly to differ.

Comparing these particular Guatemalan societies with—let us say—that of the French-Canadian villages, I should say that here education is more secular and more casual. These Guatemalan societies seem to me relatively meager with respect to organized moral convictions and sacred traditions. What the Indians tell me about the times of their grandfathers suggests strongly that the Indian societies have lost in ceremonial richness, as I suspect they have lost in the moral value and the integration of their local traditions. Because I have observed the influence of priests in other communities in maintaining a sacred tradition and in explaining symbolic significance of traditional rituals, I think it likely that, if, indeed, these societies have been becoming more casual and more secular, the lessened influence of the Catholic priests has been one factor in this change. The Guatemala of today is well regulated by secular government in the interests of public order and hygiene. My guess—which is to be tested by historical investigation—is that secular external regulation (important probably even in pre-Columbian times) has grown in later years, while that control dependent upon moral conviction and instruction and upon local tradition has declined. The school, for these rural people, is another form of external regulation rather than an expression of local tradition.

Whatever study of the history of this part of rural Guatemala may in fact show, the present situation in these societies suggests the question of whether a rich culture is compatible with a society in which the mechanisms for education consist chiefly of formal regulations and of casual conversation. The comparison between Indian and Ladino societies—alike though they are in their generally secular character—indicates a correspondence between certain characteristics of culture and certain characteristics of education. The Indian beliefs and tales have relation to current life, and more of them have moral content or depth than is the case with Ladino beliefs and tales. And, second, in the Indian societies there is a social-political-religious organization—a system of progressive public services through which all males pass—that is largely native to the community, that is a force in social control, and that involves relatively sacred things. This organization is largely lacking in the Ladino societies. These differences may be stated in terms of differences in the educational institutions of the two peoples: To a greater degree than is the case with the Ladinos, the Indians hear and tell stories that express and justify traditional beliefs; and by passing through the hierarchy of services the individual learns the ritual that is the inner and relatively sacred side of the formal civic organization. Emphasizing characteristics of those Guatemalan societies which are more evident in the case of the Ladinos than of the Indians, this paper concludes, then, with the suggestion that an education which is made up, on the one side, of practical regulation and instruction without reference to tradition and, on the other, has nothing much more compulsive and expressive in which to exert its influence than the casual contacts of everyday life is not likely to educate with reference to any greatly significant moral values.

A NOTE ON THE GENERAL AND THE SPECIFIC IN EDUCATION

ENDS AND MEANS

The questions as to general *vs.* special (particular) education have meaning only if stated in a recognized context of ends and means. The "generalization" of education may refer to the effects sought: one wants to bring about effects in those educated which are general to them all or to some identified part of them all. The "generalization" may, on the other hand, refer to the means: one asks whether a given effect (either the development of understandings general to all or of abilities special to some) can be achieved by "teaching general principles" or by exposition or practice of particularities.

The taking of a particular action (visiting the fire station) might be shown to be an efficient means of realizing general education in, say, common responsibilities of citizenship. On the other hand, teaching the general principles of mechanics might be shown to be an effective means of teaching some people to be mechanics. The controversy as to whether law can be effectively taught by the case method or by enunciation of general legal principles is a controversy as to the effectiveness of general or specific educational means to accomplish an education special to a few.

As this ambiguity is usually present in discussions of the general *vs.* the specific in education,[1] the question as to generality *vs.* specificity in

Reproduced with permission from the files of the Ford Fund for the Advancement of Education. Remarks directed toward a memorandum circulated by Clarence Faust prior to a discussion meeting sponsored by the Fund, New York, Spring of 1954.

[1] The ambiguity is present in the memorandum to which this document is a response. In paragraph 2, page 1, the question is put as a contrast in the results of effects of education: Can we bring about understandings common to all ("matters of common concern"), or can we develop powers special to some ("his potentialities as an individual")? This question recurs in the second paragraph of page 2 in terms of general *vs.* vocational education. General education is general as an effect (if not also in means taken to reach that effect): it brings about common understandings or competences on common concerns. Vocational education brings about one understanding or competence in one individual and another understanding or competence in another individual, each according to his capacities and interests.

But between the two parts of this exposition of the question, in the first paragraph of page 2, the question is raised as to the means appropriate to the end sought: to reach the effect, good citizenship, is it an effective means to teach basic principles ("when these principles are understood, the child is likely to be a good citizen"), or is it an effective means to cause the learner to take action relevant to such principles ("good citizenship may be taught through various particular experiences")?

Furthermore, the memorandum uses for the most part forms of speech that raise questions as to the effectiveness of means (". . . the process of education can be centered in matters of common concern. . . . Can the individual be taught . . ." [paragraph 1, page 1]; ". . . the nature of the human mind and its operation . . .

education can be clarified by asking him who raises such an issue the double question: What generality or specificity of effect do you intend or foresee, and what evidence have you that any defined generality or specificity of means will result in that effect?

Many of the issues raised by teachers, by professional educationists, or by social or biological scientists are with regard to the limitations of educational means set by the nature of human nature (transfer of learning, order of capacities of the developing child) or as to the effectiveness of some particular or general educational means (citizenship classes, saluting the flag, learning by lectures) to reach an end often not clearly defined. In all these issues the clarification needed is double, as to ends and as to means. To determine the relevance of some special knowledge or opinion, we must ask, first, what effects are we seeking to bring about in whom by some proposed means, and what limitations are asserted on our powers to produce those effects? It may be, for instance, that the more ultimate question of ends, What is the right education? is hidden behind ambiguous words of purpose: "education for citizenship" may mean a citizenship in which every adult shares responsibilities and understandings common to all; or it may mean a citizenship in which some are slaves and others freemen or in which special understandings and responsibilities are given to "leaders" or "an elite" but not to others.

Second, the validity of the special knowledge, in these issues brought before us by educators, scientists, or perhaps laymen, in so far as they are issues as to the effectiveness of means, is of course a question of evidence and judgment of its effect as proof. The educator or scientist is to be asked, From what observations or experiments do you draw what inferences? What is the basis for a further inference that what was learned in this schoolroom or laboratory may be generalized to a conclusion affecting educational programs, local or universal? A little experience with these issues of science and pedagogy suggests that there is no very large body of established knowledge as to the nature of human nature or as to the demonstrated effectiveness of defined educational means; that on the whole we are confronted with a varied and disordered very particular knowledge, half-knowledge and advocacy, intermixed; and that educa-

---

the nature of knowledge and the methods of achieving it" [paragraph 3, page 1]). The questions stated on pp. 3–4 under "Psychological," "Physiological or neurological," and, in part, "Philosophical," are with reference to powers and means. On the other hand, Mr. Faust's letter (page 2) puts the question in terms of what we ought to do, as a question of ends sought to be realized. Oddly enough, the only place in the memorandum where the question of ends is unequivocal is in the formulation of the questions attributed to sociology ("Should new members born in a society, etc.") although most present-day American sociologists will tell us that they are in the business of telling people not what they should do but only what they can do.

tional practice actually takes place in a context shaped chiefly by common sense, habit, immediate expediency, and human patience, perseverance, and hope.

From this point on in this memorandum education may be understood as the total effect sought to be realized in this country by organized effort to educate: education is the right over-all end in view.

THE GENERAL SEEN IN PARTICULAR

The basic question of the memorandum sent out by the Fund is stated as "The question of generalized versus specific education." Throughout the memorandum there is presented a choice between two alternatives: Can this be done *or* that? Should people be prepared for specific roles *or* should they acquire general capacity?

Let us challenge that "versus." Let us deny the mutually exclusive implication of those "or's."

"The problem of education is to make the pupil see the wood by means of the trees" (Whitehead). Special and general education may be aspects of the same end or effect and may be realized by a means which is both special and general. The implication that to give so much general education is to reduce the amount of special education may be questioned. Perhaps these are not in all respects or situations in conflict; perhaps in some they strengthen each other.

The possibility that special education may also be general education is often discussed in terms of the specificity or the generality of subject matter taught. It has been brilliantly discussed in this way by Whitehead. "Mathematics, well taught, should be the most powerful instrument in gradually implanting this generality of idea." "Work should be transfused with intellectual and moral vision."

The possibility may also be put forward in terms of special capacities and interests in relation to general knowledge. It may be argued that one effective means to the understanding of general principles is the development of the idiosyncratic and the personal. General education may in part be reached, not necessarily by telling pupils what is generally true of the world or of the people in it, but by encouraging a personal discovery in that child or young person of the universality that is represented in himself and his own particular situation. The child's realization of the consequences, now not only for himself but for others similarly situated or differently situated, of the fact that his father is a dockworker or a judge, is a contribution to his general education. The understanding of the place of his mathematical or artistic aptitudes and interests in the distribution of all aptitudes and interests in his community is a part of his general education that may be forwarded as those aptitudes are cultivated and exercised.

Education is in part a coming to see one's self *sub specie aeternitatis*. One's special nature is the seed of that development of understanding. In college many a young person experiences both personal relief and also a development of his general understanding when he sees, perhaps suddenly, the political opinions at his breakfast table as the product of general social and economic conditions, or when, for the first time, he sees, even though superficially, his own inner life in the general categories provided by Freud.

Should every child or young person receive the same general educa·tion? The question cannot receive an unqualified negative because all life is a learning and living with generalizations of different kinds. It cannot be answered in an unqualified affirmative, because every experience is fresh and tends to be related to, if not indeed to seem to spring from, one's unique nature and life. No two people read the Great Books the same way. The special qualities of individuals and of groups are to be developed both for the contribution that development makes to the division of labor and the variety of persons in our society, but also, and probably at the same time, for the insight they provide that individual in recognizing the generality of the world and human experience.

Should Negroes receive the same education as other people? Yes and no. They should be given the same opportunities to choose and guide their learning as others. Their special situation in our sociey is, however, their special basis for understanding the general nature of all things. To make an education for them which ignored their special situation would be to deceive them and the rest of us, and—as happens indeed in the higher education of Negroes—to cause them to arrive at frustration and confusion. Their special position in our society is also general: a situation of disadvantaged groups susceptible of general understanding. It provides a cause and purpose that are special to Negroes, in one sense, and common to all Americans in another. The ends and the failures of democracy are special in the Negro, and general too. Negroes can learn some important general principles with advantages lacking to others.

Should women receive the same education as men? Yes and no—as answered above as to Negroes. To talk in schools and colleges to girls and women as if their situation were in all respects like that of men is to impede that access to general understanding which their special situation provides. The understanding and cultivation of one's own special situation is to anchor the generality of education in the firmest possible relevance and motivation: the discovery of one's self.

These considerations suggest a complication—a desirable complication —in the nature of the generality sought in education. The right total education for our country is an education in which some understandings or competences are general in the sense that everybody has them and also an education in which everyone understands his own situation in relation to some generality. Our society requires that everybody—more or less— have some common understandings as to manners, the use of highways and doorknobs, and our ideals of individual responsibility and democratic justice. It is also desirable that the mind and spirit of each one of us be liberated from the narrowness of the particular into the interests and excitements of the general. As to this latter educational end it is not necessary that all people see the same generalization, although it is of course better if each has the power to understand something of the generalization of somebody else. But liberal education may be perhaps distinguished from general education in just this respect: an education is general in so far as it gives us a common language, a common means of life, and a common conception of what life is or ought to be; while education is liberal in so far as it carries forward into wider contexts of significance the powers and position of the individual.

EDUCATIONAL PRACTICE: GENERAL EDUCATION AS CONFORMITY

The foregoing is talk about what education should or could be. It is also relevant to this inquiry to ask what it currently is. The practices of any body of educational institutions may be different, both in means and in effects, from what is desired and from what people think they are. Accepting the premise of this inquiry—that problems of education may be clarified by discussion—one may also hold that clarification may be aided by better knowledge of what really goes on.

The issue now raised is, of course, one of fact. It can be answered by finding out what the facts are, by "research." As to such questions (as will at once be suggested), the research needed is not limited inquiry by formal technical methods into the measurable effects of this educational practice or that or into this mental or personal quality or that. It is an inquiry, guided by conceptions as to the *desirable* kinds of general and special effects of educational activities, into the actual kinds of general and special effects of educational activities and into the actual kinds of general and specific effects that in fact come about. The investigator begins by defining what general or specific understandings, capacities, or attitudes ought to be developed in those young people there, and goes to find out, by whatever observations and inferences seem to him persuasive, what such general or specific qualities are in fact developed in them. The choice of educational end determines the questions to be asked in studying the particular school, class, or educational practice.

We might, for instance, define as a desirable end of education the establishment in every American of a respect for individual difference and a will and courage to express, and make effective, one's own special powers and one's own judgment and opinion in fair relation to those of others. One might then inquire if current educational practice has in fact this result.

As in other research, inquiry is best guided by a "hypothesis," a sense of a special problem to be inquired into. In connection with the topic here proposed, illustratively, for investigation into the facts, one may venture to make several related, tentatively held assumptions as to the real state of things—these to be tested and supported or rejected, as particular facts in particular schools and elsewhere require.

Hypothesis: There is a tendency in current American education to achieve conformity and call it general education. In the achievement of this conformity respect for individual difference and responsibility to make effective one's own specific differences tend to be lost. In early primary education "socialization" tends to be identified with amenability to the immediate expectations of the group or with compliance and unimaginative participation in group activities. In later primary, secondary, and higher education, the pressures of class and neighborhood to conform are supported by the school's emphasis on "standards," "social adjustment," "ability to cope," and "democracy." That which makes the individual like the others is safe for him and brings apparent results to the educator; such conformities fit in well with the practical problems of organizing education for large masses, with the individual's need for security, with the current emphasis on social adaptiveness in relation to mental health, and with the anxieties and fears of Americans of the present time. The "hypothesis," in short, is that with the intention of accomplishing an education general to all we are producing our own kind of "Group Think."

Such a general hypothesis could be tested by reducing the inquiry to more special questions of fact, answerable in particular educational situations, such as: When a child is encouraged to make his own decision, what happens if he makes a decision contrary to the expectations of teacher or group? What happens to the child who prefers to be alone? Is the creative element in delinquency recognized? When habits of conformity are established is the distinction recognized between conformities which are simply usefully expedient, those which exemplify moral principles ("waiting one's turn"), and those which merely result from the demands of the group without allowance for individual difference? Are decisions put forward as those made by the group genuinely of this character; is an individual's decision a real expression of his will (fake student government is worse than academic tyranny)?

It is suggested that the most fruitful clarification of fundamental questions of education is that which is stimulated and guided by inquiry into what education actually is.

THE EDUCATIONAL EXPERIENCE: EXPLORATION, CONVERSATION, CREATION

EXPLORATION

Education is a desirable experience of a particular kind, in this respect like falling in love, joy, and the state of grace. It is a good thing that happens inside people. As a teacher, I often think of education as something I am doing to somebody else, but I must admit that I am not often sure that I have done it. In my own self I feel now and then the educational experience, and in the lives of others I see its signs.

Its causes are obscure, but I should not be a teacher if I did not think that there is much that can be done to bring about this kind of desirable experience. Formal arrangements favorable to education are more effective, I suppose, than are formal arrangements for falling in love. I would not close the schools or give up forums for adult discussion. But to judge the success of any particular such arrangement, one must be able to recognize the educational experience when it occurs.

The word "growth" suggests the upward change that is education. An inner something improves. The growth takes place in qualities of the intellect and of appreciation, in qualities we dignify with large words: understanding, insight, wisdom. In our kind of society, where all are to take part in making decisions, these qualities are needed by everyone. So we make a beginning with their development in the home and in the schools, and try to remember—although we often forget—that it is only a beginning and that education has no end. After we leave school, the world continues to affect us. The factory disciplines or hurts us; the neighbors and our associates shape us in their own image; the voice of the radio has its insistent way with us. If as grown men and women we do not trouble to continue our education, the world will make us in its own way, good or bad.

In thinking about education it is helpful to distinguish training, something also desirable and indeed indispensable, but of a lower order. Training is the formation of useful habits. In spite of claims to the contrary, there are no educated horses, only trained ones. Like animals, men form useful habits, and some are habits no animal can form, like speech and literacy. Training serves two ends: it prepares us to do useful work, and it frees the mind for education. A great deal of training is given in

A series of three lectures, sponsored by the Fund for Adult Education, delivered December 6, 7, and 8, 1954, at Riverside, Santa Barbara, and Berkeley and Los Angeles, California. Copyright 1955, The American Foundation for Continuing Education. Reprinted with permission.

that which we call "technical education." There is a conflict between technical education and liberal education only in so far as the technical education stops at training. Unfortunately it often does.

In adult life there is at least one circumstance favorable to carrying on an education: maturity. For making the discriminations and judgments implied by the word "wisdom," some years of experience are helpful. If one arrives at maturity with some training achieved, one is at least prepared for education. Training comes easier in youth than it does later. But although there is some correspondence of youth with training and of maturity with education, either can happen at any time of life. An occasional grandmother learns Greek grammar. The education of children may begin when they are very young indeed. Often its beginnings are by accident, through some book or person that illumines and gives wider significance to the world around the child.

The very young experience also education by intention. When Edmund Gosse was not yet four, he watched his father draw a chart of markings on the carpet, then of the furniture in the room, then of the floor of the house, then of the garden. The child was too young to draw the plan himself. He just watched. Gosse tells us that as a result "geography came to me of itself, as a perfectly natural arrangement of objects." This was education; the child caught an insight of fundamental worth about the nature of geographic representation.

While we are distinguishing education from things like it but different, let us acknowledge that education is not the same as the pursuit of information or even of learning. One may acquire information only and so become a bore. One may acquire learning only and so become a pedant. For a striking example of a bore, see old Joseph Finsbury in *The Wrong Box*, of whom it is written that "a taste for information had sapped his manhood." For an outstanding pedant, see Dr. Middleton of Meredith's novel, *The Egoist*. To convert knowledge into education it must be leavened with imagination and carried forward into the life one lives with others. Knowledge cherished as a private possession, learning pursued in a cell of life separated from the other rooms of existence, does not educate.

Perhaps the commonest confusion identifies education with schooling. But anyone who has had schooling, even in a good school, knows that many hours are passed there, sometimes very pleasantly, that are not educational. When we have built a school building and hired teachers, the problems and the uncertainties of education are just beginning. The abundance of schools conceals the rarity of education. One of the reasons why the education of adults is a field ripe for development lies in the fact that so many of us leave school with most of the job yet to be done. Necessary as it is to have schools and to improve what goes on in them, they

are, for some people, dispensable. Education has taken place with little
or no schooling, or in spite of it. The case of Abraham Lincoln will be
always remembered. One of our able American writers, Richard Wright,
became an educated man by extracurricular self-teaching, and accomplished this although the influences of his childhood were chiefly those of
ignorance, vice, violence, and fear. His education began with a school-
teacher, but out of school. She boarded with his family and one day read
him the story of *Bluebeard and His Seven Wives.* Wright tells us "the
tale made the world around me be, throb, live. As she spoke, reality
changed, the look of things altered, and the world became peopled with
magical presences. My sense of life deepened and the feel of things was
deepened, somehow." His grandmother beat him for listening to this story;
she called it "the Devil's work." But with it his education began. The
paths to education are various and curious. The young Negro boy, his
imagination aroused, then feasted on sensational stories in the newspaper
supplements, moved on to forge an order that got him a book from a library closed to colored people and to read his first serious novel, *Main
Street.*

Many a man who has produced major works of the mind has found
his formal schooling of no importance in his development. Henry Adams
reckoned his school days as time thrown away and remarked of his experience at Harvard that "the entire work of the four years could have
been easily put into the work of any four months in after life." This
evaluation should encourage those of us who set about educating ourselves after leaving school. In his memoirs Charles Darwin wrote of the
Shrewsbury school—outside of which he now sits in stone, a benevolent,
bearded figure—that "nothing could have been worse for the development of my mind than Dr. Butler's school . . . as a means of education
to me it was simply a blank." He regarded the three years he had spent
at Cambridge University as completely wasted; Edinburgh University
"sickened" him and the only effect on him of the geology lecture was,
he says, "a determination never again to read a book on geology." It
may be added that Darwin overcame this particular school-acquired
repugnance, for it was a reading of Lyell's *Principles of Geology* that so
stimulated his mind during the famous voyage of the "Beagle."

Of course, very many have in school more fortunate experiences.
Schools we must have, and better ones than we now have. But the dependence of education upon schooling is not absolute, and no school
and university together do anything more, at the best, than get education started. The men who became educated in spite of what happened
to them in classrooms remind us how great is the self-educability of
a determined person.

Such a person, adult and resolute, may make his own education in his own way. No particular program is right for everyone. Distrust the claim that someone has found the ultimate curriculum, the right way to learn for all men. Some elements of education men must have in common with one another so that in their societies they share common purposes, common understandings as to the good life. But formal programs of education result not so much from the nature of man, which is various enough to find many different roads to education, as from the necessities of teaching twenty adults in a room or ten thousand children in a school system. Programs are needed, but each is suspect, because a program tends to say, "Conform," when the true end is, "Be yourself." To meet together, as adults, and discuss what we have read in some of the great works of the mind is as good a program of adult education as I know. It is good because the examples of thought and appreciation are among the greatest and because the ideas offered for our consideration are among the most important. On the other hand, no list of books is sure to provide the best education for everyone, and there are times when minds go forward fastest through lesser books, even bad ones, or away from books entirely. What matters is that one find a way, orderly enough for that one, in which to promote, in pleasure and in pain, the inner growth of which I speak.

Consider the variety of the paths by which men have become educated in school and out. Some of us in America look with admiration at the achievements of classical schooling in the French lycée or the German gymnasium. When the circumstances were just right, the education resulting was indeed impressive. An example of this is provided by the account given of his schooling by André Maurois. His was a bookish family, devoted to education. His mother read aloud to him, poetry especially, when he was a very small boy; he himself learned to read very young and lay in a lilac tree and read Perrault, Hans Christian Andersen, and Jules Verne. From his sixth to his eighth year private teachers taught him the beginnings of English, German, and music. In the junior lycée he found no more than ten or twelve boys in classes instructed by teachers who were educated men devoting themselves with passion to the task of molding successive generations of young Frenchmen. So at the age of ten Maurois made his maiden speech before the class on the subject, "A Comparison of the Esther of Racine with that of the Bible." He was then studying Latin and reading Gogol and Pushkin. At twelve, no prodigy but just a rapidly educated child, Maurois composed a tragedy in five acts in verse about the mistress of Charles the Mad. Such literature as Maupassant and Anatole France he read in these years; in the senior lycée he discovered the Latin and the French poets and learned these so well that hundreds of passages remained "by heart"—Ronsard, Victor Hugo, Baudelaire. The essays he wrote weekly were on such a subject as this: letter of Conrart, Permanent Secretary of the Académie Française, to Saint-Evremond in defense of the Académie against the latter's satire. His last year in the lycée was devoted to philosophy. For ten years his attention had been concentrated on matters of form, grammar, style. "Now," he says, "the heavens were lighted up. Epictetus and Epicurus, Plato and Aristotle, Descartes and Spinoza, Locke and Kant, Hegel and Bergson, contended for mastery in our minds." And so on.

Some think such an education impossible in America where so many are to be educated, and some think it undesirable even if it could be provided. In Maurois's case it was possible and appropriate because of French culture and French social conditions. I speak of it as a contrast to the educations which have occurred without such special and fortunate provisions. In spite of Henry Adams' disclaimers, he did manage to get an education, and I suspect he is not quite right in saying that Harvard did not help. Darwin's path to education was indeed largely outside the school; he became educated in the course of his research; he held, year after year, an extraordinary private conversation with nature, asking questions and receiving answers. He began this course while still a schoolboy, and, as his record in school suffered, with collecting box and inquiring mind he was educating himself, in a specialized way, in valleys and upland.

I have known intimately at least one authentically self-educated man. He is a Maya Indian living in a remote bush village in Yucatan. His few years of schooling at a primitive school taught him only the Spanish language, and a little reading and writing. Later, while he was active in affairs of his village, leading it toward material improvement, he developed a habit of reading. He read newspapers, school primers, religious tracts, and government handouts on farming or hoof-and-mouth disease. He obtained a Bible; this was a tremendous help to him; he read the stories slowly and thought and talked about what he read. His education advanced by a sort of natural method, in which his mind moved back and forth between the problems of conduct and action in which he was himself engaged and the ideas his forceful mind found in anything and everything he read. At one time he planned to kill a man he thought was doing him to death with black magic; he discussed with himself the plan in relation to suggestions he had from reading the Gospel and decided against it. At another time he studied a pamphlet about marketing, read in the newspaper the reports of grain prices in distant stock exchanges, and worked out for himself a relationship between the price of corn in his own local market and the quotations in the newspaper. This man had a slow, powerful curiosity about everything, and the course of his education, limited as it was, was carried along in strong convictions of his responsibility to do right and to help the progress of his village. He is a really admirable example of the self-taught.

Cases such as these are not common. Even in America, a country where universal compulsory education got an early start, where public libraries began, and where lectures for laymen have been popular for generations, today the education of the adult is not encouraged by abundant good example. Very few of the people around us are pursuing their education. Very much of what goes on in public life presents examples that it would be fatal to imitate if one were seeking to develop one's own free and rational mind. And base examples are even admired by many Americans who have had what in America is called education. After we have made a tremendous effort to put every child in school and very many in college, the appalling fact remains that today many adults follow a voice that, with lies and threats, betrays and degrades education and is hateful toward the educated. On the other hand, when an unusual man in public life makes a speech that treats his audience with the respect due to reasonable and moral men, the impression on many Americans is extraordinarily bracing. Then again we see the possibilities of helping one another to grow in wisdom.

Where are men and women to meet in America to help one another with education? The Danes found the right community for continuing education in those residential groups, the folk high schools and colleges. In England the workers' education movement has achieved much. Here we may yet find, in occupational groups, in clubs, in widespread organization of adult discussion, or in further extension of college teaching into many local communities, the kinds of associations that will be right for us.

Perhaps some homes may be redeemed for the mutual education of their members. Many a home presents some favorable elements: an association of people who have a natural concern with one another and who, even nowadays, frequently meet. Moreover, some of the inhabitants may be directly involved in education already, in so far as they are in school. Intellectual and aesthetic exchange with a child, especially one's own, can be educational to both parties. Taste in literature is subject to cultivation in children's books; I can see even before my child can that *The Tailor of Gloucester* is a distinguished work of literature, although it was written as much for the child as for me. Some things one learns best from people of one's own age, but some things are well learned in family relationships because it is these that give the experiences their early significance and beauty. For the adult, too, the learning or relearning takes fresh value when the ideas and discriminations are exchanged with a younger person. When I went over the elements of Euclid with my daughter, I learned things about geometry that school had never taught me, and reading with my son some of the Federalist papers gave me understanding of our Founding Fathers that I should never have gained otherwise.

It is not safe to assume that the school is discharging educational functions that were once carried on in the home. The school is doing things notably different from what was done in the large, old-fashioned families of our grandfathers. When reading was taught in some homes in connection with the reading aloud of the Bible or of other literature, it was no doubt taught less efficiently than it is taught in schools today, but it was taught as a part of intimate and traditional life. Teachers recognize that the school cannot provide this kind of stimulation to read for the sake of what is in the book and also for the sake of the personal experience in which the reading takes place. Nowadays, thinking of reading only as a technique, the usual parent leaves it to the school. The school, too, thinks of it on the whole as a technique, for that is what it is in the context of learning which the school provides. The teacher tries, against great difficulties, to bring about in the child a set of "good reading habits," with a common result, I fear, that a bored, bright child acquires the only really serious bad habit—the habit of not reading at all. It may yet turn out to be good educational policy to encourage that occasional family in which books are read and read by one to another to teach the children to read before they go to school. My impression is that because of the plans of the school about the teaching of reading, such families are now hesitant to do so. Learning to read arises best in the context of a delight in books. And there will be no growth in such delight until it grows among the adults who make the homes where it flourishes. So the future of the children's schooling and the future of adult education are intertwined.

These preliminary reflections evoke the difficulties of identifying that kind of experience which is truly educational. If education is not training or information or mere learning, if it is not always to be found in school and may take place out of it, if most of us live lives filled with work, recreation, visits with the neighbors, and just sinking back into the Sunday supplement, and if we see around us little to stimulate the effort toward reasonable understanding of the universe—if all this is true, by what shall we know that stranger, that shy one, the educational experience?

I think that something of its nature can be learned from those reflective persons who have told us how it happened to them. These evidences may be joined with what each of us knows of how it happened, at certain times, that his mind and spirit took a leap forward. As a teacher, occasionally, and as a learner, also occasionally, I have knowledge of my own such movements of the mind to contribute to the evidence as to the nature of that inner growth which is education.

In the best book about this subject that I have read, *The Aims of Education*, A. N. Whitehead describes the education of children and young people as a movement of the mind from freedom through discipline to freedom again. The mind begins in a phase of imaginative discovery of experience. There is a free ranging of thought and appreciation. This is the first of the three periods which Whitehead sees. It corresponds with the first twelve years or so of life and with primary education. It is followed, he tells us, by a stage of precision, corresponding with secondary education, in which additional facts are put into systematic order. And this is followed by a mature stage, ordinarily begun in higher education, when again there is freedom to range but in which, now, general ideas are entertained under control of the discipline that has been acquired.

Here I look not at the sequence of stages in the mental growth and schooling of the young, but at the mind's movement in any educational experience, brief or long, in young or old. I am thinking of how you and I add to our education, now, in any effort of the kind that we may make, from striving to understand the meaning for us of a novel we are reading, to the pursuit, perhaps under guidance of a university, of some course of lectures or discussions. As Whitehead sees a cycle, I, too, see a cycle; indeed, it is probably he who caused me to see it. I see a movement of the mind that begins as a free reaching outward, impelled by curiosity, wonder, excitement. I see the mind next pass through a sort of contest, a conversation of alternatives or between this event and that idea, in difficult and fruitful interaction. And then, if education happens, there is a third phase of the cycle in which the new fact or idea or experience is made a part of me; I act, internally, with regard to it. In the rest of the present lecture I shall speak of the first phase; the second and third phases provide the topics for the other lectures of the series.

Education arises out of the universal impulse to explore the world around us. Aristotle wrote that philosophy begins in wonder. He might have added—perhaps he did—that so does education. One may receive training by merely adjusting to the expectation of the teacher, but one cannot become educated without a sense of wonder at what no teacher is quite prepared to explain. There are glimpses of significance that stir mind and soul together; these are what make education possible.

Of course one is not educated by just wondering. A zestful feeling about the universe, with nothing added, may yield, at best, a vague happiness. Education requires much more: a respect for reason and the hard and troublesome use of it. Nevertheless, in considering first the disposition to explore, I attend to a necessary precondition of the educational experience.

In children the impulse to explore, to wonder, is very powerful. Many a reminiscence connects some childhood stirring of the imagination with later development. Maurois recalls the poems read to him by his mother when he was very young. He asked for certain of these poems, one about a bugler sounding the charge and a fair-haired youth of seventeen. Many years later he writes, "Perhaps these poems were very bad; I do not want to know and I have never reread them; they gave me my first literary emotions. I could not hear them wthout weeping. But . . . they were sweet and comforting tears and I think they made me better." The English contemporary novelist Joyce Cary writes of a small child—perhaps himself—seeing an amateur performance of *The Tempest*. In retrospect, he was completely astonished and his sensations were so new that he had no comparison for them; they were experiences of a new kind. The impact of the words, "Hang, cur, hang, you whoreson, insolent noisemaker," he felt

as a real insult; they gave me a shock of delight and anxiety. I looked anxiously at the boatswain to see how he could take them, and when I saw that he did not answer at all but simply went on shouting orders to the crew, I felt a deep admiration and sense of discovery. That's the right way to behave, I felt; I thrilled to the wise boatswain, brave and independent.

He goes on to say that, except for a few lines, he could later repeat nothing of the play, but

thousands of musical phrases, of half-understood images, had fallen upon my senses enriching them as if by three or four years of ordinary seasonal falls, flower, harvest, leaf and snow, so that I felt dizzy with the weight of experience. . . . Words like beauty, death, love, took living form and sang in my head like angels.

This, Cary recalls, is the child's exploration.

It is difficult to suppress the sense of wonder in children. Even when we try to do so, it bursts forth. Edmund Gosse's puritanical mother forbade him to read any fiction. At the bottom of an old trunk he found fragments of a sensational novel. It filled him with delicious fears. Denied even a visit to the zoo, I suppose lest it stir his mind to evil thoughts, the child invented a private world of strange beliefs in which he could make the butterflies in his father's natural histories come alive, or send himself, during morning prayers, up to a cornice from there to gaze down upon his other self.

For a long time now the books that adults have produced to be used in teaching children have on the whole done what they could to discourage this essential exploration and wonder. I read in a letter he wrote Coleridge that Charles Lamb deplored the dull and formal knowledge of schoolbooks of his day which failed, he wrote, to stimulate "that beautiful interest in wild tales which made the child a man." The primers of today are still decorous and dull, as John Hersey and his neighbors found in their study this year of reading in their local schools. Tests may show that children learn to pass reading tests as well as ever, but is there important improvement in encouraging the beautiful interest in wild tales? There seems to be some doubt as to whether children's programs on radio and television have this effect. There is evidence that some children are overstimulated to nervousness or to delinquency by the sensational in comics or in television. It may be, nevertheless, that the greater evil is that they are not stimulated enough. What I am told by the very young suggests that the differences between one cowboy and another, or one space-man and another, are not remarkable; they do not send the mind into great experience and discovery. Perhaps they chiefly prepare the young for absorbing the adult equivalent of these productions—the bland and undemanding stories of the weekly supplements, the digests, and the untroubling flow of oddments in back pages of the newspaper.

It is the adult, not the child, however, who must look to his sense of wonder. It is a sense that languishes in later life. Education begins in wonder and ends in routine. In Guatemala I was struck with the freshness and alertness of the Indian children as compared with the closed, finished, undemanding mental qualities of the grown men and women. In Chicago I often have the same experience. Yet here, at least, an occasional child becomes an interesting and educated adult. The pressures to conformity everywhere are hard on the sense of wonder. In primitive society they are pressures to understand a few things, as others understand them, very well. In civilized society they require that each understand a little about more things, as the people immediately around one do. The former conformation produces individuals who are deep in a very small world; the latter produces individuals floating about on the top of a very large one.

Not many adults maintain the sense of wonder. Some do in connection with the work they care most about. One of our distinguished biologists, Professor Curt Stern, in his Sigma Xi National Lecture this year, told us that after twenty-five years of looking at the little fruit fly, *Drosophila,* each time he finds fresh delight. He marvels "at the clear-cut form of the head with red eyes, the antennae, the elaborate mouthparts; at the arch of the sturdy thorax bearing a pair of beautiful iridescent, transparent wings." He is particularly delighted by the bristles: "With surrealistic clarity the dark colored bristles and hairs project from the light brownish surface of the animal, delicate and stiff, in rigid symmetry." He finds this view fascinating and compares it, in interesting contrast, to the glow of a young skin in a human being. Now this is a persistence of the sense of wonder and delight that we can envy. With this to sustain him, it is no wonder that Professor Stern is finding out important things about the nature of life.

Perhaps a sense of wonder, a disposition to explore, is just a gift. Some men do exercise the gift. G. K. Chesterton did. He persistently looked at the world through his legs, with astonishing and valuable results. I cannot tell you how to preserve and cultivate the imagination. It will probably continue to develop if you find some enigma, great or small, and keep working toward understanding of it. You may find it in the workings of machines, or, better, of men. A good book published not long ago, titled *The True Believer,* is about a rigid and fanatical kind of mind that is at the moment making trouble for our world. It was written by a longshoreman in his spare time. He persisted in exploring; he struggled with the ideas that came out of the human nature he explored.

Adults are not confined to an imposed curriculum. If habit quiets the sense of wonder, on the other hand, the opportunities for education widen, as does experience in later life. We may explore tools, fields and woods, people, events, difficulties, and possibilities. Everywhere there is something in which to discover beauty and truth, appreciation and understanding, poetry and science. The hindrances to education are enormous; the helps no less surprising. Out of the radio and the phonograph disc came an unpredictable development in American musical taste. Now, we find a fresh field of educational exploration in, of all places, the drugstore. The shelves holding the cheap paper-bound books are a major project in adult education. Included are some of the very best books ever written and also not quite the worst. To order them in worthiness, with good reasons, would educate anybody.

I agree with the assertion (by Robert M. Hutchins) that "the prime object of education is to know . . . the goods in their order." The heart of the educational experience is to distinguish the better from the worse. This is true, whether the good is sought in books, music, politics, or men. Education is a struggle to build one's self by making clear one's own order among goods. That which is most appropriate to human beings is the sense of value. It is, as Whitehead says, "the ultimate motive power." It "imposes on life incredible labours, and apart from it, life sinks back into the passivity of its slower types." Education is improvement in judgment about values. We can take the world as we find it and accept that lower passivity. Or we can undertake the labors and pursue an education.

As we explore the order among goods, how do we know that it is a better good to which we come? There is no proof that will satisfy every seeker. There is no argument that will satisfy everyone that the pursuit of order among goods brings the seeker to the better, not the worse. There are many who have no zest for the search, because they say each order of goods is special to him who holds it, or to the tribe or nation from which he takes his directions of search. Yet simple things may be said that have weight with him who thinks, as I do, that it is at least true that some order of goods is discoverable by education.

There is the evidence of one's own private convictions: one makes judgments on one's own success in discovering better books or music. There is at least the feeling that in the course of education one has clarified the judgments which, for instance, condemn the demagogue and approve the democrat.

There is, too, the evidence provided by the sequence usual in the development of the human beings around me. The boy collects marbles or pictures of baseball players, then perhaps seeks understanding of machinery, and if he ever seeks understanding of morals and of art, he does so when more fully grown. To pursue the goods in the reverse order would not seem to us educational. It would be climbing down a ladder when you want to go up. If one remains throughout life with the marbles and the ball players, education is clearly arrested.

In every part of the world, among savages or civilized people, men and women postpone some immediate and material satisfactions for some remote moral or spiritual ends. In this, all cultures are alike. All peoples distinguish the desired from the desirable: everywhere there is an order of goods that can be explored and be more fully understood. In the more civilized societies these orders of goods come to be examined, criticized, and refined. In both the West and the Orient they are in part expressed in the form of a series of progressive stages in a man's life: in both parts of the world one is urged to conduct one's self so as to grow in wisdom and so as to leave less worthy things for nobler. Adult education has justification in every system of thought.

The differences of judgment as to what is better and what is worse, as between one man and another, or one tribe or nation and another, are of course great. But they are not unlimited. Those who compare the customs of mankind are nowadays more and more inclined, I think, to recognize the wide and general similarities among the orderings of values that have been reached by peoples in all parts of the world. For instance, capricious violence against a person of one's intimate group is everywhere regarded as an evil; very generally loyalty, hospitality, and courage of some kinds receive positive evaluation. And certain broad trends of development have occurred in men's ideas of good and evil: the condemnation of slavery; the rising, widening recognition of human dignity and individual growth. The judgment that Hitler had the wrong order of goods is not likely to be reversed; and it is at least an open question if his victory by arms would have much delayed that verdict. Very few people who have given up cannibalism return to the practice, and when torture is re-introduced in modern times, the practice is, after the event, even by the torturers more often deplored than admired.

If one seeks education as an effort to seek excellence, in work and play, in art and in ethics, one thereby widens the circle of those whose judgments as to these matters may support or may test his own. Education multiplies the minds in communication with our own. Alone we are not; we may find him who shares our struggle to judge well our present ordering of values almost anywhere—next door, across the world, or speaking to us from the past out of a book.

None of these considerations may keep this man or that from throwing up the whole business as too uncertain. Why seek so indeterminate an order of goods? Nevertheless, the simple observations I have just made set forth the fact that on the whole the human race has kept at it. I am one of many today who neither seek nor hope to find a source of authority for ultimate judgments as to the good. I think each must struggle to find it for himself. I am sure that you and I shall never agree on the same detailed order of goods among many things. And if one says that there is an order of goods that is true for all men, there is another who says it is not so. For the pursuit of education I do not see that it is necessary that either view prevail. I think it will be generally admitted that all human beings recognize some hierarchy of values and that those who recognize education as an organized activity see its desired course as a movement up the hierarchy. Education will serve either to discover value in the universe or to create it. Education is to make the soul grow.

In this lecture I have talked only of the first surge of the mind in which the educational experience begins. Alone, this movement outward does not assure growth in understanding of excellence. The surge may simply ebb again, the gleam die, the interest sink to nothing, or become no more than excitement and pleasurable sensations. To understand fully the nature of education we should have to go on to see what next the mind does as it educates itself; how alternative considerations, or facts and ideas difficult to relate to each other, are taken up in a disciplined struggle. We should go on also to examine the outcome of this struggle in the improved understanding and discrimination achieved by the learner, so that what is learned is thereby added to the learner, changing, and by that much, however little, improving him. We should be talking about the entire cycle of effort and achievement which is the educational experience.

The surge outward is, however, an indispensable beginning. How free are we nowadays to take advantage of it if it occurs? We may look about us to see if minds are ready and willing and unrestrained to look into the remarkable universe. We may ask ourselves if ideas are freely entertained in America, in our local communities. Are we encouraged to pursue adventures of the mind? Are we restrained from pursuing those adventures in certain directions? The possibilities of educating ourselves are as wide as the climate of freedom allows. I think it must be admitted that in recent years the climate has taken a turn for the worse. In this period of fear and danger, the ceiling of permitted visibility has, I think, somewhat closed down. We are discouraged from looking in certain directions. We Americans, free as we are in comparison with many millions of other men, are far from perfectly free to undertake adventures of the mind. This is the year in which many teachers admit that they avoid talking about subjects that might get them into trouble, in which books have been taken from public shelves because the opinions of the writers are suspect, in which takers of public opinion polls report a growing reluctance of citizens to express their views on many a public issue. We just do not want to get into trouble, and trouble can come from expression of an opinion or an idea. These are times when heresy, once a matter of religious doctrine, has been seen to arise again, now in connection with political orthodoxy. Safety is to be found in the middle of the road of thought; and if the mind moves too far in that direction that is seen by people not merely as leftward but also as sinister, one is in danger. Reputations and careers are threatened or destroyed by the fact that one once had opinions over in that direction, or even that one consorted with others who had them. Advisors to the government are excluded from counsels of public policy chiefly because they were once wrong, or because their opinions on some issues coincided, but for quite other reasons, with the views of Communists. Many a man finds himself in some situation of action or employment or mere uneasy association with his fellow workers or neighbors in which he is not free to explore such questions as world government, or the employment of Communists, or the ideas of Karl Marx, or even simple political issues of the moment. Speakers with opinions unpopular to local minorities are denied a hall in which to speak; discussions of the United Nations in public schools come under criticism and are restrained or suspended.

This is the year in which a bill was introduced in Congress that would deny mailing privileges for publications and films which contain material that "explicitly or by implication favors the political, economic, international, and governmental doctrines of Communism or other totalitarian government." This is the year in which four American colleges refused to allow their students to debate the question whether American diplomatic recognition should be given the Chinese Communist government. As the Japanese in the days of their authorization rule forbade the publication or utterance of ideas that were "dangerous thought," so now we avoid or even forbid anything that is "controversial." Forgetting that the United States of America could not have come into existence without controversy, and that controversy, ruled by reason, is the very breath of American life, we now make the mere participation of a citizen in discussion or advocacy of a politically sensitive issue a cause for putting him aside. In many places we do not trust ourselves to reach wise judgments by free and open discussion of issues. Even the special committee of the Atomic Energy Commission, in reviewing the Oppenheimer case, reported to the American people that the regulations under which they worked prevented them from the exercise of a mature practical judgment. In all these events we see a growing disposition to curb the minds of Americans, to prevent ourselves from using imagination and intelligence to reach answers.

It appears, then, that if the surge of the mind to explore even the unpopular and the dangerous idea is subject to restraints, the effort to do so is not only a contribution to one's own education, but an effort on behalf of the freedom of us all. Freedom and education depend on a common principle: that as the mind grows it may dare any idea, try out every speculation, consider every issue, so that reason and fact sort the better from the worse and bring us a step nearer truth. We are as free as we allow ourselves to be. No, we are as free as we allow others to be. If I deny the right of my fellow citizen to debate such an issue of real importance to us all as the political recognition of Communist China, or to discuss with entire openness of mind the worth of what Marx wrote, I am in effect limiting my own liberty. For we are committed to the making of a society through intelligent and informed opinion. The policing of ideas is abhorrent to our principles. Education can go forward if we keep ourselves free to explore and to test ideas. Education is both the exercise and the defense of freedom.

CONVERSATION

The experience that results in education is a successful adventure with difficulties on the way. Impelled by the wonder and puzzle of things, the mind and spirit start out toward destinations not clearly seen. But soon the way is temporarily blocked. Across it lie ideas, facts, possibilities, and implications that demand to be dealt with before the traveler may go on. There is a period of struggle, mixed of pain and joy. The struggle is a give-and-take; this confronts that, a position is corrected by another position. There seem to be two sides, or more, to the engagement. But the outcome, if it be education, is not so much destruction as creation. That which lay across the path has made the traveler grow, and he proceeds, now taller than he was.

This metaphor suggests the movement of the mind in the education of child or man. The three parts of the tale fit the three lectures of this series. In the first I spoke of the outward impulse to explore. In this one I consider the struggle on the road. The growth that results is my subject in the third.

The struggle on the road is the effort to make sense of an idea or a fact that makes difficulties or opens possibilities for a view of things that has already entered the mind. So the struggle is a talking back and forth. It is not a contest in which A tries to destroy B; it is a conversation in which A and B each speaks for himself while attending to the other. The struggle arises in the traveler's mind: how is this B to be taken into account, to be arranged with reference to A? We are educated through conversational struggles in which nobody loses.

"The Socratic dialogue is the mirror of pedagogy," writes Robert Hutchins. Is this true?

It is said as to education, not as to learning. One learns some things by sitting down and memorizing them. The combinations of the multiplication table are best learned, not by discussing their merits, but by repetition and the formation of habitual associations. In learning much grammar, some elements of geography and chronology, and many other things, conversation would be merely troublesome. Some things are best learned without debate; these are the tools of the mind. They are acquired by training; they are not education but are important means thereto. Such things, once learned, are "put out of the mind."

On the other side, in qualification of the importance of dialogue, it is to be recognized that some understandings come to us swiftly and directly, without explicit discussion. In reading a history or a biography, an insight may appear within the mind as an instantaneous apparition. A vision is vouchsafed; a significance is grasped. We have no rules for assuring the discovery of order in the universe. The great insights of scientist and artist alike come unpredictably, capriciously. So it is with the course of ordinary understanding. Exploration and creation may seem to come one immediately on the other.

Nevertheless, it is in arranging for conversations that there is possibility of education as an organized effort. The truth of Mr. Hutchins' statement is its recognition of the importance of deliberate and guided discussion for making mind and spirit grow. "Teaching, like midwifery," he adds, "is a co-operative art."

The Socratic dialogue is not so much a mirror of education as it is a model (as Hutchins, indeed, elsewhere calls it). There are many educational conversations that do not rise so high. People with little to guide them enter into exchanges of views that move their minds. I remember conversations between peasant women in a village in Yucatan; in one the topic of the dialogue was the nature of the soul. Doña Francisca set out the view that the soul is an immaterial something that gives life and personality and that at death passes to God. Doña Tereza identified the soul with the breath and argued that the cessation of breathing at death showed that the soul is no more than this. Neither woman could read or write. They were debating an ancient issue that had entered the tradition of their isolated village from sources they did not know. So too in many a dormitory and tavern the "bull-session" carries onward an education that began in a book or a lecture. Informal conversations are a growing edge of more formal educational arrangements. The *Euthyphro* and the *Phaedrus* are Plato's compositions; they do not transcribe verbatim what Socrates and others said. But they are models in two senses: they propose both a line of thought on principal questions and a form of reasonable exchange of ideas for the uses of education with respect to many other subjects.

In further explication of the educational dialogue, one must admit that people still attend lectures—even when not required to do so. One may occasionally have educational experiences in listening to lectures. Even Socrates often fell to lecturing. I suppose that if a lecture educates a listener at all, it is because there are conversations in it. As I listen, I may carry on a conversation with myself, considering and debating what the lecturer says. Often this takes place later. At breakfast next day there come to the mind the considerations that show the lecturer's position to be mistaken, or not mistaken. Or the lecture itself may take the form of a conversation, a report of a past dialectic into which the listener is drawn, as a lover of a sport or an art enters into the performance of the sport or art, imaginatively, as he watches. The teacher who educates us is in many cases the one who stirs up unspoken dialectic in the pupil. André Maurois writes of one Alain, the teacher who most influenced him. Alain conducted classes in which there was no discussion; he did all the talking. But he taught by asking questions of each thinker whose work he discussed; moreover, he drew from each philosopher that aspect of his work which the others could not so well provide. The lecture was, I suppose, something of a symposium, a multiple dialogue moving to culmination.

Maurois grew up among educated people, read many books, and had very good teachers. The educational dialogue appears in very different form in the case of one Alexander Somerville, whose life and autobiography played a part in the history of the Reform movement in England. When a small boy, Somerville was an ignorant cowherd, with no reading, living in rural Scotland in the early part of the past century. His first education came to him in the person of an old blind man who walked, talking to himself, into the valley where the child watched the cows. The old man, his mind a little turned, yet retained vivid memory of many books of history he had read when he had eyesight. I tell the story in Somerville's words:

> On a stone at the foot of Ogle Burn . . . James Dawson used to sit down and call to Sir Walter Raleigh, Essex, Burleigh, and other courtiers to Elizabeth, to come to him, and when they came he sent them to fetch her majesty. He would then go into a political argument with them about Philip of Spain and the other personages and subjects of Elizabeth's reign. He would listen as if someone spoke into his ear, for their observations, and would interrupt them at times impatiently, if they did not seem to be holding a sound argument.

Then the old man would ask some shepherd or farmer he knew (who was of course not really present) what he thought of the issue under discussion, and then turn to the young cowherd for an expression of opinion. "Thus," wrote Somerville many years later, "did I first learn anything of the world which is laid before us in books—anything of countries beyond our own—anything of other ages and other classes of society."

There are, then, many kinds of educational dialogues. The dialectic of mental growth is organized or unorganized, led by a teacher or pursued among those equally prepared, carried on within one's self, or exhibited in a lecture, a book, or a dramatic representation.

It is important to recognize that the conversations of education are not only those in which abstract idea confronts abstract idea, or opinion challenges opinion. There are also the dialogues in which it is the facts that speak, talking, as it were, with one another, or with the theory or other general conception which guides them and which they, in turn, affect.

Experimental science has its own dialectic. The hypothesis proposes a question; the experiment or the observation confounds or confirms it or, more commonly, leads to putting the question in a new way. When we are not able to take part in this kind of conversation by direct experimentation and observation in the laboratory or in the natural world, we can at least retrace, in our own minds, the courses of these scientific conversations as they are presented to us in the records of experiment and observation. The history of genetics, for example, is a course of persistent, reasonable argument of fact and theoretical idea with each other. The question is asked, for example, whether in the course of the first cell division in the embryo the determinants of future particular structure are separated off, that which is appropriate to the part of the body to arise from the one cell going to that cell and that which is to govern the development of the part of the body to come from the other of the two cells going alone to that other cell. To answer this question Wilhelm Roux destroyed one of the two cells of the two-celled frog embryo, and only half an embryo developed. The question asked seems to have received an affirmative answer. But later Driesch performed a more refined experiment: he removed one of the two cells from physical contiguity to the other; and the remaining cell, entirely alone, developed into a complete frog. The argument has shown that the first tentative conclusion was wrong; the position of the cell destroyed by Roux next to that left undestroyed had something to do with the power of a cell to develop all or part of an organism. The first cell division, in this class of cases, does not separate the determinants of future particular structure.

And the dialectic of theory and experiment continues. You may find it illustrated in many a field of natural science. At one time a course in general education with regard to the natural sciences at the University of Chicago made excellent use of the educational value of the dialectic of experiment and theory. The texts for the students were the scientific papers in which were reported the results of that long series of experiments that led up to our present understanding of the effects, interacting and complementary, of several hormones in regulating the normal balance, the homeostasis, of carbohydrate metabolism. The scientific mind, beginning with the fact of the disease diabetes, constructed a dialogue of fact and theory that led to understanding and control of the disease.

Rarely it happens that, to the good fortune of education, a record is made of the movements of one man's mind in carrying on, within himself, the dialectic of science. Such a record is given us in Charles Darwin's *Journal* of his famous voyage on the "Beagle," when as a young man he spent the years 1832–35 as the naturalist member of a voyage of exploration and scientific observation in the South Atlantic and in the South Pacific. We have this *Journal* in a later form after Darwin had rearranged the record to bring together matters bearing on the same topic and also in a form closely corresponding to his notebooks. Comparing these, one sees how his mind went while he was in the field and something of how it moved afterward. It is a record of a prolonged, private, and immensely productive conversation with the facts of the natural world. When it begins, the idea of natural selection was not at all present in Darwin's mind, and even the idea that species might come into existence by small progressive modification, rather than by instantaneous divine creation, was hardly conceived by him as possible. When the conversation is broken off by the ending of the *Journal,* the elements of idea for the theory of natural selection are almost all present, although not yet assembled.

Reading this *Journal,* one's mind is stretched and strengthened in following the course of Darwin's long conversation with the facts. So many curious and yet related facts struck into his mind. He notes the strength of a monkey's prehensile tail that supports the body's weight even after death. He feeds raw meat to a glowworm and observes how the insect applies to the meat with his tail a digestive juice. He is amazed by the hosts of arthropod species in Brazil: "the variety of species among the jumping spiders appears almost infinite," he writes. The reader begins to understand that from hundreds of such observations there were forming in Darwin's mind two ideas of immense power: the idea of variation and the idea of adaptation. He sees a snake that has the form of a viper but bears on its tail an enlarged point that is struck against grass and brush with an effect like that accomplished by the rattles of the rattlesnake. The snake is intermediate between viper and rattlesnake. Darwin sees how every character has a tendency to vary by slow degrees. Might the variation go so far as to change one species into another?

In this mood of wondering and doubting Darwin continues his journey up into the Andes, where he is struck by the marked differences between the vegetation and the animals in the eastern valleys as compared with those of the other side. He sets down his judgment that this is no more remarkable than that animals and plants differ on opposite sides of a broad strait of a sea. But then he adds a curious footnote in which he apparently accepts the view that the distribution of animals, created as immutable species, has been affected by geological changes, but to which he adds a portentous sentence: "otherwise the changes might be superinduced by different circumstances in the two regions during a length of time." So the facts talk to Darwin, and he replies, now with the expression of the possibility that species might be transformed into other species by the accumulation of small changes naturally induced over "a length of time." The facts are talking to Darwin because he listens to them, and his mind conceives the generalizations which their talk to him obscurely hints: that it is almost impossible to tell a species from a variety, that life-forms are closely adapted to their life-conditions, and that the evidences of slow variation of life-forms in response to the influences of life-conditions are all about him.

The conversation reaches its climax as Darwin explores that little cluster of tiny islets, the Galápagos, off the coast of Ecuador. Darwin is at once impressed by the fact that many of the species on these rocky islets are, as he calls them, "aboriginal creations, found nowhere else." "Yet their general form strongly partakes of an American character." Why should the creative force create species on the Galápagos that resemble, but are not identical with, those on the nearest mainland six hundred miles away? Why not create them to resemble, say, the species found in Africa? Darwin, rewriting these passages of his *Journal*, puts this question in plain words and remarks that the animals of Galápagos resemble those of America, where the physical conditions are very different, more than they do the animals of the far-distant Cape Verde Islands, where the conditions are similar. The dialectic is rising to its resolution and conclusion: through variation and adaptation life-forms once the same as those then on the American continent became differentiated into new species and genera on Galápagos. The animals on the islets are like those of America because they and the animals of America are descended from common ancestors. What Darwin has still to add to this interaction of fact and idea is the conception, which he apparently found in Malthus, of the struggle for survival in an expanding population. And he is to test the theory of natural selection in many years of painstaking study of barnacles and other animals and plants.

Darwin's conversation with the facts is, in its quiet and unnoted way, a sort of *Euthyphro* of empirical science, a model of the dialogue of idea and specially investigated fact. In other fields of learning the dialogues from which we may learn take different forms. In the study of human beings in their many societies, primitive and civilized, we rarely find that particular fact and theoretical generalization are so closely and influentially interrelated as in the study of carbohydrate metabolism. It is true that experimental psychology does give us a dialectic of observation and hypothesis to tell us, among other things, how rats or people learn. But these dialogues do not reach into the complex realities of many people doing many things as they appear in tribes, cities, and whole personalities. Those talkers with the facts who begin by looking at the tribes, cities, or personalities develop a dialectic in which one vision of the whole offers itself to us for comparison with some other vision of the whole. Freud's way of explaining neuroses, dreams, the development of personality, mythology, and religion, is one more or less coherent vision of all these things, seen as related to each other in one conceivable way. There is presented to us a conception of the human being as a creature of powerful inborn impulse, meeting early experience with transforming, even damaging, effect, and expressing in religion, art, and dreams the images of thwarted impulses. If we read the book *Folkways* by William Graham Sumner, we are given a different vision of man; here he is seen as a mere creation of the tradition of his group, a mechanical product of custom, incapable of doing anything much to change his state of affairs. If we read recent anthropology, still a third vision, also fact-connected, arises. The human being that is now shown us is not thwarted; he is freed, so it seems, by the customs around him; they fill his material and spiritual wants; they offer him those explanations of suffering, death, good, and evil that make existence and a degree of happiness possible. To seek to understand any one of these viewpoints of man's nature thoroughly is an educational adventure. To consider, thoughtfully and returning always to the facts about men's behavior and institutions, how two or more such viewpoints differ from or resemble one another is to take active part in this other kind of dialogue. It is a dialogue in which we wait until one speaker has told us at great length his view of things, and then listen to another speaker with another view, while we hold in mind the facts and arguments of the first speaker. In this kind of dialogue the argument does not move from point to point, leaving behind disproved hypotheses. Rather we see a subject matter illuminated from different points of view as first one light, from one angle, is turned upon it, and then another. We feel ourselves a long way from resolving the differences between the visions or theories. For the time, we learn by trying out each whole conception on more particular fact. Two or three conceptions contribute to an improved understanding; no one is put entirely away.

The conversations of learning and education are various, according to the nature of the relation between the general idea and the particular fact. I suppose it would be possible to conduct a highly educational conversation about the many explanations that historians have offered for the fall of Rome. We would not, at the end, decide how Rome fell. But we might stretch our minds. Another conversation would review the same work of literary art, guided by the several kinds of questions asked of it by different literary critics. A series of Supreme Court decisions interpreting the equal protection clause of the Fourteenth Amendment with regard to racially segregated schooling offers a basis for another kind of educational conversation.

A conversation in some form is an indispensable part of that education which makes mind and spirit grow. One may learn truth as somebody else has thought it without the troubles of argument. But to develop the power and responsibility which are the pleasure and the burden of educated men in a free society, one has to struggle with idea and fact. It is much easier not to. In certain isolated universities of North Africa the principal qualities required of students are attention and memory; no attempt is made to train their critical powers and their judgment; they are in school to learn the Truth and not to think for themselves. So these students learn texts by heart and never participate in lecture or discussion. Nor do they ever, we are told by Professor Le Tourneau, take any part in their country's political life.

To take useful part in public decisions is to seek understanding through a struggle of alternatives. In America, too, it is sometimes found easier not to struggle. In some of our schools and colleges rote learning is less formally taught than in Africa. In many courses the student reads a textbook in which things are asserted about something without any invitation to argument. The paragraphs are short, brightly written, and conveniently captioned. Perhaps the instructor wrote the textbook. Then we have a monologue repeated. The long, difficult, strange, and beautiful dialogues of idea and fact that led up to that book are quite hidden beneath its bland and easy surface. Let us rejoice that in leaving school we may escape from such books. They contain no visions to stir the explorative spirit. They provide no line of disputation on which we may exercise our critical faculties. "What is the use," asked Alice, just before she fell down the rabbit-hole, "of a book without pictures or conversations?"

As adults we may choose from many recorded conversations in arranging, for our own education, the conditions for carrying on our own further conversations. We bring to the enterprise the experiences we have had in work or in play. We are freer than are children to choose the approach congenial to our special nature. One may relate his ideas closely to action, as that one knows action in factory or politics or profession. Another may consider the topic philosophically, for general ideas and aesthetic appreciation. A third is more interested in the methods for observing natural phenomena and for drawing general descriptions from the observations. Whitehead says (in chap. iv of *The Aims of Education*) with respect to technical, liberal, and cultural education that each should contain the others. I agree; and we may choose that beginning that suits us. But the technical and the liberal are not equals in education; the great end is the growth of the self, the effort to know, with reason and knowledge, the goods in their order; and the technical is educational only as means to that end.

Among the difficulties of carrying on such a conversation in America today is the prevalent separation of work and play. Stated roughly, business is troublesome activity without reference to the works of the mind and spirit, and play is ceasing that troublesome activity without reference to the works of the mind and spirit. Relaxation, the ceasing to be troubled, is a good and necessary thing. But it is not education, which is effortful and goal-directed. When education is taking place in a grown person, we probably find that for him the distinction between work and play begins to disappear. The work tends to be related in his mind to the ideas and facts which he is pursuing, and instead of merely relaxing all the time when he is away from his work, he finds pleasure from time to time in pursuing the same ideas and facts. A program of adult education in which the participants think only of what they read on the fortnightly occasions when they meet to discuss it has serious limitations. It may turn out to be more recreational than educational. Effective educational conversations are carried on, intermittently but persistently, as one argues with one's self while apparently cooking dinner or shaving. It takes a series of many little efforts to advance education. Yet relaxation has its part in education too. For the mind to grow, it must struggle, and then must abstain from struggle. "So now you must labour with your brains, and now you must forbear your activity, and see what the great Soul sheweth," wrote Emerson.

Perhaps the most serious difficulty in the way of conducting conversations that are educational is the confusing, the almost shattering, influence of most of the talk around us. As extremes, we have on the one hand Plato and Darwin, on the other the calumny and vituperation of much current public utterance. In between and all around are other kinds of speech quite distinct from the dialogue that is educational: the empty and plausible oration, the pretentious, ugly, and muddy language of many a so-called scientific paper or official document, the sleazy words of ephemeral light fiction, and the bright and completely false-sounding utterances of those who would have us buy something they have to sell. What a chorus of bad example! The heaviest price we have to pay for that incalculable good, freedom of speech, is listening to the uses to which the freedom is put.

Each kind of talk has its purposes and its implied rules. I may talk to express myself; then it matters only that I am occasionally allowed to do so; a sympathetic listener increases my pleasure but does not assure a dialogue. A social conversation has only the simple rules of common decency: that each speak; that nothing too distressing be said; and that obedience be given to whatever conventions are special to the occasion. At a large cocktail party a quite successful conversation can be carried on by merely repeating the same bit of utter nonsense, and I believe that the experiment has been tried. Where the end is pleasure, the rules are simple. Where speech is used to bring about a sale, or in diplomacy to allay fear or mislead an opponent, or in ruthless politics to terrorize a victim, there are other rules or none at all.

The educational dialogue, Socratic or otherwise, differs from all these other kinds of utterance in its ends and in its rules. The rules are those appropriate to mutual enlightenment, to growth for all participants. There is first of all the recognition by all participants that the end is insight and understanding. So what is said is taken seriously. Light as the touch may be—and in learning humor is very welcome—in conversing for education there is the sense of the significance of what is said. I speak, or I listen, because the speaker means what he says, and believes it a contribution, however small, to the effort up the ladder of important understanding. So the utterances that move toward education are vitiated by insincerity and diminished by triviality or mere show of personal skill.

In the next place we may recognize the educational dialogue by the fact that it is truly a dialogue. The duty to appear at least to listen in the social conversation is replaced by the duty in fact to listen. No serious conversation takes place unless first I speak to one who attends to what I say for the dominant purpose of understanding it, and unless then I listen, seeking understanding, while he speaks with the same purpose. One may be silent in a circle of friends, or in a discussion of a book, and yet learn from the discussion of others. But then I carry on within myself an unspoken conversation in the same spirit and with the same rules as prevail in the spoken discussion. When the new idea entering my mind meets a difficulty or a conflicting view or fact, I talk, internally, for one side and then for the other of the possibilities I may begin to see for dealing with the view or the fact. To make reading educational I give the writer every chance to tell me what he is saying. And it is not yet fully educational unless then I meet what he says with my own idea, or the idea or experience of another, and make the effort of seeing what comes of trying to entertain both or first one and then the other.

There is a balance, which the scientist, the scholar, the judge, and the wise leader all know, between the personal and the impersonal in the educational conversation. To be wholly closed within one's self is, obviously, to make education impossible. But to attack the educational experience with the complete impersonality of a machine, even if this were possible, would be equally defeating. One gives of one's self in conversing for understanding. One commits one's self to positions. One says, "Yes, just now, so far as reason and experience tell me, this is what I stand for; I will risk myself on this until shown something better." And to this position one adds whatever support comes from one's own life, personal as it of course is. Yet, on the other hand, the end, understanding, is not mine alone; it is shared with others. These others and I are communicating about a something impersonal, a something which, though expressed in some small part by the experience and insight of each, is above us both. Its names are many: common sense, truth, wisdom, the right. In Michael Polanyi's fine phrase, the effort to understand is made "with universal intent." The speaking in an educational dialogue is personal but disinterested, self-committing and self-transcending.

So we see that the educational dialogue calls for a large measure of good will. It begins in an act of faith: the assumption that those who converse speak in honesty, for the purpose of reaching understanding, and with generosity toward each other. The liar and the malicious speaker at once disqualify themselves, but the conversation begins with the assumption that they are not present. Such a dialogue flows on mutual respect. In certain kinds of utterance, as in legislative bodies and in debates, formal rules keep the talk going even when, between particular individuals, the respect is lost. In talking with friends to reach understanding, we do not need the formal rules. In talking, silently, with a book, we need the habit of mind which attends to what is said to us with friendly receptivity and yet with suspended judgment.

The educational dialogue requires balance also between assent and denial, agreement and disagreement. Needed is a certain willingness of the mind to reach out to that which is not yet understood, even to that which at first repels one. Those who only show the other wrong do not learn. Alain, the teacher whom André Maurois so much admired, said that "refutation is a dull game." Simple refutation is rarely educational. On the other hand, if one's agreement with the idea comes too easily, it may come before it has met the tests of judgment. If the new idea is a good one, it will be strengthened by doubt and restatement. There are people whose first approach to a new idea is negative. There are others in whom affirmation prevails. But there are only two dispositions of the mind that allow it to grow: one may say neither, "Yes, yes," nor, "No, no"; one must say either, "Yes, but—," or else, "No—and yet—."

In this series of lectures last year, Lyman Bryson said that we are embarked in the United States on the attempt to build a civilization in which as many as possible of our problems will be solved by each of us using what he has of the power to think. Often it does not seem that we are actually doing this, but of course Mr. Bryson is right; this is our purpose; and this is why universal education and democracy go together. We want not only government by the people; we want government by a people who make the effort to think.

No one citizen can think about everything. No one of us can form considered judgments as to the thousand problems of our common life that one day's issue of the *New York Times* brings to our notice. But there is something that we can all do; we can come to recognize a reasonable discussion when we hear it. We can, through practice of the dialogue in our own unending education, come to distinguish that man in public life who takes up problems with disinterested consideration of the alternatives, guided by reason and fact, from that man who is just talking for effect. We can support the one and reject the other. The former is carrying on intelligent conversation with universal intent. We can trust him. The latter we cannot trust; he may be a knave, a blatherskite, or a fool.

A representative democracy, in a world grown so complex as this one, depends, at the least, on common understandings as to the rules of reaching decisions. It cannot depend on common understandings as to what ought to be done about every particular matter. It cannot depend, safely, on trusting only the objectives of its representatives. The ends of our common life are inseparable from the means we use to get there. We want freedom and government by the people. We can get it by supporting men who themselves think with universal intent, and who respect the power of the people to do so also. If we support men in public life who offer to reach ends we seek by means opposed to those ends, we will get what the supporters of Hitler and Stalin got.

The implied rules of the educational conversation are both intellectual and moral. They say, "Use reason," and they say, "Be fair and generous." They are a commitment of faith in man's rational nature and his power to develop it. This morality of the educational conversation is also the ideal of public life in a democracy. Its application in public life gives courage to those who strive to improve education. Its exercise in education strengthens its practice in public life. An autocratic teacher, an instruction which does not accord respect to the intelligence and to the person, even a thoroughly dull school or course of instruction—these are not merely bad education, they are in conflict with our democratic principles. But where the conversations of organized education are conducted under the rules just described, there is preparation for citizenship in the kind of society we want ours to be.

The fearfulness that infects us today is bad for freedom and bad for education. We cease to trust the power of our minds to deal with problems in fair and intelligent discussion. High-minded speech is often platitudinous or evasive; we cannot accord full respect even to those whose intentions are fully honorable. They have failed to exercise the educational dialogue. And much other speech is irresponsible or downright malicious. Those who speak in malice and self-interest corrupt the reasonable dialogue and inure us, I fear, to lying and deceit. We are intimidated, or at least dazed. The effort to keep the public conversation going in this time of troubles becomes too heavy a burden. We accept the suspension of some of the freedoms of honest conversation on which a healthy common life is based. We are encouraged secretly to report on the activities and thoughts of our neighbors. We hesitate to commit ourselves to positions lest our own sincere utterances prevent us from serving our country at home or abroad. We exclude from the councils of the nation experts because, it appears, we fear they may give us honest advice that later on we might come to think mistaken. Speaking for American scientists, Vannevar Bush has written that in the administration of security regulations the scientists "see only slightly concealed an inclination to exclude anyone who does not conform completely to the judgment of those who in one way or another have acquired authority," and asks "whether we are treading the path that will lead us into the fallacies of totalitarianism." These words are his, not mine.

Yet the American ideal of public intercourse remains what it has always been: the reasonable conversation. It can be restored and strengthened here at home. It can be extended to the international community. The Voice of America may yet become an educational conversation of the world's peoples. We can show an example by talking rationally and by stopping to listen to what other peoples have to say to us. Just because it is too difficult just now to carry on a conversation with Russia is no reason to abandon the attempt to converse with India or Iran. It is not a reasonable conversation to shout our virtues at them through a transmitter. It is not a reasonable conversation to assume that they will buy our way of life as if it were a superior-model automobile, and then talk fast about our model. A world of democratic peoples is possible if peoples talk to peoples reasonably, and conversationally, attending to what each has to say in thoughtful respect for the other's views.

An ideal is a picture of the place you will never quite, but always strive to, reach. Its attainment happens in little pieces of the striving. We shall never have a world of perfectly rational and fair-minded men, just as we shall never have an educational system in which everyone learns to think with the excellences of intellectual conversation that I have imagined. But the great good is contained within the small; the civilization of the dialogue is set forth, however humbly, in any one small piece of honest intellectual exchange, with my neighbor, with my book. A new beginning toward the unattainable is forever right at hand.

CREATION

Education is of course learning something. More importantly, it is becoming something. Although knowledge is needed for education, an educated person is not the same as a man who has knowledge. An educated person is one who is at work on his enlargement. If we learn things that become parts of us, if we make efforts to develop our own particular understanding of life and of the order of life's goods, it is education we are doing. A person is something that it takes time to make; there is on everyone an invisible sign, "Work in progress"; and the considered effort to get along with the work is education.

Thought of in this way, education is not as common as one might suppose. The institutions that we call "educational" are engaged only now and then in the development, in children and young people, of understanding of the order of life's goods. Schools and universities provide care of the young, offer recreation and pleasant associations, teach many useful skills from reading and writing to surgery and the preparation of legal briefs, and occasionally, desirably, indispensably educate.

So much of life goes just to keep things running, to police action, to bolstering the dikes against catastrophe. In our national life we have small freedom to decide how to spend the income of our immense national wealth. Most of it is firmly committed to paying for past wars and to trying to protect ourselves from, or in, future wars. In the schools we have got ourselves into a situation where we have only limited freedom to educate. You will see a schoolroom with fifty children and one teacher; the teacher uses most of her energies in keeping some kind of order. In a high school or college, also, much that goes on is merely custodial. Part of the budget goes to keeping the young people out of trouble and reasonably happy. If parents feel sure that this much is being accomplished, they are thankful and content.

If an occasional adult turns to the task of making himself grow in understanding of the order of life's goods by way of books and reasonable discussion, he meets a world and often a neighborhood that are unfavorable to his effort. Time and the will for education are in short supply. There are the pressures of immediate circumstance; there are work, entertainment, and the enjoyment of life in other ways. There are the innumerable problems of personal and public life. Many people today are passive or pessimistic; the tone of much public life is harsh and threatening; the danger of war by indiscriminate slaughter continues.

Nor is there much encouragement for education by adults, of themselves, in the examples and expectations that we encounter in our communities. What appears in most current print or broadcasting is for the most part irrelevant or ignoble. And one's neighbors are not likely to expect one to start work on one's own development through the pursuit of learning. Education, being a growth of the self, is in nature endless and hardly begins in the schools, but there is a widespread mistaken idea that all that sort of thing is over in school and college. Thoughtful people, who read a good many books, are today sometimes looked upon as a little queer, possibly as dangerous. The pursuit of learning by grown men and women is not very popular.

I state these difficulties so that we may take them into account in judging the worth of what I say here about what education is and how it goes on in men and women. No doubt I have overemphasized them. To the peasant of India wanting to learn just to read and write, America is vastly fortunate. Compared with other peoples, we are blessed with unusual material provision for such education as we may want to undertake. Where else is the working day so short? Where else have people such means to enjoy books, travel, and time to think?

In the very general sense of becoming something, everybody gets educated; everybody becomes something in the course of his life. The questions are: How good or bad a something? Who decides what I become?

To meet the necessity of becoming something or other as one grows up and grows old, there are at least four distinguishable possibilities. The first way is no longer open to us; it was the way in which, in primitive societies, education was brought about merely through living the expected life. Taught by the example and the simple instruction of those around him, the American Indian or the African tribesman arrived at such wisdom as he needed in his well-integrated and largely stable world.

The other three ways are open to us in these later and more difficult times. Each is called "education" by those who approve of that way of making people.

One can become what a dictatorial authority decides that one should become. This is education in a Nazi or Communist state; it has had its full demonstration in George Orwell's book, *Nineteen Eighty-four*. In such a making of people, the choice of what to make is taken away from each individual, and the sense of freedom, so far as it exists, comes from identification with the nation, or the race, or some principle of history. Just now we are struggling both against the Communist way of making people and also against the rise of the same tendency among ourselves to take this way of becoming. We are submitting to this tendency when in response to a demand from some indignant faction we exclude favorable mention of the United Nations from a schoolbook, or when we become afraid to study the writings of Karl Marx. This struggle on two fronts is noise and bitterness rather than thought; it is one of the difficulties that today impede any effort to make one's self as one wants to be.

A second way of meeting the necessity to become something or other is to become whatever at that time the people living around one are, changing to something a little different as people around one change. This, on the whole, is what many of us in this country do. It is sometimes called "adjustment" or "adaptation" or "socialization." This method, like the preceding one, leaves most of the work to others with a result that one is moderately comfortable and fairly acceptable to those who made one what one is.

In this country we will not choose the first of these ways and will defend ourselves against both foreign and domestic antagonists from having it imposed upon us. The lesser danger and the harder to avoid is the second way of becoming something. It will take some little thought and effort to avoid becoming the chameleon of the world's peoples, the easy adjuster to the immediate expectations of the suburbs or the neighborhoods in which we live, creatures whose characters are in their skins, not in their selves.

The third available way of bringing about the making of one's self avoids both dangers. It is the path I imagine us to choose in so far as we turn our interests and energies to our own education, as grown men and women. It is to take charge of one's own education, to put work into it along lines of one's own choice, and so produce something of a self-built self. This is, in fact, occasionally accomplished. It is a way open to anyone who wishes to give himself a good deal of interesting trouble.

For one who takes this responsibility, the experience that is education comes to be recognized, as it occurs within one's self or as one sees it occur in another. Education is to be distinguished from such other experiences as excitement, pleasure, and having an opinion. I have ventured to identify its characteristic, distinguishing cycle of development. It begins in a reaching out of the mind and spirit, an entertainment of possibilities of significance and value in things seen, heard about, imagined. If this exploration of a universe that thereby begins to expand for one is to become education, it requires, as Whitehead so well presents the matter in his book, *The Aims of Education,* the discipline of order and precision. Further facts must be considered. Ideas must be doubted and tested. In describing this phase of the cycle, one emphasizes the interaction of mind and mind, idea and idea, fact and fact, as forms of that conversation by which the cycle of the mind proceeds. And finally, there is an act of appropriation, a taking to one's self, on one's own terms, the piece of knowledge that has been offered. Although teachers are needed, education is always in part one's own act. As the child grows older, there comes to be more awareness of one's own effort to learn and to become, the third phase of which is an experience of growth by an act of affirmation. Something—an idea, a fact—is offered by book, teacher, or the experience of life. If it flows over and past one, there is no education. If it sticks to one, and becomes training or habit, nevertheless there may be little or no education. If one deals with it, thoughtfully and reasonably, in terms of what one already is and with a result that thereafter one is by some degree more than one was before, there is surely education.

It is this third aspect of the educational experience that concerns me now. For it, the word "participation" might be used to suggest the sharing of the act of learning by both teacher and student, or the part that is taken by the reader of a book in the ideas of the book. The word "incorporation" might emphasize the way in which something learned is built into one's self. And "application" points to that involvement of learning in the life of action with our fellows of which I shall speak later. But I choose the word "creation," because man is a maker, and the making of his better self, through learning, is the end of that activity which I am now examining. It is by trying to make something which we feel to be part of us, and yet something which we can give to another, that we make ourselves.

Creation, not always connected closely with education, is an experience that all may have. Sara, age three, creates a song by changing one word of a song her mother sings to her. Now she sings a song that is "her very own." The Pueblo Indian potter varies one line of a traditional volute and knows herself an artist. I read today of an American who devotes his life to improving the effectiveness of the handles we grasp on the tools we use. Such creations are narrow, but they provide the sense of being a creator.

Greater creations may be achieved not only by the professional artists or scholars but by other people who are carrying on some private study for the joy it gives them. That part of the Maya hieroglyphic writing known as the Supplementary Series was deciphered by an American chemical engineer in the course of the journeys by train that he took in connection with his business. The glyphs had been for years a puzzle to specialists. The ancient Mediterranean script known as Linear B, written by the Greeks of Crete and Asia Minor, was recently made readable by the efforts of a young English architect.

The great creations of art and science and scholarship no doubt con-tribute to the education of those who achieve them and also provide works and ideas which become materials for the education of others. The coming to understand something—to understand it in that degree and kind which makes the thing learned a part of one's mind and self—is a creation, too. In this case the thing made is more private and personal. It is never wholly so. Education is an exchange in which each learner helps build the other as he builds himself.

Learning that educates includes an element of invention. In anthropol-ogy we speak of a process called "stimulus diffusion." Peoples learn from other peoples not only by imitating one another but also by observing one another and then doing something in a different way that reaches the same end. After Chinese porcelain had been coming to Europe for al-most two centuries, European potters, stimulated by the beauty of the Chinese product, set themselves the task of finding a way to make it and succeeded. In the early nineteenth century a Cherokee Indian, who was entirely without schooling or knowledge of English, was impressed by the white man's writing and was stimulated to invent, single-handed, a syl-labary. He had not grasped the alphabetic principle, but the example of writing that he saw and only partly understood was enough to cause him to invent. It seems to me that my own experience as a teacher might pro-vide examples of learning by stimulus diffusion. More than once I have been a little startled to hear some old student of mine thank me for the wonderful insight I gave him years ago: he then tells me I said something to him which I am sure I never said. I said something, and he was stimu-lated to think something else. I do not recommend this method of instruction; I mention it only to emphasize the element of originality in educative learning.

In the self-educating learner, the imagination, working on the infinite suggestiveness of the world around one, moves the mind to arrangements of idea and value that are both new and old. An idea is not the same when it is learned by you as when it is learned by me, provided the learning be more than mechanical repetition. I am a different learner; the thing learned is thereby different; therefore there is creation. Montaigne made the point when he wrote to the Countess of Gurson advice as to how her son should be brought up. He wrote, "For if by his own discourses he embrace the opinions of Xenophon or Plato, they shall be no longer theirs, but his. He that merely followeth another, traceth nothing, and seeketh nothing." I accept Whitehead's assertion that "the appreciation of literature is really creation." He goes on to say that the words we read and the music we hear are not mere stimuli to evoke an equivalent response. Learning that is educational is more of an original production, a self-modifying act, than is suggested by the words "stimulus" and "response." "No one, no genius other than our own, can make our life live." Whitehead therefore deplored the deadening weight of what he called "inert ideas" in so much schooling. In contrast, to take a thought, a judgment of appreciation, or the significance of a fact into one's own thoughts and feelings, is to give it the place there which one's self feels to be just, is to perform an act of creation in the self. I think of this distinction between inert ideas and the self-modifying creative act when I read a bad textbook and elsewhere listen to a good teacher. The textbook offers me inert ideas. The good teacher—man or book—offers me something of which to make something of my own. I am led along a course of fact and thought with which I am compelled to struggle, which I am compelled myself to order and reform.

When we try to learn in company, or with one companion, this struggle with its creative result is thereby helped along. The efforts of one to understand and to appreciate are provoked and tested by the efforts of the other. This may happen among schoolmates, between husband and wife in an adult education class, and even between people of very different origins and natures. I count among my teachers a certain Maya Indian whom I knew in his remote village in Yucatan. He talked with me about common human problems out of his own very different experience. When Tolstoi was teaching in his school on his estate, he was one day stirred to excitement in recognizing literary ability in an eleven-year-old peasant boy. A creation akin to his own appeared when the boy insisted that the old peasant in the story he and his schoolmates were writing should be made to put on a *woman*'s cloak on hurriedly leaving the hut. Tolstoi saw that the detail was right; Fedka's imagination suggested "the picture of a feeble, narrow-chested peasant . . . the late hour, the peasant undressed for the night . . . the women going and coming, getting water, feeding cattle, the external disorder of the peasant's life." Tolstoi found this revelation of creative power terrible and delightful. He learned something then about children and about art. And the boy Fedka learned as he created.

It follows that education is in opposition to imitation and conformity. These have their place in learning: one conforms in order to learn rules of grammar; one imitates the teacher when he shows how the lathe is to be used or pronounces the French word that one is to repeat. But in education the learner, by his own efforts, by so much makes himself over: there comes about in him a rearrangement of the understood, the important, and the desirable. The rearrangement is not permanent; mind and feeling, with developed discriminations, are now a base from which the cycle begins again. With widened powers to understand and appreciate, the work in progress is resumed.

Sometimes when we try to educate we only regiment. Consider the children who after viewing an educational television program on clay modeling all proceeded to make the clay rabbit exactly as the demonstrator had made it. We should have applauded this uniformity if the attempt had been to teach the combinations of the multiplication table. For the modeling of rabbits the standardized result was not what was wanted. I fear that many a school talk about freedom and experiment covers hidden pressures to do the thing as the formal method or immediate convenience suggests. Schools are such busy places; schoolteachers have too much to do.

In spite of the report as to the clay rabbits, I have the impression that on the whole children are more spontaneous, more easily original, than are adults. It would probably be better for adult education if in this respect grownups were more like children. I have some sympathy for that man who, after the lecturer had finished explaining some experiments with a white rat in a maze and had invited questions, arose to ask, "What, in later life, became of the rat?" To pursue, with real interest, even an irrelevance is a step toward education. To accept without question is not.

On the other hand, grown people, if they choose, can find times and places for creative learning. They are freer to make their own arrangements for the effort in such a way as to meet their own needs and interests. They are not so busy with mere training, and they do not have so closely to obey the teacher. Indeed, they can well be teachers of one another, as they are in many an organized discussion group today.

As adults we bring to the educational effort something that children cannot bring: the experiences of adult life. Recently I joined in a series of educational discussions in which twenty men took part. Each of us had read the same texts, on one day pages from John Winthrop's history of the Plymouth Colony, on another, a short novel by Melville. But each man brought to the discussion something of his own: that which he had himself lived that bore upon what had been written. Was Captain Vere right in condemning Billy Budd, a youth he knew to be innocent of soul? A man sitting at our table had had comparable responsibility as an army officer. We read a debate as to Communism in the schools and asked the question: Is there anything that should never be taught to anybody? At once one said that theft and murder should never be taught to anybody. But then another spoke, saying that in Counter-Intelligence during the war *he* had been taught theft and murder. We read a paper by William Graham Sumner in praise of capitalism and an economic enterprise absolutely free. The members of this discussion group, executives in growing and successful corporations, brought to Sumner's view an experience that apparently confirmed what Sumner wrote; they adopted his words with no little enthusiasm. But then one pointed out that Sumner's position was strongly unfavorable to all legislation with regard to wages and hours, and, indeed, unfavorable to private charity. And some of the men present thought well of laws protecting some wage-earners, and many had worked hard at raising money for charities. It seemed that the position they had first adopted had to be reconsidered. The issues of life and the issues of books are united in adult education because the learner has met some of the hard questions in his own experience.

I am struck by Sir Richard Livingstone's statement that "the young, whether they know it or not, live on borrowed property." They borrow, with incomplete understanding, the experiences of older people. In a widened sense, the proposition is true of everybody, young and old. We all live on mental property borrowed from our predecessors. The accumulations of our forefathers' experience, as recorded in books, we only partly understand. We have not had their experiences. As we live our somewhat different lives, we learn again the truths they learned. But they are not quite the same truths. Or, you who find this form of words unacceptable may allow me to say that we come to know the same truths in the contexts of our different experiences.

The learning of the individual may be compared to the learning of each generation, each age. As the age creates out of the knowledge of the past its own new form of learning, so the individual takes from books and discussions parts of an accumulation and creates his own developed self therefrom. I think of how you and I learn, when I read Henry Osborn Taylor's account of how medieval Europeans took and made over classical and patristic learning. He stresses the long time that it took for the medieval thinkers really to assimilate, to make their own, what they read:

With each succeeding generation, the subjects of medieval study were made more closely parts of the intelligence occupied with them, because the matter had been constantly restated and restudied in terms more nearly adapted to the comprehension of the men who were learning and restating it.

At length they made the ancient thought "dynamically their own . . . they could think for themselves in its terms, think almost originally and creatively, and could present as their own the matter of their thoughts in restatements, that is, in forms essentially new." This is, I think, the outcome that is education also in the individual. As life is so short, it is not often that one reaches, in more than a few matters, this complete assimilation into one's own mind and feeling, of that which is given one to learn. The period of schooling is surely too brief. As one continues education throughout life, this assimilation, this conversion of another's learning into one's own creation, is more nearly reached.

Taylor sees, in the literature of medieval times, three stages in the assimilation of the earlier learning. First, what he calls "conning": the ancient book was read, and hardly more than repeated. The theologian copied an early text and added only a simple commentary. Second, "its more vital appropriation." This stage Taylor finds expressed in medieval works in which, with little form, the writer set down an opinion he had read in one authority, then a contrasting opinion from some other authority, and finally offered his own attempt at adjustment of the two. I have seen the equivalent in many a good student's notebook. In this stage education is occurring. The third stage—still following Taylor—is represented by the few really great medieval writings, notably the *Summa* of Aquinas, in which a great body of learning, thoroughly considered, is restated with added elements of thought. This last stage of the assimilation of "borrowed property" is, in small degree, represented in our own separate educations in so far as we restate parts of others' learning with elements of thought drawn from our growing structure of judgments of the relevant, the important, and the good.

I would cling a moment longer to this comparison of education with the assimilation by a whole people of the learning of earlier times. Taylor emphasizes the important part of emotion in the development of medieval learning. He says that the transformation of classical and patristic culture was accomplished as much by artists as by scholars, and that the emotions, the passions, of the scholars were involved in their recasting of earlier thought. He reminds us of the cathedral of Chartres, of the devotional prose of St. Anselm, of the chivalric romances, and especially of the passionate feeling that imbued religious thought. I think that, in its own minor form, learning by the individual which educates is also carried along in a current of feeling. Teach your pupil to think? Livingstone replies, "Teach your pupil to think and feel."

It seems to me that feeling is a part of thinking, that we learn easily when we care strongly about what it is that we are learning. The feeling is itself something to be enlarged and disciplined. The passion with which one approaches a topic is both a hindrance to learning and a great strength. It makes it difficult to think clearly but it provides an energy for thinking at all. I felt both the advantage and the disadvantage of strong feeling in intellectual exercise in the course of that series of discussions with business executives that I just mentioned. These men came to the discussions with strong and favorable feelings about the free enterprise system and the importance of increasing material production. They also had strong feelings about taxes. As these were two subjects in which my own feelings were somewhat less forcefully mixed, from my point of view the emotional involvements of these men were something of an obstacle to their clear and critical examination of productivity as an element in the good life. On the other hand, it was their very passion with regard to these questions that carried them into the subject, carried them into it with a fierce intensity. Then it was that I was reminded of the strong feelings of the medieval churchmen and thought for a moment that the disputation in which I was taking part was as much theological, in a broad sense, as it was economic. Someone indeed raised the question if there was not a religious quality about faith in free enterprise and material production. The discussion became a very good one.

In talking about the place of feeling in education, Livingstone's principal point is that the discipline and the cultivation of appreciation are essential objectives. The making of the better self is not only a training of the intellect. It includes also the improvement of those discriminations by which we see that a thing is beautiful and good and admit it not only to our understanding but to our delight. One attends to something in the world about us not always to act upon it, not always to analyze it, but sometimes with an attitude of simple openness to its goodness. This attitude is itself subject to development, to refinement. In it feeling is a strong component. In this aspect of education passion is controlled, and feeling enhanced and made sensitive to disciplined judgments. Livingstone refers to this part of educated men as the "other eye . . . the eye which enables them to contemplate, enjoy, and adore." And Whitehead puts it roundly when he says that beauty is the "aim of the universe."

In this lecture I have spoken of education as a making, through learning, of a better self. I have put forward a conception of education that identifies it with the growth of the individual. In the process whereby we try through study and discussion to effect that growth, I have emphasized what is personal, original, creative. It would almost seem, from this emphasis, that education is something that any man should be able to do out of his own unaided experience, as if the attempt had not been made before.

Of course this is not true. Education is possible only because we have access to the learning achieved by those who lived before us, and the making of the self that is education finds its building materials in that older learning. The comparison of the education of the individual with the mastery of classical knowledge by the thinkers of the Middle Ages is not only a comparison. The education of the individual and the transmission of the common heritage are aspects of the same thing. The learning of each one of us is a part of that learning whereby our age takes over, and yet remakes, the learning of the peoples who lived before us. While we seek our own education, we also work at the transmission of knowledge through the generations.

Therefore becoming educated is a social obligation as well as a personal privilege. If all the books were burned and no one told us legends of the past, education and civilization would collapse together. Our studies make our times as well as ourselves.

If, then, I send my child to school, I am concerned not only with what the school helps to make of him but also with what the schools—and all other efforts to educate—make of all of us. I am involved in decisions as to what to study, and what kind of person is to be made by the studying, both for myself or my child and for all of us, everywhere.

As I think about what I have said here, it seems to me that I have evaded a question that lies behind the matters that I have talked about. I cannot answer the question, but I can point out the direction in which I think we can go in continuing to struggle with it.

I have said that education is an individual enterprise. And also, in talking about the intercourse we have with one another in the course of education, in admitting that we borrow the intellectual and moral property of other people, living and dead, in our studies, I recognize that education is a social experience. How much is individual, and how much is in common with others? I have said that in education mind and feeling explore, converse, and then create. Of what material is this creation accomplished? I have replied: Of two experiences, my own and that stock of experience which has been accumulated for me by millions of predecessors.

Then should I not be told: Define, then, this common stock. Tell us what books we are to read, to what learning we are to attend. Does it matter whether we all choose different books? Shall I study Sanskrit literature while another studies mining and metallurgy in America? I made a comparison between the assimilation of ancient learning by scholars of the Middle Ages and the education of the modern American. But is not the comparison more than a little misleading? Modern Americans are not in the position of medieval scholars. Then the Western Europeans had but the Western heritage to consider, and hundreds of years in which social change went but slowly, as compared with the explosive changes of today. Today we have the world's traditions open to us; the people and the problems and the heritage of every people and nation impinge upon us; and the rapidity with which changing circumstances demand instant decisions makes it impossible to find an exclusive basis for an education of a hundred and sixty million people in the deliberate reconsideration, throughout a dozen generations, of a few related books. Your description of the educational experience is all very well, I hear it said, but what, today, shall we teach in the schools? And what shall be the content of adult education?

The question I have failed to put until just now may be expressed in terms of the problem of choice of the more ultimate values, the conceptions of goodness which education helps us to form. I spoke of education as the rearrangement of the important and the desirable. Is each to decide for himself what is important and desirable, and is each resulting program of education as good as any other? I said that education is the making of a better self. What is "better"? If my neighbor chooses to educate his children for better delinquency, or to revive naziism, is his view of education to carry as much weight as my own?

What shall we study? For what moral end, if any, shall we study it? For a long time education was conceived as the inculcation of common values through the reading of the great books of the Western tradition. It is so conceived by many today, although the books are not widely read, and although many people are troubled by a lack of common values in America. In Livingstone's essay, "Character and Its Training," there is an eloquent statement of the view that common culture and common values are indispensable and that the source for these is still to be found in the exhibition of intellectual and moral excellence in the great men and the great works of the West. Others have expressed similar views, and Robert Hutchins and Mortimer Adler have more than stated this position: they have done something about it in effecting uniform publication of certain of these books and in getting thousands of Americans to read them.

I think that my own position is the same, with variations. I share the view that education requires reasonable discussion and that the best basis therefor is a good book that everybody in the discussion has read. I think, too, that many good books have been produced in the Western world. And I agree also with the men I have mentioned in supposing that it is part of the good life to share with one's wife or neighbor or fellow citizen strong convictions, born out of common experience or common learning, as to what is good and what is beautiful. I think that to

live together without common values may be possible, but that it would
be a life lonely and bare. That I think so I have been helped to see
by David Riesman who in some pages of his stimulating writings has
suggested a different position. (I do not think he has advocated it.)
He tells us that people may live together in peace, may co-operate,
without sharing common preconceptions. He reminds us of those social
inventions, such as the market and skills of negotiation, that allow each
man to get along with all the others by putting forward only some part
of himself. To get along, he goes on to say, requires procedural consensus, "some shared values of a very general sort like due process, and
among sufficient people in strategic locations, some less-than-fanatical
attitude toward compromise and even corruption." Reading this, I tried
to think of myself sitting somewhere reasonably secure from war and
crime because of the market and procedural rules, like traffic regulations, and because other people somewhere were compromising skilfully
with corruption. I tried to think of a nation and a world held together
by these things and nothing else. And, passing the question whether in
such an America I should in fact be safe, I felt pretty sure I should not
like it. I should feel more than a little cold. A nation run only by traffic
rules and the convenient compromising expediencies of other people is
not the kind of nation I want, hardly more than it is the kind of family
I want.

So I am for continuing the quest for values. I even see no harm in
using the word and in sometimes talking about the subject. But I think
we can promise each other only a quest. The alternative to more co-
operation through the market and procedural rules is not a return to a
real or imagined condition of agreement as to values "based on choice-
lessness." Choice is the condition of man today and for the future, so
long as man is free. The alternative to a life of expediency is not to turn
back to some moral authority of the past but to press forward, each now
seeking that part of the good which he finds he needs and which he finds
he shares with others.

The books of the West will continue to help us. But we cannot expect
them to do for us just what they did for those who read them in times
when the meaning of life was found in an education and an experience
more nearly the same for a few people in all Western Europe than it is
today for many people in the whole world. We shall read those books
against the questions and emphases of today: against the impact of our
discovery of man's irrationality, against the involvement of all nations in
a common fate, against the evil we have come to see that men can do,
against the hydrogen bomb. The old books were written without knowledge of the profound alterations in man's condition. Yet the books of
the West record a magnificent conversation. And now the conversation

continues; things said before need to be said now in different ways to meet the questions of the changed condition of mankind. And to the conversation of the West come now to be joined the conversations that other peoples—Chinese, Indians, Muslims—have had, each within that tradition. Already a set of Great Books of the Western World appears just a trifle parochial. Many an Oriental has read some of them as well as great books of his own tradition, and soon we of the West shall find it quite natural to read his books as well as our own. For all traditions are becoming common property. The conversation becomes world-wide.

It seems to me that the state of education in our times and for any future which I should like my children to enjoy is one in which many choices are open to him who seeks to make himself grow. We shall continue to talk with many kinds of people who have different heritages from the past and who take different positions with regard to the content and the source of moral authority. There will be some who find an ultimate authority in some chosen expression of ethical and religious rule. There will be others who are seeking certainty. There will be still others who do not carry on the search, finding that they can decide to do this and not do that, with satisfaction to themselves, but without certainty.

In one of the stories written by the Swedish poet Pär Lagerkvist, mankind, moving through eternity, fail to find God when they all set out to seek certainty, and find him only when they go "to demand of him his boundlessness, his anguish and his space without end." And when God, an old man sawing wood, replies, to their question as to why he did all this to them, that his only intention was that men should never be content with nothing, the wood-sawyer seems to grow tall, immense, and mankind move on in eternity having found a kind of peace.

This is where I suppose that we are now. Some of us will continue to search for certainty. I think that those who hope to find it and those who do not are together in so far as they ask questions about the ends of life. That has always been the human quest. Education is part of the pursuit. When we talk to each other in the course of the pursuit, we help each other in the common effort.

The Indian or the Chinese who reads his own book asks these more ultimate questions, and when he does so, he is closer to me, more helpful to my own education, than is my American neighbor who never asks them. It is a curious fact of modern life that one can sometimes find immediate understanding with someone born and brought up in a part of the world remote from one's own, and yet find a gulf of misunderstanding with an American neighbor close at hand. I think this is because the more ultimate questions, of happiness, virtue, and the nature of the good, are the same questions in every tradition, while the seekers and the accepters are more different from each other than are the seekers from one another. There is nowadays some talk about the lack of understanding between intellectuals and other people in America. Mr. Edward L. Bernays, in an address he gave this year, referred to the current glorification of the doers and the scorn for the thinkers. "Doers" are with us mostly businessmen, and "thinkers," I suppose, are in many cases professors. Mr. Bernays' remedy for the bad relations between the two is to urge the doers to use the special knowledge of the thinkers in getting done the things the doers have to do, such as solving problems of distribution and of what is called "industrial relations." It seems to me that this solution ignores the real difficulty. I do not think the misunderstanding or lack of confidence is so much between thinkers and doers, as it is between the people who ask only, "How shall we get this done?" and the people who ask, "Why should we do it?" It is a separation between the questioners and the takers-for-granted. In our country it is mostly material productivity and individual initiative that are taken for granted; in Russia it is a narrow doctrine policed by the state. But when, anywhere in the world, one asks, against some background of experience, some tradition of questioning and answering, the same questions as to the ends of man and the nature of the good, one has joined a conversation and a quest in which all humanity can ultimately share.

The end of man's existence is not co-operation. It is not even safety. It is to live up to the fullest possibilities of humanity. And man is human only as he knows the good and shares that knowing with those to whom he is, in humanity, bound. It is not necessary that we begin with the same assumptions. It is not necessary that we read the same books, though it is very helpful to do so, especially when we meet to carry on education. What, I think, is most necessary for pursuing the conversation is that we ask the same ultimate questions. The question, "Can we all, on this earth, get along together?" is, of course, an immensely important question because it has to be answered successfully if we are to ask any other. But even more important is the question, "Why should we try to do so? What should we work for, live for? What is the good life?"

Lagerkvist's story, about the talk of mankind in eternity in the course of the search for God, seems to me to describe the historic stages of this conversation. Once men talked only each of his own experience, his own local life. But, as civilization took place, discontent seized us and we began the thoughtful search for meaning, truth, certainty. In the West we associate the beginning of this search with Socrates. Thereafter, for a time, Western mankind seemed to find certainty in some unity of thought. But the movement of man cannot be stayed. We go forward, even toward uncertainty and doubt. Indeed, as our minds grow, so does "the soul's longing"; we must be free to question, to seek, though it is anguish to do so. So we come to a stage in our journey when we are aware that we gather together the experience each has had. In this later stage, when we speak, the words are not about ourselves, "but about the meaning of life, as each sees some part of it, on behalf of everyone." Now, some of us, even in the bad state of the world, begin to ask each question, not as its answer affects only me, or America, or the West, but as it affects all people.

If I should choose a few words to describe the endless act of creation that is education, I should choose these: Education is conversation about the meaning of life, as each sees some part of it, on behalf of everyone. The words are too large for your needs and mine when we prepare to discuss a reading or a topic in some class or discussion group. Though we have in fact joined the quest and entered the "dialogue of civilization," we do not have then to think of our small places in the great enterprise. It is enough if we find the effort a significant joy.

REFERENCES

ADAMS, HENRY. *The Education of Henry Adams.* New York, 1931.

BERNAYS, EDWARD L. "A Thought for Doers," an address given before the Third Annual Institute for Public Relations Directors, University of Kansas at Lawrence, February 26, 1954. Lawrence, Kansas: William Allen White Foundation.

A "Bill to prohibit the transmission through the mails at less than cost of publications, books, other printed matter, and films containing material contrary to the best interests of the United States," introduced in the House of Representatives on May 25, 1954, by Mrs. St. George and referred to the Committee on Post Office and Civil Service.

BRYSON, LYMAN. *Reason and Discontent: The Task of Liberal Education.* The Fund for Adult Education Lectures of 1953. Pasadena, California, 1954.

BUSH, VANNEVAR. "If We Alienate Our Scientists——," *New York Times Magazine,* June 13, 1954.

CARY, JOYCE. *A House of Children.* London, 1941.

DARWIN, CHARLES. *Charles Darwin and the Voyage of the Beagle.* New York, 1945.

DARWIN, FRANCIS (ed.). *The Life and Letters of Charles Darwin.* New York and London, 1925.

FREUD, SIGMUND. *An Outline of Psychoanalysis.* Translated by JAMES STRACHEY. New York, 1949.

GOSSE, EDMUND. *Father and Son.* London, 1912.

HOFFER, ERIC. *The True Believer.* New York, 1951.

HUTCHINS, ROBERT M. *The Democratic Dilemma.* The Gottesman Lectures, Uppsala University. Uppsala and Stockholm, 1951.

KROEBER, A. L. "Stimulus Diffusion," in *The Nature of Culture*, pp. 344–57. Chicago, 1952.

LAGERKVIST, PÄR. "The Eternal Smile," in *The Eternal Smile and Other Stories*. New York, 1954.

LE TOURNEAU, ROGER. "The Muslim Town: Religion and Culture." MS.

LIVINGSTONE, SIR RICHARD. *Education and the Spirit of the Age.* Oxford, 1952.

MAUROIS, ANDRÉ. *I Remember, I Remember.* Translated by DENVER and JANE LINDLEY. New York and London, 1942.

MELVILLE, HERMAN. "Billy Budd," in *Selected Tales and Poems*. Edited by RICHARD CHASE. New York, 1950.

MEREDITH, GEORGE. *The Egoist, A Comedy in Narrative.* New York, 1906.

MONTAIGNE, MICHAEL LORD OF. *The Essayes of Michael Lord of Montaigne.* Translated by JOHN FLORIO. London, 1904.

Natural Science II, Syllabus, The College of the University of Chicago. Chicago, 1947.

ORWELL, GEORGE. *Nineteen Eighty-four.* New York, 1949.

POLANYI, MICHAEL. Unpublished lectures, University of Chicago, 1953.

POTTER, BEATRIX. *The Tailor of Gloucester.* New York, 1931.

RIESMAN, DAVID. *Individualism Reconsidered, and Other Essays.* Glencoe, Illinois, 1954.

SOMERVILLE, ALEXANDER. *The Autobiography of a Working Man.* London, 1854.

STERN, CURT. "Two or Three Bristles," *American Scientist*, XLII (April, 1954), 213.

STEVENSON, ROBERT LOUIS, and OSBOURNE, LLOYD. *The Wrong Box.* New York, 1923.

SUMNER, WILLIAM G. "The Challenge of Facts," in *The People Shall Judge*, II, 82 ff. Selected and edited by the Staff, Social Sciences 1, The College of the University of Chicago. Chicago, 1949.

———. *Folkways.* Boston and New York, 1940.

TAYLOR, HENRY OSBORN. *The Medieval Mind: A History of the Development of Thought and Emotion in the Middle Ages.* New York, 1919.

TOLSTOY, LYOF N. "Who Should Learn Writing of Whom?" *The Novels and Other Works of Lyof N. Tolstoy*, XV, 301 ff. New York, 1904.

WARD, HENSHAW. *Charles Darwin: The Man and His Warfare.* Indianapolis, 1927. (Mr. Ward's quotations from Darwin's own writing with respect to his education have been used in these lectures.)

WHITEHEAD, ALFRED NORTH. *Science and the Modern World.* New York, 1925.

———. *The Aims of Education.* New York, 1949.

WINTHROP, JOHN. Extracts from *The People Shall Judge*, I, 11 ff. Selected and edited by the Staff, Social Sciences 1, The College of the University of Chicago. Chicago, 1949.

WRIGHT, RICHARD. *Black Boy.* New York, 1945.

SAID TO THE STUDENTS IN 240
AT THE LAST CLASS MEETING,
DECEMBER 6, 1957

You will, I think, be interested in some things I have been learning about introductory courses in social anthropology. I have recently been making a small investigation of such courses. There are three of them about which I should like to speak: Anthropology 24, Anthropology 240, and Anthropology 2400.

Anthropology 24 is a well-known course. It is given in many colleges and universities and is generally popular. A student who takes it finds himself comfortable there. He begins by buying a book, one book; this costs him about four dollars, but anyone would pay four dollars to avoid the reserve collection in the library. It is true that other books are mentioned in the course, and the correct references are provided to most of them, but it soon appears that no attention need be paid to them. During the quarter or the semester the student rests comfortably between the covers of the book he has bought. The instructor is comfortable too, because what he is to teach is provided to him also. In some cases he wrote the book, and then, of course, the instructor is very comfortable. When he meets with his students, he adds to the material in the book some facts which he worked up while he was writing his doctoral dissertation; these sometimes enliven the course, and if they don't, they too tend toward restfulness. When the student comes to prepare for the final examination, he has his notes on the remarks made by the instructor, and he has his book. The preparation can be accomplished without much strain. All in all, this course is highly successful, and the real basis of its success, I have found, is that it never presents more than one idea at a time and not too many of these. One is never asked to consider the same facts from contrasting points of view or to perform the exercise of thinking first as one anthropologist has thought and then as another has thought; in this course the anthropological line appears very clearly in the chapter headings of the indispensable book.

In Anthropology 240 none of these conveniences are provided. It is an uncomfortable course. One can never be sure what one ought to think because no one ever tells you and because one is asked to read—or to read in—quite a number of books. From this course one gets an impression of social anthropology very different from that given to those who take Anthropology 24. In 240, social anthropology appears as many kinds of contrastingly original powers addressing themselves in different, and yet somehow not entirely different, ways to a bewildering range and variety of facts about people. Social anthropology in this course is, as one student told me, very hard to get your teeth into. One might get one's teeth into it and perhaps shake it into making sense, if only there were not so many kinds of troubles and discomforts mixed up with the effort made by the mind. Take, for instance, the difficulties in getting books. And the unbelievably concentrated and overcrowded schedule. But, of course, this is nothing I have to tell you about.

It is mostly about Anthropology 2400 that I want to speak. In this course social anthropology appears as it does in Anthropology 240—as many beginnings to construct mental forms for the understanding of society and culture in a very wide context of comparison. The students who take Anthropology 2400, like those who take 240, are given many books and many ideas with which to think. In 2400, also, the instructor is an interlocutor, a leader of that thinking that begins with the student as he reads and thinks about what he reads. As in 240, social anthropology is not one line of thought but many lines, pursuing similar objectives of understanding by way of different conceptions. As in 240, the student's task is not to reflect and repeat but rather to learn to think, first as one anthropologist has thought and then as another, and, one hopes, to begin to make judgments of his own. If he is successful in the course, he has come at the end to know something about social anthropology while also coming to know how little he does know.

But Anthropology 2400 is different from 240 in important ways. In the first place, the reserve book collection is a collection of books for occasional and special reference. It is used by the student whose interest in the subject rises to such a degree that he just has to go find out for himself. One cannot predict exactly where or when that interest will arise and for some it probably never does arise; but the reserve collection is there to make it easy for the student to propel himself forward into matters with which he comes to be specially concerned as the course goes on. The basic readings in the course consist of not many books, all of which the student can buy or rent for the whole period of the course. Most of them can probably be found in the paperbacks. They are books the student can always have with him; as his mind returns to a question, there is the book to take down and to read again. It follows, of course, that the student will have the book with him in class discussions to consult or to use to confound the instructor.

The other great difference between Anthropology 240 and Anthropology 2400 lies in the fact that 2400 is, for all its relentless pursuit of understanding, a leisurely course. It is leisurely in the sense that there is time in which to read the same book twice, to come back to a passage again and again. There is time in which to think about an idea once, and then again, and then again. I hear that in this course the same topic is taken up or reviewed in November, in February, and in April. It seems that those who designed this course understood that learning is a slow fermentation; the brew has to be kept and stirred up again from time to time. These designers also understood that minds do not work best when doing two or three things at the same time, on the same day, or even in the same study period. So, I hear, in Anthropology 2400 the preparations for discussion of texts in class meetings may receive the undivided attention of the student in that share of his time which he gives to this course; he is not at the same time required to write exercises or papers that receive grades on which his fate depends. When he writes something in the early part of the course, his production is not graded, but it is reviewed and criticized, in some cases in class meetings. Only after the student has assimilated some facts and thought some ideas—thought them once and then again—does he write papers that are judged and evaluated in comparison with the like productions of his fellows. In short, the main difference between 240 and 2400 is that while the former course is a steeplechase at full gallop, the latter is an educational experience.

I should add that I have not yet found any place where they give Anthropology 2400. The traveler from whom I heard about the course neglected to tell me that. If ever I find it actually given somewhere, I will let you know. And then, if you go there, you will find me there too, arrived among the first to enrol.

PART II

EDUCATION AND THE
SOCIAL SCIENCES

THE PLACE OF THE SOCIAL SCIENCES IN A GENERAL EDUCATION

The place occupied by the social sciences in schools and colleges that offer a general education is a large one. I do not have to emphasize this. It can be seen from a glance at the catalogues and heard in the loud complaints uttered by proponents of other subject matters, longer established in the curricula, who find their places crowded by these recent invaders—the social sciences.

The place occupied by the social sciences is not only a large one; it is also a hot one and a tight one. Nor does this fact need demonstration. In the current attacks upon colleges and universities claiming subversion and radicalism, the social sciences are the center of the target.

Questions of academic liberty arise chiefly out of utterances about social, economic, or political matters. In any college or university requiring it, the oath of allegiance to the Constitution must be taken by *all* the professors. It is, however, only the social-science professors whose essential task it is to study our Constitution and all constitutions. If a professor is charged with communism or with teaching calculated to undermine the American family, it is social-science subject matter that is involved, and probably a social-science professor.

These are familiar facts. It is more important to consider the questions: Why should the social sciences have a place in general-education training programs? What should they do to deserve the place they have?

I find an answer to both questions in the very fact that popular moral judgments attach to matters of the state, the family, and the market, rather than to photosynthesis, or the laws of thermodynamics. It is just because, in the everyday world, this subject matter is so closely bound by prejudice and practical interests, that to free it from that prejudice and to set it apart from those interests is to liberate the intelligence and contribute to general education.

From this it seems to me to follow that in schools and colleges offering a general education, the social-science materials must be set forth thus: As subject matter to be studied for the sake of studying it, objectively, and in order of matter and problems that seem to the scholar to arise out of the essential character of that matter itself, and not out of the practical concerns of men.

Reproduced from *Growth and Development: The Basis for Educational Programs* (New York: New York Progressive Education Association, 1936), pp. 145–51.

A general education, it is agreed, is something that should stay with the individual and continue to serve him after he has received it. It should provide him, we say, with the means to further understanding. These means are differently named and emphasized—independence of thought, objectivity, accuracy, and the ability to make a reflective synthesis out of knowledge and experience. These capacities are not demonstrated in the treatment of social-science subject matter by untrained persons. They must be learned. But just because objectivity, accuracy, and synthesis are not apparent in social matters, the learning of them is a great achievement of education. Further, these capacities must be learned in connection with social-science subject matter in order that the individual may be able to apply them to social-science subject matter.

It may be true that objectivity and accuracy are more apparent in the physical and biological sciences. But that does not mean that to learn them there is to be liberated from the confusion and the bias which attend matters of society. Biologists and physicists do not show the greatest objective and orderly understanding of social problems. To become free of inherited attitudes about society, one must study society.

A general education, it is also declared, is to orient the individual with regard to his world. By its means he should for himself rework knowledge and ideas into a whole acceptable to his intellect and congenial to his temperament. A general education is, then, synthetic. The subject matter of the social sciences is that part of the individual's world that most concerns him. To an orderly understanding of it—if to anything—a general education should conduce.

But the argument is made that the study of family, market, and state breaks down the faiths and standards with which the student comes to college, turns him to cynicism and endangers his personality. To this I reply that it is life that is confusing, not the college. It is in the world that contrary winds of doctrine blow.

We live no longer under a simple religious faith. If the young person has illusions, he will in life find plenty to disillusion. If he has faith, he will find many to scoff at his faith. And if he seeks security in a new religion, it is likely to be one of the illiberal political-economic dogmas to which he will turn.

A college or university, however, that has realized its essential character is not confusing. It rests upon a single principle of being—the search for an ordered understanding, for its own sake. And the general education it provides is a weapon the young person can take with him into life. With it he may deal with that confusion and resist the dogma.

A general education in the social sciences brings the realization that human behavior and institutions may be considered as natural phenomena and can be compared and distinguished one from another as objects of study and dispassionate reflection. To equip a young person with the viewpoint and methods of scholarship and science for use on the subject matter with which his life as a man and a citizen is most closely involved is not to take something away from him but to add something to him.

I am saying that the theoretical and orderly study of social-science subject matter has a place in a general education. The corollary is that, to deserve the place they have, the social sciences should be theoretical and should be orderly. I think they are often neither. I think it is their responsibility to become both. I think that in failing to define their essential nature as theoretical and orderly they are unready for a struggle with social and economic dogma.

We have recently received a report of the Commission on the Social Studies. The basic document of this report bears the title, "A Charter for the Social Sciences." The language of that report blows hot on one page and cold on the next; but, if I have read its essential conclusion correctly, it includes findings which show that the existing teaching of the social studies takes place within a bias of indoctrination of ideals of individualism and acquisitiveness and that these doctrines are out of step with the economic and political trend of the times. It accordingly recommends that the bias of indoctrination be changed to a bias in favor of collectivism and the conception of the distribution of goods for the welfare of all.

Whatever may be done in teaching the social studies in primary and secondary schools, I think that the way of social science in colleges and universities is not the way recommended by that report. It is the task of social science to seek an understanding of social-science subject matter. It is not the task of social-science teachers to indoctrinate in terms of any philosophy of social or political practice.

Social scientists do inculcate, and they inculcate values. But the values they inculcate are those of theory, scholarship, and science. We call these values objectivity, precision, tentativeness, theoretical analysis and synthesis; or, more briefly, truth.

I think that social scientists *as* social scientists make a mistake if they choose as the essential issue the question as to which bias is more congenial to the times. Whether the next economic organization will be individualist or collectivist is an interesting question. It is an important question. But in defining the causes of social-science teaching in a college or a university, it is entirely irrelevant. That is not the issue for social science. The issue is: "Shall it be recognized that the essential task of social science is the pursuit of understanding of social phenomena for its own sake?"

If we do not make that clear, we have not chosen the *only* ground upon which a struggle for academic liberty can be fought. We may not take refuge in a declaration that there is always some social bias within which social-science teaching takes place and in the false conclusion that social science, therefore, should find and teach within the bias supported by public opinion, or by "enlightened opinion," or by some other opinion as to social policy or program. When one talks in those terms, one is talking the language of those who speak of "Marxian ethnology," or "Jewish physics."

To say that the social sciences, as they form a part in a program of education, should be theoretical is not to say that they should be speculative. They will be as empirical as social scientists find it fruitful to be. They will deal with particular facts of social life and social institutions. But they will set their smaller problems within their larger and build their more comprehensive descriptions, without being bound by a concern for social action.

If the principle for which I declare is sound, it is not enough to declare it. It should be realized in the teaching programs that offer a general education. I think that in many cases it is not realized. The social sciences, as expounded in colleges and universities, are not always unified by the conception that social phenomena may be studied to understand their nature. What represents the social sciences in such programs is in some cases a mere reporting of current events. In other cases, it stops with an explanation of the forms or workings of local and recent institutions. In others, it is even persuasion that this social policy or that practical end be accomplished.

I recognize the contribution which is made to the solution of practical social-economic problems by scholars. I hope that contribution will continue and grow. I say only that what endures in the general education derived from a study of social-science subject matter is the knowledge that such matter may be studied simply to understand it.

What is learned is the means by which to accomplish such ordered understanding. What is important for general education is the capacity to put social phenomena in frames of reference dictated by their nature, to assign them to classes, and to determine relationships felt to be inherent in them.

Therefore, I say, social science must be orderly. It is not enough that social-science teaching free the student from the prejudices with which he grew up. Simple debunking is not good social-science teaching. The student should gain the capacity to see the relationships of parts of social phenomena to wholes, of examples to classes, of causes to their results, of events to their nexuses. He will be interested in his own political and economic problems, but he will see the facts involved in relation to other related or comparable facts of other times or places. His education may work a Copernican revolution of his conception of his social cosmos.

It seems to me that the social sciences are prevented from realizing these objectives by the conventional boundaries which separate them. The existing division of labor among the departmentally recognized social sciences perpetuates the accidents of their several historical developments. It does not favor an orderly presentation of the subject matter and methods with which society may be studied. The social sciences entered the period of specialization of knowledge and the multiplication of courses and departments when they were hardly more than born. This has tended to fix their early and illogical outlines for teaching, administration, and research. Knowledge of social-science subject matter has since advanced, but we are prevented from taking full advantage of the advance for education because conventions of organization have been established, departmental interests have become vested, and teaching has become ritualized.

To look at social-science curricula from this point of view is to see the confusions in their prevailing presentations. It is also to discover how clarity may be achieved. Courses under different names and in different departments cover the same subject matter, or make use of the same method of description. Specialized subject matter is presented without reference to the more general context in which it is a special field. The particular interests of particular teachers—perhaps the extensions of their doctors' theses—are taught as if they constituted social science. And concern with the rightness or wrongness of social policy or with means to accomplish immediate social ends obscures the essential nature of social science.

I do not see how this situation may be remedied without a reordering of social-science curricula. It seems to me that this implies freedom to depart from the groupings of subject matter defined by the traditional disciplines. Just how new groupings will be made will depend, of course, on factors peculiar to each faculty and college. I will suggest three general guides for those of us who think the end worth the effort:

First, social-science training for a general education will center upon the study of society simply to understand it. Vocational and technical instruction will be eliminated from the basic curriculum and elsewhere plainly distinguished from the theoretical work. Universities may also

train persons to deal with practical political, economic, and social problems; but instruction in such terms will be subordinated or segregated.

Second, the selection of the subject matter to be included in the
social-science curriculum will be made because of its general relevance
to all educated persons or to all social scientists. It will not be chosen
on a basis of equal departmental representation. The curriculum will
not be made up simply by sticking end to end the topics which the
participating professors happen to be interested in. It follows that the
social scientists who make this selection must be willing to represent
more than their special fields.

Third, subject matter that belongs logically together will be presented
together. Allied elements will not be kept apart because it has been the
custom to include them in different departments. Such a reordering of
what is now thrown together as "social science" should at once clarify for
the student essential matters, such as the distinction between history and
an inquiry of generalization, the setting of recent Western institutions in
a comparative framework, the applicability of the quantitative method to
various kinds of social data, and the relation of statistical method to other
social-science methods.

These are examples offered as suggestions; I would not venture alone
to rewrite the social-science curriculum. The reordering cannot be done
by administrators. It can be done only by social scientists. The administrators can give the social scientists time in which to put their house in
order and encouragement for the task.

It is the responsibility of the colleges and universities to do this reordering. It is there that social science is being made and remade. It is there
that common problems among social scientists are discovered. The fact is,
however, that the secondary schools are engaged in converting the social
sciences into something called the social studies and are doing it to the
dissatisfaction of many people in the colleges. If teachers in colleges and
universities do not like the way it is being done, they have themselves to
blame. It is because social scientists in higher institutions are too busy
with the perpetuation of their vocational specialties to consolidate the
gains of social science into a common base.

In this country, social scientists are sometimes accused of inculcating a
social doctrine that somebody does not like. They are not yet required, as
they are in other countries, to inculcate a social doctrine that somebody
in authority likes. The way is still open to social scientists to make it clear
that if they inculcate any social doctrine they are not social scientists at
all. They have the opportunity to clarify their teaching so as to remove all
doubt that they have one objective—an ordered understanding of society
and human behavior.

RESEARCH IN THE SOCIAL SCIENCES: ITS SIGNIFICANCE FOR GENERAL EDUCATION

A fable, which Aesop somehow neglected to record, tells of a hen who was making an effort to instruct her chicks about their future sources of food supply while she and they were balanced precariously on a chicken coop which was being carried down a river by a flood. It was a long time since the hen had studied the forests on the bank, and the account she was giving her chicks of forest resources was none too good. So she called to a wise owl on the bank for help. "You know the woods, oh owl, for you stay in this forest and study it," said the hen. "Will you not tell me what to teach my chicks about life in the forest?" But the owl had overheard what the hen had been telling the chicks about the forest as she came along, and he thought it was scientifically inaccurate and superficial. Besides, he was just then very busy completing a monograph on the incidence of beetle larvae in acorns. So he pretended he had not heard the hen. The hen, turned back upon herself, proceeded as well as she could to prepare and put into effect an instruction unit on the food resources of oak forests, meanwhile struggling to keep the chicks from falling off the chicken coop. The chicks took the instruction very well, and later the chicken coop stopped at a point far downstream, and the chicks all went ashore—to begin their adult lives in a treeless meadow.

The problems of the teaching of social science in connection with general education are chiefly two: how to get the owls to help the hens and the hens to make use of what they learn from the owls; and how to take account of the fact that the chicken coop is constantly being carried along the current of events. The first problem is chiefly one of effective organization. Effective organization will help to solve the second problem too, but only if it rests upon a sound philosophy of general education and an understanding of the place of social science in general education. The first problem I will here merely state and then will applaud some recent steps taken to deal with it. To the second problem I can hope to contribute only my own views as to what there is in social science that is most significant for a general education.

The need for closer collaboration between social scientists and teachers of the social studies arises from a number of circumstances. Among these is the demand that has come from educators for an education that deals with contemporary social life. This demand was early filled by a trivial sort of instruction in current events. More recently the tendency has been to organize instruction in the social studies around social problems, that

Reproduced with permission from *Social Education*, V (December, 1941), 568–74.

is, around topics of wide current practical importance to our citizens. In the meantime, the more theoretical social sciences, emphasizing research, have grown in power and competence in the universities and have exerted some influence on the curriculum of the secondary schools and junior colleges. But what little science of government, economics, and sociology has entered the intermediate educational institutions has got there by a sort of osmosis through the cell-walls of school and college.

There has been no organization of social scientist and teacher to deal with the problem. Indeed, the collective wills and interests of the two groups have remained diverse. The social scientists are, on the whole, disinterested in general education and seldom take pains to develop secondary school teachers. The teachers are rarely specialists in those frontiers of social science where new knowledge is won. To the teacher, the social scientist is inaccessible, unco-operative, and ignorant of the problems of teaching. To the social scientist, the teacher of the social studies is confused, superficial, and inclined to debase the currency of science. The teacher continues to write textbooks for the social studies which the social scientist condemns, while the social scientist continues to write monographs which the teacher can hardly read.

The teacher and the social scientist will come to develop common interests in the problem of the social studies and adequate ways to deal with it as they work together on enterprises connected with the problem.

A direct attack upon the problem was initiated by the General Education Board in the spring of 1939 when it invited a group of social scientists interested in problems of social-science education to meet with a few experts in the field of social-science education to discuss the possibilities of improvement in the teaching of the social studies. There resulted a printed document in which it was attempted to define the nature of a social problem and to illustrate the sort of contributions to general education which social scientists might make by formulating three sample social problems for the use of the teacher. In a second edition, this document was revised so as to retain only one of the three specific problems earlier chosen, that dealing with housing. The objective of the writers of the document was to show teachers of the social studies how social scientists of today define, analyze, and study a topic of scientific research that is also a problem for the citizen. The publication was used in, and subjected to criticism by, a number of social-science workshops. The entire enterprise was truly a collaboration between teacher and research worker, for it was the teacher who required that social-science knowledge be given in manageable units for consumption by the teachers and that the units coincide with problems of practical concern to the individual, while it was the social scientist who wrote out the definition of the problem and showed how it was not merely a problem of action but a problem for scientific study.

The history and outcome of this enterprise are probably well known to most of you. You no doubt know that it was followed by action taken jointly by the National Association of Secondary-School Principals and the National Council for the Social Studies leading to the preparation of a series of what are now called "resource units" to be used by teachers in improving instruction in social-science fields.[1] These resource units are now being prepared under a grant from the General Education Board. They will later be tested in the schools. They will differ from teaching aids now issued by various publicity and pressure groups in that they will not attempt to indoctrinate any point of view. They will not be written to promote international peace or safe automobile driving or anything at all except intelligent understanding. They will differ from instruction units now published for the use of progressive schools chiefly in the fact that they will be prepared by leading scientists in the fields in which fall the topics selected. And they will emphasize—at least I hope they will emphasize—the characteristics of the problems selected that make them scientific problems. The analysis will make clear to the teacher and through him to the pupil how the social scientist objectifies that problem, looks all around it, and shapes methods for getting better understanding of it. The manuscript written by the research scientist will then be submitted to specialists in education for additional implementation to make them of the greatest possible use to teachers.

It really seems as if something is being done to bring the owls to the help of the hard-pressed hens. If this undertaking prospers and is followed by others like it, a great deal of what the owls know about acorns and other such subjects will be communicated to the hens, and, after proper translation into simplified clucking, which I am told is appropriate to chicks, will reach the chicks.

But meantime the chicken coop is going on down the river. Will there be any acorns when the chicks go ashore? Writing about the problem of bringing social-science knowledge to teachers in the intermediate schools, Professor Erling M. Hunt says that it "is further complicated by the unceasing change in subject matter to be taught due to new discoveries of scholars and research workers and to new developments in the political, economic, and social scene. Even if it were possible to prepare teachers for the social studies, they could not possibly keep abreast of new developments without help from specialists and popularizers."[2] I will add my

[1] *See* Paul B. Jacobson, "Resource Units for Teachers," *Social Education,* November, 1941.

[2] Louis Wirth (ed.), *Contemporary Social Problems* (2d ed.; Chicago: University of Chicago Press, 1940), p. vi.

opinion that it will be difficult to keep abreast even with all the help they can get and will add my advice that they do not try too hard to keep abreast in all subjects of the degree of particularity represented by acorns.

Any list of social problems which is selected will have to be revised at intervals that will not be very long. The list recently made in connection with the writing of resource units about which I have just been speaking begins with Democracy and Dictatorship and ends with Agriculture. It is certainly a timely list. It includes also American Defense and Recreation. It is a safe guess that as American Defense grows as a topic of current importance, that part of the subject of Recreation which deals with the use of leisure time is likely to decline in importance. And what the next five years are likely to do with the subject of Consumer Problems it would take a hardier prophet than I to venture to say. As there will certainly be consumers in 1946, there will be consumer problems; but will they be the same as face consumers today?

At last I find myself confronting the subject that was assigned to me to discuss. What is the significance of social-science research to a general education? I offer an answer that I believe simplifies the problem presented by the fact that we can't stop the chicken coop from going on down the river. I think that problem is only in lesser part met by the perfection of organizations which more promptly communicate to the teacher the results of research done by the expert. Such organizations will take advantage of the *particular* results of social-science research. But a more radical attack upon the problem, in my opinion, comes about when there is clarification of the *general* significance of social-science research for general education. I say that the primary significance of social-science research for general education lies in the nature of social-science research itself, as that method is applicable to any and all topics. I say that it is more important for teacher and pupil to understand that a social problem can be also a scientific problem and what universal considerations attend the scientific way to attack it than it is for them to be up to date on any chosen list of timely topics. I say that it is better for the chicks to understand that one can get objective, generalized, verifiable knowledge of either meadow or forest than it is for them to be up to the minute on what the owl has found out about acorns.

I am not saying that every citizen should be made a social scientist. Such a suggestion would be ridiculous. I am merely saying that one of the elements of a modern general education is understanding of what is involved when one studies a social problem scientifically, just as understanding of the great forms of literary expression or of the essential nature of matter and life is a part of a modern general education.

I am not saying that we should abandon instruction in the form of units organized around practical problems of current interest. That method should be retained, because those subjects are both interesting and important. The demand will continue that we teach our young people about the problems of unemployment and public revenue and good government, and it is a desirable thing that they learn about these things. I am merely giving my opinion that there is something in the teaching of the social studies that is more important than having the right topics and more important than including in their treatment all the most recent knowledge on the field. It is more important that the nature of social science, its powers and limitations, be understood. This seems to me worth declaring because I do not believe that social problems are, on the whole, taught in high schools and junior colleges as scientific problems. I think they are chiefly taught to give information, or to awaken a social conscience, or to indoctrinate some point of view approved by some teacher's college committee or by public opinion. However desirable it may be to inform and to indoctrinate, neither information nor indoctrination is the contribution of social-science research to a general education.

A general education differs from a professional or a vocational education in that it is general. It is concerned with those aspects of knowledge which are relevant to all men and women and to many situations and experiences. The aspects of social-science research which have this general characteristic are recognizable in any well-conducted piece of social-science research, whether it deal with housing, population, business cycles, or the religious beliefs of the Navajo Indians. I will attempt to state some of them.

It is part of a general education to understand, in the first place, that there is a social science, as distinct from common-sense knowledge about society and as distinct from social reform. Every educated person should know that to a great extent society can be studied objectively and systematically, as can starfish or the action of glaciers. One can get impersonal, organized, verifiable knowlede about housing, crime, and race relations, as one can get such knowledge about any other phenomena of nature. An educated person will know how to distinguish the scientific way of attacking a social problem from those ways of attacking it which are more generally practiced around him. He will understand that in a great many instances people do something about a social problem because they feel badly about it rather than because they understand it and that what they do corresponds with their feelings rather than with the facts underlying the problem. He will understand that this is true, whether the action taken be to write a letter to the newspapers, to pass a law, or to demand changes in the school curriculum. It is a part of general education to understand that scientific knowledge is different from feeling strongly about something and from common-sense knowledge and that it is a more secure basis for social action than either.

The successful teacher of the social studies will make clear to his pupils that there is a difference between the analysis of processes, which are matters of efficiency, and other objective judgments. The citizen must know what are his values, and he should understand how to act so as to protect or realize them. The uneducated person confuses values and processes, ends and means; a good education in social science will help to keep them distinct.

As a part of this understanding, the educated man or woman will have been taught that a social problem is not a simple thing. Social problems are closely intermeshed with one another. If one makes a beginning with the problem of housing, one finds that it is only one aspect of the larger problem of national insecurity. It is also related to the problem of the national income and to that of the national health. The solutions given in the form of new housing projects or in zoning laws encounter the problems of racial intolerance. It follows from this that a social problem does not mean the same thing to everybody. A striking feature of that memorandum on housing which was recently prepared as a first experimental resource unit for teachers of the social studies occurs in the introductory pages where it is pointed out that the problem of housing looks very differently to laymen, land-owners, builders, tax officials, and city planners, and where it is shown that full understanding of the problem depends upon special scientific knowledge of economists, sociologists, and students of government. The contribution of social-science research to a general education is not made use of when a social problem is presented to young people as if it existed with simple reference to some social ideal. It is not made use of if the problem is presented as if all one had to do was to take note of the social injustice attending the present state of things. That is not functional education; it does not prepare the young person for life.

A further contribution which social-science research can make to general education is the understanding that although social science is like physical or biological science in that it is objective, systematic description of the world around us, it differs from physical and biological science in that all the facts and all the problems are controversial. The social scientist is studying, chiefly, to put it strongly, himself, and one cannot help feeling and caring about one's self. We, as human beings, care about the institutions and social problems which the social scientist studies. Therefore it is harder for the social scientist to maintain objectivity than it is for the physicist, and it is harder for Society, with a capital "S," to keep from interfering with the social scientist than with the physicist. This is one of the elements of understanding of social-science research which belongs in a general education. If social problems are presented by the teacher of the social studies so as to communicate this general knowledge of the nature of social science it will be made clear to the learner that the mere facts of social science lie within a realm of controversy and prejudice. As Professor Wirth has pointed out,[3] even the number of people living in a given city of the United States is a controversial matter in the sense that if the city has been losing population the Chamber of Commerce will not want the fact to get abroad. The number of people unemployed in this country is a controversial fact, first, in the sense that various interest groups care as to what criterion is selected for determining who is unemployed, and, second, because even if it is decided who are unemployed, various groups will interpret the fact according to their interests. For some employers there will be just enough unemployed to assure a labor reserve, while for other of our citizens these same unemployed constitute a problem of providing relief.

At the same time the educated man or woman will understand that this special difficulty under which the social scientist labors has its compensation in a special advantage enjoyed by the social scientist and understanding of the nature of social-science research is not complete until another general characteristic of it is recognized. It is a peculiarity of the scientific method as applied to man in society that the investigator can get a more intimate knowledge of his subject matter than can the physicist of his, just because he is part of it. The physical scientist learns of his subject matter only as caliper and scales can tell him about it. The social scientist can ask questions of his subject matter and get answers, and he can project his own humanity imaginatively into the subject matter and so increase his understanding of it. The contribution of social-science research to a general education is provided in part by an understanding of the advantages and the dangers of this essential characteristic of social-science research. The social scientist does not abolish his own prejudices any more than he abolishes his own human nature. But he controls prejudice by making it explicit. So, too, he develops controlled use of his human insights. It is more important to a general education that the individual knows that there is a problem of using and controlling the human faculty of insight as a scientific instrument than that he know the latest facts with regard to any problem studied by that method.

I say again that the primary significance of social-science research for a general education lies in the nature of social science. The nature of social science can not be taught in abstract terms. It is conveniently and

[3] In "Biases in Education for Business," *Business Education for What?* Proceedings of the University of Chicago Conference on Business Education (Chicago: University of Chicago Press, 1940), p. 2.

appropriately taught in connection with particular social problems. I think that it can also be taught by direct participation of teacher—and ultimately of the young student too—in elementary sorts of social-science research. The way to do this is pointed out to us by the recent development of the workshop as a method of instruction of teachers and other mature people. When Jones looks at the social world immediately around him and at the problems with which Jones has to deal, objectively, and relates these to larger and more theoretical considerations, then Jones learns something about social science. The future teaching of social science will include opportunities for Jones, while he is still a pupil in a secondary school, to get some direct understanding of how social facts are collected and ordered in the elementary aspects of social-science method. The community around the school is at hand, ready to be considered from the point of view of the social scientist, and it will be used more systematically than it is now being used in the future teaching of the social studies. This is one reason for the significance of the topic to which today's program is devoted.

In so far as the teaching of social problems, whether by book or by direct observation of social life, contributes to the fundamental and lasting broadening of knowledge and intelligence which we call a general education it will show how social science, rather than doctrine, or wishful thinking, or common sense, deals with those problems. It will show that social problems have many sides and are interrelated with one another. It will show how these difficulties are surmounted. It will make clear that there are ways of making social knowledge verifiable. It will show something of the methods of proof used in establishing social facts. It will develop respect for those conclusions in the realm of the social which depend upon the consensus of the competent, and it will do this by showing the methods by which these competent ones arrive at consensus. If the teachers of the social studies are able to communicate some of these matters to the young, it will not matter much if the list of problems which they teach is not perfect or if their knowledge of the results of particular research in particular fields is not up to date. It will not then be so serious a matter if the chicken coop comes ashore in a meadow instead of a forest. For then the young person will have learned what there is to know about social science which will help him as an adult citizen under any circumstances of life.

A CONTRIBUTION OF ANTHROPOLOGY
TO THE EDUCATION OF THE TEACHER

This is far from the first time that an anthropologist has spoken as such about education and teaching. Two other such occasions have fallen within my own direct experience in recent years, and I have consulted the records of these occasions to learn what I should say on this present occasion. The first occasion was a symposium on "Education and the Cultural Process" held at Fisk University in March, 1941, and the other was a symposium on "Environment and Education" held at the University of Chicago in September of that same year. Altogether nine anthropologists contributed ten papers (**2, 3**) to these two symposiums—all on some aspect of education or teaching as looked upon by an anthropologist. On reading over these papers, I receive a strong impression that, in spite of their apparent diversity, all these anthropologists, are, at bottom, saying the same thing. Consequently I am led to entertain the idea that this is perhaps the only thing that anthropologists have to say, or perhaps that it is the most important thing, and that in either case it is what I had better try once more to say.

BASIC IDEA OF "A CULTURE"

This basic anthropological idea is that every individual lives within something called "a culture"—a body of customs and beliefs which provide satisfaction to his human needs and adjustment to his environment. This culture is thought of as something special to each of the many societies in which mankind lives, and it is the many special cultures, separable and comparable, which these anthropologists are usually thinking about when they talk about education. The people of the Trobriand Islands live within or in terms of a culture which is notably different in content from the culture of the Dakota Indians, and yet it is reported or assumed by these anthropologists that the Trobriand culture does the same thing for the people who happen to live as Trobrianders as that which is done by Dakota culture for the people who happen to be Dakota Indians.

A reading of these ten papers makes it evident that all the contributing anthropologists regard each of these cultures as having a necessary and important character: integration, or wholeness. In words used by Malinowski in his paper, each culture is "an organic unit." The customs and

An address delivered July 25, 1945, at the Fifth Annual Conference for Teachers of the Social Sciences in Secondary Schools and Junior Colleges at the University of Chicago and reproduced with permission from *School Review*, LIII (November, 1945), 516–25.

beliefs which are the parts of the whole are consistent with one another and depend on one another. Mekeel refers to such a culture as "an operational totality" and declares that every culture has "a matrix, a configuration, into which the pieces fit." He denies that a culture "is an index of easily movable items" and tells us that 'it must be viewed as a meaningful whole." The Dakota Indians serve chicken and dog meat at a wedding feast, not simply because the two are palatable and available, but because chicken symbolizes the American way of life and dog meat the Indian way; in their situation, marginal to two cultures, both configurations are represented by meaningful symbols in the form of food. Mekeel goes on to tell us that even the ways in which very young children are trained in their excretory habits are consistent with the type of character which is adaptive to, or consistent with, their adult life and that, therefore, these ways of infant training are also parts of the culture, the integrated whole.

Plainly these anthropologists regard integrated culture with favor. They are not indifferent to it; they think it good that there be consistency and wholeness in the culture in terms of which the individual lives his life. The thing which it is thought that a culture does for an individual is a good thing. It is thought that the culture provides the individual with goals, with purpose and significance for his actions, and with the sense that all the activities he carries on are contributory toward realization of these goals. In such a culture the individual knows what he ought to do and finds himself doing it. Conversely, these anthropologists view with alarm attempts to educate without due reference to effects of the education in making the culture less integrated, less whole. Malinowski writes that "the anthropologist recognizes more and more fully how dangerous it is to tamper with any part or aspect of culture, lest unforeseeable consequences occur." As an example he chooses sorcery among African natives, advises caution to anyone trying to educate the natives out of a belief in sorcery, and tells us that, examined in its cultural setting, African sorcery turns out to be a crude but often effective way of managing misfortune, disease, and death and that the natives would be worse off without the sorcery than they are with it. He advises the teacher in Africa to abstain from trying to teach natives not to believe in sorcery, but rather to leave it alone until, by gradual introduction of hygiene and other security-giving modifications, the culture no longer has any place for sorcery, which will of itself disappear. Thus the picture we get of a culture is that of a complex structure in which all the parts are fitted together. The anthropologist tells us not to try to pull out a few pieces that we do not like lest the whole come tumbling down; he wants us to understand the relations of the parts to the whole and, guided by this knowledge, to accomplish a change in manner of life through gradual substitutions.

This conception of "a culture" is, it seems, a peculiar contribution of anthropology to the understanding of human behavior. It is a conception certainly related to, but not the same as, the conception of "human culture"—that aggregate of invention and institution which began when the first stick or stone was kept and its use was explained by one ancient primate to another. Culture in the general and singular serves to set off all mankind as against all animals. Culture in the particular and the plural serves to set one society off as against another. The idea of separate and comparable cultures, one to a local community, is an outgrowth of intimate study of tribal and peasant life in the past two or three generations. You do not find the conception in the pages of Edward Burnett Tylor or in those of Sumner's *Folkways* (4). It appears in the detailed accounts of special primitive groups, finds its most eloquent and persuasive statement in the works of Malinowski, and is expressed also simply and compellingly in Ruth Benedict's *Patterns of Culture* (1). As it is an idea that would naturally develop out of the study of the various primitive societies, it has been anthropologists who have developed it.

SIGNIFICANCE TO EDUCATION OF IDEA OF INTEGRATED CULTURE

If this is *the* important, or at least *an* important, contribution of anthropology to the understanding of human living, my assignment is to provide an answer to the question: What is the significance of the conception of integrated cultures to the training of teachers? Fortunately there is guidance in the papers of the symposiums to which I have referred. I will, however, state the matter as I see it and use the suggestions of these other anthropologists without making them responsible for the formulations that I reach.

In the first place, I assert that, merely because each of us, with few exceptions, grows up in one of these cultures and by this fact is limited in his understanding of his own conduct and that of other people, the coming to know another culture than our own should be a great liberalizing experience. I think, therefore, that the giving of this experience is a task of those who shape the programs of general education. The point I here make is thus a point for teachers in so far as teachers, like everybody else, should have a general education of which this element should be a part, and also for teachers in so far as teachers make the programs of general education for other people.

The end in view here is to bring the young person to understand that every normal human being is reared in a society with ways of life characteristic of that society; that these ways "make sense" as one way is seen to be related to the next, consistent with it and supporting it; that the motives which people have and the values which they embrace are derived, generally speaking, from this traditional culture. The further objective is to lead the young person to look back upon his own culture from the vantage point secured in the understanding gained of other cultures and thus achieve that objectivity and capacity to consider thoughtfully his own conduct and the institutions of his own society which are, in part, a result of thinking as if within another culture. On the one hand, the end is to cause the individual to see that there are ways other than his own which are compatible with human needs and with the dignity of the individual; on the other hand, the end is, through comprehension of another way of life, to develop the power to think well about one's own way of life so that that way may be improved. To some degree the study of anthropology provides this liberalizing experience through the acquaintance it gives with cultures other than our own, and much of the appeal which anthropology has for young people in schools and colleges comes from the fact that it provides such experience. I think this contribution primarily belongs, however, not in the training of anthropologists but in the general education of everybody. How to get it there is something that is yet to be determined.

Because we cannot move a tenth-grade class every afternoon to China or Central Africa, we shall have to teach about these countries chiefly through books and pictures. A principal requirement is time: vicarious acquaintance with, say, Chinese village culture might be sufficiently achieved in one or two years of persisting attention to the subject. I am sure that almost nothing is accomplished toward the end I have in view by the current practice in primary and secondary schools of dividing a year of social studies into short periods in each of which a new subject is taken up, at fortnightly intervals, from Russia to money or minority groups—and, indeed, I doubt that anything very important is accomplished toward any good end. In place of this succession of bowing acquaintances with miscellaneous subjects which are connected, I suppose, in one way or another with the modern world, I suggest the possibility of substituting a persisting and penetrating consideration of some society and culture notably different from our own and well provided with documentation. This might be a principal part of the social-studies curriculum at some place between the ninth and twelfth school years.

SIGNIFICANCE TO TEACHERS OF IDEA OF INTEGRATED CULTURE

This suggestion is an application of the conception of integrated cultures to the making of a curriculum in general education. I turn now to other ways in which the conception may be relevant to teaching. An application may be made of the conception of an integrated culture to the teaching activity itself. If cultures consist of an integration of customs and institutions, then teaching itself may be looked at as one such element more or less integrated in the culture of the community in which the teaching is carried out. This point is, indeed, made in several of the anthropological papers contributed to the two symposiums that I mentioned at the beginning of my remarks. Seeing formal education in its relation to other aspects of culture, these anthropologists are struck by its relative unimportance. They remind us at the beginning of their discussion that schooling is only a small part of education in the broad sense, "the process of cultural transmission and renewal." By the time the child comes to the teacher, he has already passed his most formative years, and the informal instruments of education have already largely shaped his world. What the school can do after that is correspondingly limited. Furthermore, what the school can do continues to be limited by the more powerful influences of the home, the play group, and the neighborhood. Do not expect to accomplish more than is possible, say these anthropologists to the teacher, and you may successfully teach that which finds some support, some basis of consistency, with the culture as it is transmitted in informal communication outside the schoolroom. So Mekeel is not surprised that Indian children, after many years of residence in government schools, in which attempts are made to teach the ways of white men, so often return to Indian life. So Malinowski warns the teacher in Africa not to separate, by his teaching, the child from the native community where he enjoys the warmth and security of life in an integrated culture. The lesson for the teacher from such observations is that teaching is not to be regarded as a technique of inculcation or of stimulation learned from books or from other teachers and thence applicable to a classroom, as medicine may be administered to a sick man, or fertilizer to a farmer's field. The suggested application is that teaching is effective in so far as it tends toward the development in the young person of a coherent body of attitudes and values adequate to the life-needs in his particular community. The classroom is important only as it is understood in its relation to the society and culture of the children who occupy it, and teaching will be effective only as it is related to society and culture.

Being established in the viewpoint of culture as an organic unity, anthropologists seem to be calling upon the teacher to understand, not so much teaching methods, as the community in which the teaching takes place. The real nature of effective teaching, these anthropologists are in effect declaring, lies, not in ways of preparing instruction units nor in devices for testing reading comprehension, but rather in the part played by the school and by what goes on in the school in the cultural life of the children's community. I suspect that in this the anthropologists are telling the teachers to look to matters which teachers in fact do constantly look to because they cannot help it, even though these are not matters that bulk large in the formal training of teachers. In one of the symposium papers Warner looks at the school in the community as he would look at initiation rites in a primitive society, as from the outside. He finds that the high school in the American towns that he has studied is one of many institutions which express and maintain, among other things, the system of ranking according to social status which characterizes the society. The lower-class pupils study commercial and technical courses. The upper-class children take courses that prepare them for college. The children of each class are taught what will fit them for the station in life which it is expected they will assume. Moreover, he finds a marked tendency to classify children in supposed intelligence groups according to the social positions of their parents, so that a child from the upper class is not put in the lowest intelligence group even if his individual performance might put him there. Still further, he finds that what teachers do to warp theoretically impartial educational procedures to fit the local cultures is done largely because the same result is accomplished anyway by the informal groupings of children in and out of the school. The children's cliques bring about an assorting of children according to their parents' social positions, and the school, in effect, is conforming to these other less visible institutions. Warner is thus applying the conception of an integrated culture to the school and its community. "Understand these," he seems to say to the teacher, "if you would understand what your teaching does, can do, and cannot do."

SIGNIFICANCE OF IDEA OF CULTURE IN MODERN SCHOOLS

The possibility that teaching will not be integrated with the rest of the cultural life of the child is, obviously, increased to the degree that the teacher represents a way of life different from that of the child. The possibility will be very great when an outsider comes to teach in a native community, whether the community be one of Africans or Indians or Kentucky mountaineers. Missionary teaching is often ineffective or disintegrating because it is not related or is unwisely related to the local culture. But the same danger exists, in compound form, in urban schools where the children represent not one integrated culture but many disintegrated cultures, and the teacher not only does not, but could not, teach to develop a single coherent integration if he wanted to. What, then, is the significance of the conception of the individual in one integrated culture in connection with teaching in a society where there is no integrated culture? What is the value of this anthropological conception, developed in primitive society, in modern urban society? It is all very well for the anthropologist to advise the teacher what he may do or even should do in teaching Indians or native Africans, but what can the anthropologist helpfully tell the modern teacher in a modern school?

Half of the answer depends on the extent to which the modern city community is like an Indian tribe or an African village, and part of this half of the answer is given by Warner when he, in effect, urges the student of teaching to study the school in its community. If the student does so, he will find the extent to which the school in integrated with other institutions and helps to perpetuate a local culture. Part of this same half of the answer is expressed in Mead's paper read at the Fisk University symposium. This anthropologist considers the function, not of the school in the community, but of the whole institution of education in modern society, as if she were studying warfare in New Guinea. She finds that its function is different from the function of education in primitive societies. In primitive societies education depends, she says, on the will to learn something that everybody assumes one would want to learn. In modern society it depends on the will to teach something that somebody thinks ought to be taught, even though not everybody wants to learn it. This different nature of education in modern society leads, she goes on to tell us, to a conception of education as something that may not so much perpetuate an old society as make a new one. The society it may make is so new that none of us living now is able to say what it will be, and yet it is supposed that these children whom you and I educate, or their children, will make that society and that the kind of education we give them will somehow fit them for doing so. This is indeed a far cry from the way in which a tribal Indian or isolated African native would look at the educational institutions of his own society. He thinks of education, so far as he thinks of it at all, as something that will perpetuate the kind of life which he has always known. Mead is telling us that, just as modern society is different, in kind, from all primitive societies, taken as another kind, so education is and must be different.

What is this difference in the two kinds of societies or cultures? In the paper that she contributed to the Chicago symposium, Mead enumerates three differences: (1) Primitive cultures are homogeneous, while ours is heterogeneous. (2) Primitive cultures change very slowly, while ours changes rapidly and constantly. (3) The population stocks of primitive societies are relatively less diversified than are ours. Mead thereby recognizes that modern urban culture is different in kind from all primitive societies. As the culture is changing rapidly and constantly, there cannot be one well-integrated culture. What children do is different from what adults do, and indeed adults come to think—some of them—that it is right that children do something different. Moreover, the changes come so rapidly that during the school years of one individual he may be taught completely inconsistent ideas. Benedict, in her paper, makes this point. There are periods when we tell children to be saving of money; there are others when it is a public duty to spend. There have been recent periods when war was unexceptionally evil and "the earth was unanimous for peace," and there have been more recent periods when, as she says, you might go to jail for saying so. As our culture is always changing and is never integrated, Benedict concludes that "education in our world today must prepare our children to adapt themselves to unforeseeable conditions."

At this point is is apparent that the conception of an integrated culture has undergone some significant alteration. The anthropologists to whom we have looked for guidance began by telling us that every individual lives in a well-integrated culture. Now some of them seem to be confirming our suspicions that, in the case of our own society, no individual does. The question may then be repeated: What is the significance of the conception of the individual in one integrated culture in connection with teaching in a society where there is no one integrated culture? Again, the first half of the answer may be repeated: In some degree, as in Warner's studies of the place of the school in the status system, there is integration in modern society, and the school is part of that integration. But the other half of the answer may be given also. The value of the conception of the individual in a well-integrated culture lies, in part, in the suggestive contrast between our own case and the case of the stable primitive societies. We should not so well see the peculiar problems and responsibilities of modern education if we did not see modern education as a special and variant case of education in all societies. That it is special and variant is expressly stated by Mead. In stable societies with well-integrated cultures, all educative influences, she says, operate simultaneously and consistently upon the individual, and she has illustrated this fact vividly in her series of photographs showing the treatment accorded babies in Bali. But in our heterogeneous and changing society there is a qualitative difference, she says; what the radio says may be quite unrelated to what mother says to baby, and what mother-in-law over in the corner manages to convey by a gesture is emphatically in contradiction. It is the inconsistencies, the lack of integration, that make our society different from stable primitive societies. In a sort of definition by indefinition, it is this lack of integration which gives our society its character. Interestingly enough, of all the contributors to these two symposiums, it is not an anthropologist but a psychiatrist, Franz Alexander, who says this most plainly. "Paradoxically stated," he says, "the pattern of our world is that it has no fixed pattern." For the psychiatrist the significance of this conclusion lies in the need to study individual careers in terms of individual life-histories. For the teacher the significance lies in the need to develop the capacities of the individual to deal with circumstances which the teacher cannot foresee.

THE TEACHER'S TASK

The conception of one integrated culture leads, therefore, to a view of the task of the teacher which sees it as double. The conception is helpful to the teacher, in part because it is directly applicable to the child in "this" school in "this" community. The conception is helpful, in part because it is not directly applicable. The apparent contradiction is resolved by distinguishing the short run in time and the local setting from the long run in time and the wider setting. So far as the short span of years is concerned, and in the local neighborhood (especially if that neighborhood be in one of the more stable towns and not in a community of rapidly changing population), the school will be found reasonably well integrated with the rest of the cultural life, and what can be accomplished by the teacher will be limited by these relationships which it is, therefore, necessary for him to understand. On the other hand, the school is an instrument for social change and is accepted as such, both by laymen and by educational leaders. For example, while it is true, as Warner says, that the high school perpetuates the status system of the community, it is also true, as Mead says in her paper read at Fisk University, that education is a recognized means by which the individual may leave his social rank and move to another. For the more remote future, education, to us, exists to develop powers to deal with contingencies beyond our powers of prediction. Children are to be educated so as to find what personal and cultural security they can find in the communities that now exist, and they are also to be educated to make, by effort and understanding, new integrations out of whatever pieces of living the future may bring them. The teacher today is both a perpetuator of an old integration and a builder of the power to meet disintegration. If a paradox remains, it is not one that I have invented; it exists in the nature of modern life.

REFERENCES

1. BENEDICT, RUTH. *Patterns of Culture*. New York, 1934.
2. *Education and the Cultural Process*. Papers presented at a symposium commemorating the seventy-fifth anniversary of the founding of Fisk University, April 29–May 4, 1941. Edited by CHARLES S. JOHNSON. Reprinted from the *American Journal of Sociology*, XLVIII (May, 1943). Individual papers of special interest to educators are:

MEAD, MARGARET. "Our Educational Emphases in Primitive Perspective," pp. 5–11.

REDFIELD, ROBERT. "Culture and Education in the Midwestern Highlands of Guatemala," pp. 12–20.

MALINOWSKI, BRONISLAW. "The Pan-African Problem of Culture Contact," pp. 21–37.

WATKINS, MARK HANNA. "The West African 'Bush' School," pp. 38–47.

MEKEEL, SCUDDER. "Education, Child-training, and Culture," pp. 48–53.

BENEDICT, RUTH. "Transmitting Our Democratic Heritage in the Schools," pp. 94–99.

HERSKOVITS, MELVILLE J. "Education and Cultural Dynamics," pp. 109–21.

POWDERMAKER, HORTENSE. "The Channeling of Negro Aggression by the Cultural Process," pp. 122–30.

3. *Environment and Education.* A symposium held in connection with the fiftieth anniversary celebration at the University of Chicago. *Supplementary Educational Monographs,* No. 54. Chicago, 1942. Papers presented at the symposium are:

BURGESS, ERNEST W. "Educative Effects of Urban Environment," pp. 1–15.

WARNER, W. LLOYD. "Educative Effects of Social Status," pp. 16–28.

ALEXANDER, FRANZ. "Educative Influence of Personality Factors in the Environment," pp. 29–47.

MEAD, MARGARET. "Educative Effects of Social Environment as Disclosed by Studies of Primitive Societies," pp. 48–61.

ALEXANDER, FRANZ. "Additional Remarks," pp. 62–66.

4. SUMNER, WILLIAM GRAHAM. *Folkways: A Study of the Sociological Importance of Usages, Manners, Customs, Mores, and Morals.* Boston, 1907.

ISSUES FACED IN THE IMPROVEMENT OF UPPER-DIVISION CURRICULUMS IN THE SOCIAL SCIENCES

The man who sets out to improve the teaching of the social sciences in the upper division of a university has already turned his back—to use a manner of speech attributed to the Irish—on many of the important issues that he faces. Decisions have already been made in the lower division and in the secondary and primary schools which, in effect, determine what he may do in making a social-science curriculum for the Junior and subsequent years. Some of these prior decisions fix a general policy as to the role of upper divisions in the providing of opportunities for kinds of education—general or special, liberal or vocational. Others concern the content of earlier education and so shape the capacities and

Excerpts from an article in John Dale Russell (ed.), *Emergent Responsibilities in Higher Education* (Chicago: University of Chicago Press, 1945), pp. 95–106.

interests of the Juniors and Seniors and post-Seniors for whom the curriculum-maker of the upper division is to plan. Therefore it does not seem possible to consider the topic assigned me without talking also about education in the fourteen years that come before the Junior year of college, and it seems possible to talk about issues faced in the improvement of upper-division curriculums in the social sciences only after making some assumptions as to how prior issues have been decided. . . .

If, then, I am to consider what to expect every social scientist to know about society and the scientific study of society, I must have some view as to what he should know about these things already as a generally educated person. My ideas on this are far from certain or complete, but I will mention three elements of a general education which I imagine might conveniently be acquired before the end of the twelfth year and one or two which I imagine to be appropriate to general education in the twelfth to fourteenth years.

I imagine, first, that it is part of general education to come to understand the difference between fact and opinion as to matters of man's society: to recognize the expression of a wish or of a norm when it appears and not to confuse it with a verifiable decription of an institution or of human behavior; to know some of the most elementary ways in which one can get objective special knowledge as to man's society; and to command the use of some common source materials for getting such knowledge, such as census reports and the records of deliberate and tested observation. This I should think could be learned before the end of the twelfth school year.

I imagine, second, that it is a part of general education to come to know one or more cultures different from that in which the individual has been raised; to come to see that this other culture is a way of life providing, with inner consistency, for human needs and for the dignity and worth of the individual, and so to look back on one's own culture and see it, freshly and as an educated person does, as from the outside. I am bold enough to suppose that this, too, could be learned before the end of the twelfth year. It would take a year or two or three of persisting vicarious acquaintance with the chosen culture, or perhaps two of them. It would mean eliminating a great many of those fortnight-long doses of instruction which go by the name of "instruction units" and which follow a two-weeks study of China with a two-weeks study of minority groups, money, or the British Empire.

In the third place I entertain the thought—entertain it in the face of discouragement but with desperate fidelity—that the educated young person might by the end of the twelfth year have learned how to read a few good books having to do with society and man's human and social

nature, by really reading them, deliberately and thoughtfully, over sufficient periods of time.

To these three desired elements of early general social-science education are to be added some knowledge of places and the course of past
events; this is more nearly realized in existing curriculums, and therefore
I do not stress it. I want it included.

In the thirteenth and fourteenth years, and perhaps also in the twelfth,
I suppose that the study of man in society becomes more penetrating
and sophisticated and, in the extended analysis of a few major selected
social problems, employs the capacities and competences that I have
assumed to be acquired in earlier years. It is here that the young person
is led to analyze, in adult fashion, the choices and responsibilities that
he must face as a citizen. History and the special social sciences, not
necessarily separated out according to their names, are present in a
consideration of a chosen topic from many sides and with all available
sources of illumination. The subjects are such as younger persons could
not well comprehend: the transition from non-industrial rural society
to urbanized industrial society; the issues that arise in preserving chosen
ultimate values, such as freedom, along with other and partly inconsistent values, such as order and security. (The examples chosen are
taken from social-science curriculums in the thirteenth and the fourteenth
years of my own institution; others could be substituted.) In these years
social science makes its last contribution to the education of men and
women whose formal education here ends or who continue their education as biologists or students of the humanities or something else.
Therefore the treatment is addressed to the needs and interests of the
general citizen; the topics are the issues that face us all, in a world of
living and action, and they are treated not at all so as to inculcate attitudes—other than the intellectual virtues—but to achieve the greatest
ability to think well about the issues of contemporary society.

If this be the end sought in the social-science contribution to a general education, then the end sought in the upper division must be one
appropriate to more specialized education. What should a student of
social science know about social science that is beyond that which is
known by any well-educated citizen? I am concerned here with that
question so far as it relates to all students of social sciences, whatever
their fields of specialization within social science. I suggest that the
answer is to be found through attending to the difference between the
citizen and the social scientist. The need and the interest of the citizen
are necessarily connected with issues of action and are less concerned
with systematic theory. The need and the interest of the social scientist
are less necessarily connected with issues of action and are more concerned with systematic theory. The one is farther removed from method

and theory than is the other. So it would follow that the social-science curriculum for social scientists should be concerned with method and with theory. I think of a presentation of method and theory, not in the abstract, but always in terms of illustrative problems concerning concrete subject matter.

In studying his field of specialization, economics or social psychology or political science or some special field that is not departmentally defined, the student will learn the ways of doing research that are appropriate to that field and the concepts and generalizations that are found useful there. One of the things he needs also to know is the relations of these to techniques, concepts, and generalizations elsewhere in social science. A second thing he needs to know is the philosophical bases of knowledge as to man in society. A third thing he needs to know is the principal attempts that have been made to provide systems of thought for the understanding of man in society. These three—methods and concepts, the philosophical or metaphysical bases of knowledge as to society, and social-political theory—are not, of course, separate things but merge one into the other. In large part they seem to me to have no conspicuous place in the education of the citizen but to belong to the education of the social scientist.

These matters might be presented to the student in the upper division by representatives of the social departments acting separately, or they might be presented as the joint enterprise of the faculty of the social sciences. If the former way is chosen, the general curriculum for the social scientist will consist of largely independent courses, one in each of the social sciences. The student will learn something as to resemblances and differences between the methods and the theory in his field of specialization and the methods and the theory in other social-science fields, but he will not be much helped to see the relationships, to discover the logical connections or lack of connections. If the second way is chosen, the general curriculum for the social scientist will take the form of a collective effort at instruction representing method, the logic and philosophy of social-science knowledge, and social theory and its history. There is no pretense here that the making of such a collective effort by a faculty representative of several social sciences would produce a single, integrated, all-inclusive social science. It is merely suggested that, if the professors of the several social sciences should together make the general part of the curriculum in the upper division, some of the more fundamental and inclusive aspects of method and theory would become more apparent than if each social science offers a separate course. I think the making of the collective effort would greatly improve the curriculum.

The many assumptions, one contingent upon another, which I have ventured to make in this paper, bring me at last to very particular issues as to the order and emphases of subject matter in the general social-science part of the curriculum. If four-ninths of three years is to be devoted to the study of something outside the field of specialization, then it might not be too much to claim one-half of this four-ninths for instruction in the general or comparative aspects of social science. This amounts to one-third of the student's time during two years. We might think, therefore, of putting this instruction into two year-long courses. This in turn, suggests dividing into two parts the subjects referred to as appropriate to the more general education of social scientists. I propose, as merely one possibility, a year-long course in method in social science and a year-long course in history of social science. One course would treat the subject analytically, the other historically. The first course might begin with a consideration of the nature of the social as subject matter for science; go on to consider principal concepts as to the individual, society, the group, and economic, political, and social behavior; introduce the characteristic assumptions and procedures of the special social sciences; and raise the philosopher's questions as to these matters. The other course would be a history of the social sciences and of social, political, and other theory as to society. In this course social science and social theory would be set against the changing societies in which they arose and developed. The student would meet the special social sciences as events in a nexus of events, and he would read classic works of social sciences against a background of intellectual history.

Probably such two courses should be separated in time: the one I have first indicated coming at the beginning of the three-year curriculum and the other coming at its end. In the meantime, and throughout the entire three years, the student would, it is to be remembered, be spending most of his time studying in his field of specialization and probably some part of his time studying something outside of social science altogether. The proposals I have made as to the more general parts of the upper-division curriculum have been made with reference to the student who has decided to study social science. This part of the curriculum has another function also, of course: it may serve the occasional upper-division student working in fields other than the social sciences. It seems to me that the joint effort to produce one or two comprehensive courses having to do with method, theory, and the history of social science would serve the needs of such a visiting student better than courses fixed by departmental faculties acting separately. But I have made enough assertions of personal judgment to bring this paper to a close.

THE STUDY OF CULTURE IN GENERAL EDUCATION

An anthropologist may be expected to talk about culture, and he will be understood to mean by that word the whole integrated traditional body of ways of doing, thinking, and feeling that give a social group its character. The burden of my remarks today can be put in a single sentence, and I may well put that sentence first: Understanding of the nature of culture and of human nature is something which the social studies can contribute to general education.

In the latter part of this paper I hope to say more of what I mean by culture, and also of human nature, why I think that understanding of these conceptions is a part of general education, and how the communication of that understanding might be accomplished by teachers of the social studies. I am assuming that I may talk, not only about the social studies as they are now taught, but also as we might like them to be taught. As a teacher of the social studies in a four-year college including the eleventh to the fourteenth school years—an occupation which just now takes almost all my time—I am well aware of how far what I am doing falls short of what I would like to do.

This is not all I assume, and to state some further assumptions I am making will help to show how I come to the principal proposition about the place of an understanding of culture and human nature in a program of general education.

In first place, perhaps, is the assumption that there is an education which is substantially the same for everyone, an education that is independent of the sex, class, race, or occupation of the educated individual. Perhaps your agreement with this assumption—a sort of central axiom in general education—may be taken for granted. The assumption allows us to change our teaching to take account of individual differences, but it holds that much of what is taught in those years of schooling which most children and young people pass through ought to be the same for all and ought to be directed not to preparation for any special task but to the freeing of the mind and spirit and to preparation for the common responsibilities and opportunities of citizenship.

A second assumption is also one you will probably share with me. It is the assumption that in our changing and unpredictable world general education must somehow combine two objectives which appear antithetical: it must develop individuality and adaptiveness to change, and it must also provide us with common understandings. The individual

Reproduced with permission from *Social Education*, XI (October, 1947), 259–64.

must be able to make decisions on matters which tradition cannot and should not control. On the other hand, we have to have some common tradition to begin with, or we cannot act together at all. In the words of the Harvard report on general education: "this . . . raises . . . one of the most fundamental problems of education, indeed, of society itself: how to reconcile this necessity for common beliefs with the equally obvious necessity for new and independent insights leading to change."[1]

Perhaps we can find elements for a program of general education which do both. This is my view. I think, as a third assumption, that there are elements of that education, which everybody can and should have, which both make for consensus in society and also develop in the individual the power to make free rational choices. In a moment I shall mention some of these.

A fourth assumption requires a fuller exposition than the others and may well be the point at which some of you will separate yourselves from my views. It is the assumption that our task is to identify some of the elements of this education for everybody in a form more general than particular courses or instructional units but in a form more special than is provided in the usual definitions.

At one extreme, we define general education in terms of education for the good life, or for citizenship, or as effecting the development of very general qualities of mind and character. The abilities identified in the Harvard report as those toward which education for everybody should move fairly represent, I think, this manner of defining it in general terms. The report says that the aim is to bring it about that the generally educated are able "to think effectively, to communicate thought, to make relevant judgments, to discriminate among values." No one can object to such a statement, but it does not tell us very much.

At the other extreme, we define general education in terms of courses. Yet such definition of a program in general education is a definition for a particular school, because it is an allocation of resources within the powers of that school. It cannot be a definition for all schools.

Nevertheless, if general education is to provide for the common enlightenment of all, it should be possible to say of what this enlightenment is to consist, more specially than is said when it is defined in terms of general qualities of the mind, and more generally than is proposed in a series of courses.

Imagine, if you please, young people exposed to, say, fourteen years of general education, and imagine examiners set to examine these young people in the field of the social studies. I do not advocate a uniform national examination system to be applied to all schools; I evoke these

---

[1] "General Education in a Free Society," pp. 46–47.

examiners merely to help find the middle ground of definition of general education as to man in society. What would these examiners use as their guides in preparing the examination? They cannot use the courses of any one school, because these courses do and should differ. The definitions in terms of preparation for citizenship or of the ability to think, communicate, judge, and discriminate do point out the direction in which they are to inquire and test, but are still too general to give them much guidance. One thinks, communicates, judges, and discriminates about something, and what is that something in the case of the social studies?

Can we not help these imagined examiners, and so, more importantly, help ourselves, by stating what kinds of understanding or thinking about what subject matter do we believe to constitute elements common to all our efforts to bring about general education in the social studies?

We can come to a recognition of such elements either by looking at what we are teaching in different schools and colleges to see what in fact are its common elements, or we can reflect upon what we know about man in society and try to determine what elements of that knowledge would best meet the double need of modern education: the establishment of consensus and the capacity to adapt and to change. Today I am doing a little of both.

Looking first at the program of general education in the social sciences which I know best—that of the College of the University of Chicago—and casting a look or two at programs in other schools, I seem to find at least two principal elements. There is nothing startling about these. I suppose them to be present, more or less, in many programs of general education in the social studies and to find more or less explicit recognition. I hope merely to make the recognition a little more explicit.

For one thing we are trying to communicate understanding of the historical development of contemporary society, especially of our own Western and American society, and still more specially of some of the principal values of that society. This is to say that an element of general education contributed by the social studies is knowledge of how we, in this society, came to hold precious liberty, equality, government by the people, and other conceptions which go to make up our way of life both as it is and as we wish it to be. In this element of general education the emphasis is upon the past thoughts and the past events which have shaped present thoughts and present events.

For another thing we are trying to convey some understanding of the scientific spirit as applied to social problems of the present day and the capacity to address oneself in that spirit to such a problem. The social problems we have in mind form no fixed list; we suppose the generally educated person can show his competence with regard to almost any of them: the problem of maintaining control by the people of their government under the conditions of mass publics which attend us today; the problem of choice among various policies with regard to free or controlled economic competition; the problems of means and ends involved in assuring in our society a chosen combination of freedom and of regulation. The educated person will be able to use the thoughts of those who have written best on such questions in the past and will know what sorts of particular relevant facts need be taken into account in the seeking of solutions. Further, he has a moral as well as an intellectual attitude toward such problems: it is part of general education to develop the will to do something about these matters, to work out one's own views about them—whatever convictions they may lead to—and then to act on those convictions.

While in the first element of general education in the social studies the emphasis is on the historical development of our institutions and values, in this second element the emphasis is on a problem of common living and on analysis of the assumptions and particular facts which go to make the problem and to limit the terms of the possible solutions.

I say again that I suppose these two elements to be in fact represented in many curriculums of the social studies. They are in effect represented in the report of the Harvard Committee in those pages where it is recommended that the high school teach something about modern civilization with focus on Europe, American history with understanding of modern problems, and a course dealing with the nature of contemporary society, and in other pages where it is proposed that Harvard itself offer as part of a program of general education courses in Western Thought and Institutions and in American Democracy. How the courses are to be arranged is secondary. What is primary, in my view, is identification of those differentiated capacities to do what with what subject matter, toward the attainment of which any program of general education in the social studies ought to be directed. Historical knowledge of the development of our values and analytical understanding of facts and assumptions relevant to the formation of reasoned convictions on important contemporary social problems are, I think, two of these.

These two are rightly present in programs of general education in the social science. By communicating and restating important parts of our own heritage and by developing a common responsibility to realize common values, the presence of these two elements in a program of general education helps to bring about consensus. By throwing responsibility on the individual to work out his own convictions through reason and the use of special knowledge, they develop capacities to deal with the vicissitudes of rapid social change.

The task of this paper is to identify another such element of general education as to man in society in the study of culture and human nature. Before dealing with this third element directly some observations may be offered relative to the two elements just defined.

If general education in the social sciences were to include these two elements and no others, then such education would be exclusively concerned with our own traditions, our own history, our own system of values. The history that is taught to bring about the understanding and capacity these elements call for is a history of the Western world—especially of the United States—and of the values that characterize our particular tradition. When comparisons are made in courses in history or on social problems, the comparisons are likely to be within the European-American tradition. The world in which we now live, however, is one in which account must be taken of many people with many different heritages and different systems of values. If general education were to be concerned exclusively with our history and with our problems seen only in the light of our tradition it might be a dangerously limited education. It might not provide the individual with the elements of understanding of other ways of life than his own, or with the means of sympathetic understanding of other peoples.

In the second place it may be observed that the two elements of general education just identified attack the subject matter of the social in only two of what I take to be the three ways in which it can be attacked. One considers the subject matter as history, as events that have produced something known today. The other looks at the social as problems to be dealt with, as particular issues of policy, as choices to be made by actors in the world's affairs. The third way of looking at the subject matter of the social is by analysis with the use of concepts. By this third view the social consists of genera of natural phenomena—societies, social relations, customs, institutions, states, economies, and so forth. If the social is so regarded, one sees the common characteristics of many or all societies, of many or all men, and sees the differences among them as representing sub-classes of natural phenomena. The histories of societies are themselves compared and generalized upon. And the problems of our own society are merely the points at which this generalizing form of regarding the social may make a fresh beginning.

The conceptual way of looking at the social is of course a characteristic viewpoint of research, especially as research seeks comprehensive generalization. But it is also, I think, necessary to approach the social through history or through analysis of social problems. We do not communicate anything about the particular except through common understanding of general terms. We need, even for the simplest teaching of the social studies, some common language about the social. The question here to be considered is how far is the exposition of a language for describing the social to go beyond common speech in the giving of a general education.

The instruction in the social studies in which I take part does include exposition of concepts, but my impression is that the concepts are not well developed in relation to concrete facts. In one course known to me too many concepts are presented too formally and too briefly. Concepts are like friends; you have to work with them for some time before you have them at their best; and, like friends, concepts are best when you do not try to have too many.

These considerations prepare the way for my main proposal: that some understanding of human nature and culture is an element which the social studies may contribute to general education. The line of thought may be summarized. In seeking other elements of general education to be provided by the social studies we may try to supplement historical knowledge of our society and its values, and analytical competence as to social problems. The supplement called for should provide some of the elementary conceptual language in which the social is understood in its universal aspects. It should also provide access to understanding of peoples and ways of life other than our own. The suggestion is that some exploration of culture and of human nature meets these requirements. I think we are now providing this element to some degree, but not clearly and explicitly.

Do the schools that organize instruction around the culture of a certain people at a certain epoch give an understanding of the nature of culture? What do I mean by "an understanding of culture"?

I mean in the first place, acquaintance, familiarity, penetrating sympathetic comprehension of one culture other than one's own. From this first point of view the coming to know another culture is like coming to know a personality. The culture, like the personality, is seen as a persisting integration of dispositions to behave. It is unique, complex, self-consistent. A culture, like a personality, is a way of life. It is the way of life of a particular society. Seen so, it is just one thing, that one way of life. To come to know it takes much time, as it takes much time to know a personality intimately. But while we all have abundant opportunity to come to know personalities different from our own and in this knowledge come to see our own persons freshly and more wisely, not many of us have the opportunity, in ordinary living, to come to gain a good acquaintance with another culture.

The culture I am thinking of is one among many cultures. It is not culture in the generic of which I am thinking, the inventions, arts, and ideas of all mankind, those characteristics which set off man from the animals. I am thinking of the local and special forms of "culture," of culture in the sense in which the culture of the Andaman Islanders is one thing and that of the Chinese peasants is another. A contribution to general education which can be made by the social studies is the provision of opportunity to come to know one such culture more or less well. What culture is chosen is a secondary matter; it is more important that the fact and nature of "a culture" be undersood than that any particular one be understood rather than another.

The understanding had of the unfamiliar culture, in my view, must reach the point where the educated individual begins to think how he would act in given situations if that other culture were his own. The individual educated as to another culture recognizes that the institutions and ideas of the other people are coherent and provide those who live in terms of them with a system of values which give, for them, worthy meaning to effort and provide goals toward which to strive. Further, the understanding must reach the point where one sees human nature freshly. One must get beyond the culture to those elements in the behavior of the people which are, after all, the same as one's own. For as one comes to understand people who live by institutions and values different from one's own, at the same time one comes to see that those people are, nevertheless, at bottom quite like one's own people. The alien culture at first appears to us as a mask, enigmatic or repugnant. On closer acquaintance we see it as a garment for the spirit; we understand its harmonies and appreciate them. Finally, as acquaintance goes deeper still, we do not see, or for a time forget, the culture but look only to the common humanity of the men and women beneath.

To describe this process of getting acquainted with people with a culture different from our own is to recognize the experience as liberalizing. We are all limited in our understanding of our own conduct and that of our neighbors because we see everything by the preconceptions offered by our own culture. It is a task of education to provide a viewpoint from which the educated person may free himself from the limitations of these preconceptions. We are all islanders to begin with. An acquaintance with another culture, a real and deep acquaintance, is a release of the mind and the spirit from that isolation. It is to learn a universal language.

There is another way in which acquaintance with another culture is a major contribution to the education of every American. This is because the people of our country do not live in terms of a culture in quite the same sense in which the Andaman Islanders did or the Chinese peasants do. Cultures differ, not only in their content, in what values they emphasize; they also differ in the degree to which the values and institutions they provide are consistent and harmonious and in the extent to which they are uniformly acceptable to the people who live by them. The culture of the people of the United States is an entity much less well defined than the cultures of most of the peoples of history and of the world to-day. In this sense contemporary Americans need acquaintance with a well-integrated culture because they have never had any. And rational understanding of contemporary social problems—another element in general education—requires, it seems to me, some understanding of this fact. Ability to address oneself in the scientific spirit toward a problem of American life requires understanding of the fact that the consensual basis for common agreement found in a well-integrated culture is here lacking in no small degree. And one can talk about this in general terms for hundreds of hours, I feel, without conveying real understanding of it. If one has intensive acquaintance with one society in which the culture is well integrated, the difference between that situation and our own is really understood. I doubt if one can come to understand it in any other way.

Is it possible to get this kind of acquaintance with a culture by study, in the schools? I really do not know. But I am hopeful. I do have some views as to some of the decisions one would make if one tried seriously to provide intensive acquaintance with another culture. One would devote a long time to one culture. I am sure that it is better to devote much time to one or a very few than to spend a short time with each of many. Two years seems to me a short time in which, at secondhand, to come to know a culture. If the program of teaching the social studies were planned as a whole, from the first to, say, the fourteenth year, one might be able to make the understanding of one principal culture, with interruptions and digressions to consider comparable materials from other cultures, a major business of the entire period of fourteen years.

The primary teaching materials would consist of personal accounts of life in the society chosen for special study. Included would be autobiographies, letters, accounts of personal relations between Americans and members of the foreign group, and good fiction about the society. There are several reasons why one might choose a literate society, such as China; one reason lies in the availability of books written by members of that society. If China were chosen, one would read the classic and popular Chinese novels, as well as collections of popular lore. There is a great deal of such literature in English now, from many unfamiliar societies. Even the pre-literate societies are now represented in intimate and revealing personal accounts of life as seen by Indians, Africans, Laplanders, and as written or spoken by members of these societies. I need only refer to the plastic and graphic arts. The pupil would make his acquaintance with the unfamiliar people through every kind of record expressive of their ways of living and thinking.

This becoming acquainted with culture would involve at the same time a becoming acquainted with human nature. This means that the young person is encouraged to recognize two kinds of universals having to do with human nature: one, the presence in our own and other societies of recurrent social types; and two, the presence under all cultures of a common humanity which makes it possible for all people to understand one another in some degree, about some things. Therefore the accounts of the alien culture will be read not only to get acquaintance with that culture, but also to meet again the types of personality which one meets in Boston or Chicago, and the common humanity one knows at home. Turi's *Book of Lapland* is a personal account of Lapp culture; it is also a self-portrait of a prudent and practical man. The Chinese novel *All Men Are Brothers* is an account of life among those forced to the edges of the more stable Chinese society of the thirteenth century; in it also we meet types of adventures known to us from the literature of our own tradition. So this early study of culture and human nature will gain contributions from literature of our own heritage which illuminates human nature and defines social types. It can be imagined that *The Egoist, Fathers and Sons,* and Plutarch's *Lives* could be read in comparison with novels and autobiographies from China or other cultures foreign to us. So would understanding be gained of humanity in its two basic organized forms—culture and personality—against their common element, human nature.

I have just had in view the understanding of culture and human nature as it might be reached in the earlier years of schooling. In this first acquaintance the subject matter would appear in its concrete individuality. The first objective is the enrichment of experience with these basic aspects of the human. At this level little or no formal language of analysis is needed; the terms of common sense are sufficient. Nor is it needful at this beginning to think of the study as definitely the business of social science or as that of the humanities. It is both.

I suppose, however, that as the pupil moves from the earlier years of schooling to the secondary school and then to the first years of the college, the treatment of culture and of human nature may become, so far as the social studies are concerned, more abstract and systematic—in a word, more scientific. Indeed, the basic concepts of culture, personality, and human nature are needed in the minds of those who make the program of teaching and carry it into account from the very first primary grades. They come to the pupils as they develop capacity to use scientific concepts, and as—and this is the important point—they have gained such intimate and rich acquaintance with materials as to make the concepts really useful in the ordering and control of their world. I repeat the observation that concepts talked about away from materials are mere word-play.

I suppose that the more abstract and systematic consideration of culture and human nature may be developed in the tenth to the fourteenth years into a consideration of the subject matter of the social in the third of the three ways, which have been identified already in the course of my remarks. This is the way of social science considered, not as history, not as a rational and empirical consideration of problems of social action, but as a more or less systematic description of social phenomena as orderly aspects of the universe. So may the study of human nature and culture provide understanding of a few fundamental concepts.

You will see that not only do I suppose that human nature and culture are elements of understanding of our world which enter directly into the substance of a general or liberal education, but that I also think of them as primary concepts in the scientific description of man in society. So does common sense. We hear it said, "People are all alike." On the other hand it is said that East is East and West is West and never the twain shall meet. It is perhaps enough to add that "culture" and its closely related term, "society," are more inclusive conceptions than any such more special term as "government," "state," "market," "tribe," or "family." An understanding of culture and society, as concepts, should lead to understanding of related concepts in the books of social science that are read in the latter part of a program of general education: the works of such social philosophers and social scientists as Aristotle, Machiavelli, Locke, Mill, Maine, and Sumner. The imaginary examiners of young people exposed to fourteen years of general education in the social studies might be imagined to ask questions as to the relation of "culture" to "the mores," as to the relation of the concept of "institutions" to that of "culture," and as to the translatability of the primary terms used in one great work in the social-science field to terms used in another. It would seem appropriate if the examiners asked questions including such other related or dependent conceptions as to culture and society as "value" and "status." In the same way the conception of human nature, beginning as an awareness of the varied and yet stable characteristics of men in societies, might become a part of the more abstract and interrelated body of terms and general ideas by the aid of which understanding is extended and systematized, so the developing analysis of human nature would lead to the distinction between original nature and human nature, to the varied assumptions about and to some of the observations that have been made about differences between individuals and groups as to original nature; to the sharper determination of elements of human nature which exist in all cultures; to understanding of the nature and genesis of personality. My impression is that the young college people I know who, as a part of their general education, read Locke and Bentham and Sumner, become aware of the fact that assumptions as to human nature underlie the views of these writers. But I also have the impression that they are unprepared to judge these assumptions and that some acquaintance with human nature as a scientific subject matter would make their reading of these works more enlightening to them.

The examples I have given as to directions in which the understanding of culture and of human nature might be developed in the latter part of a program of general education in the social studies point to anthropology and sociology or social psychology as sources of help in the development of this part of a program of general education. I admit to supposing that these sciences are concerned with some matters more fundamental for general education than are some of the others. I think, indeed, that a part of what these sciences have been saying does not properly belong in the upper division where they have been saying it, but belongs in a properly planned program of general education.

But I should not like my remarks to be taken as essentially advocacy of any particular science in the making of a program of general education in the social studies. I will state the points I wish to emphasize. I think that progress will be made in improving the contribution of the social studies to general education as we identify the elements of understanding and capacity, referring to just what subject matter we decide to be of first importance. I think that historical knowledge of the development of the values of recent Western society, especially of our own, is one such element. I think that the ability to analyze present-day problems with the use of reason and special knowledge is another. I do not know how many other such elements of comparable importance we shall come to recognize. I would think that the social studies would be doing their task not so badly if they developed these two elements of knowledge and capacity, and if to them they added, more effectively and explicitly than I think they now do, one more. This third element is the intensive acquaintance with the facts of integrated culture and the fact of human nature and the development upon this acquaintance of a basic generalizing knowledge of society and human nature with some primary scientific concepts for the description and further understanding of that subject matter. To bring about the better weaving of this third thread into the texture of general education in the social studies, I would hope for the power to plan the curriculum of the entire group of years devoted to general education as one task. For the improvement of the work of the earlier years, where acquaintance with culture and human nature is extended, I feel pretty strongly that the reading of much firsthand personal and humanist source materials is demanded. These, in my view, are to be read as they come to us in translation; they are to become source books, not textbooks; we must have the words in which people express themselves as they said or wrote them. The task of bringing these materials together will be a pleasant one; I hope I may join with you in performing it.

SOCIAL-SCIENCE RESEARCH IN GENERAL EDUCATION

How can we make a general education which, in the field of social science, will continuously express the influence of research upon knowledge? My answer to the question is double: First, we may do so by seeing to it that teachers of general education in social science themselves do research. Second, we may do so by including in teaching of social science as a part of general education understanding of how, in social science, research is done.

Before we consider these answers, let us see if we have ourselves an understanding of the nature of research in social science. I think it will be well if in this hour we do not hold too tightly to that word "research." Like the word "science," it is a word somewhat jealously guarded. One is almost tempted to say that scientific research is what I do, whoever I may be, but that it is not what other people are doing if what they are doing is less precise in its procedures than are the procedures I use. To avoid these sensitivenesses, I suggest a restatement of the question I have just made immediate; the question becomes: How is new knowledge obtained in the comparative study of culture? Whether or not we are to call the activity "research," we are interested here in the ways in which social scientists—people so known and so trained—in this field (and others) make "the effort to remove a gradually growing body of knowledge from the realm of speculation and subjective opinion to the realm of demonstrated facts and principles about which it is no longer necessary to argue."[1] These words, characterizing social science, are those of Elbridge Sibley, a social scientist. In the same passage he adds the efforts to make predictions in some fields, and to formulate and test hypotheses, as part of social science as he sees it. I accept these characterizations also. But there may be some question as to how nearly these efforts must approach success for Sibley and me to recognize social-science research as already present. So, in substituting the phrase "effort to get new knowledge," I hope to be allowed to include today a good deal of what goes on when trained minds consider facts about man in society and attempt, in a really surprising variety of ways, to relate particular special knowledge about certain men in certain societies to general propositions or principles.

I have chosen a given field of advanced research—the comparative

Reproduced with permission from the *Journal of General Education*, VI (January, 1952), 81–91.

[1] Elbridge Sibley, "Education in Social Science and the Selection of Students for Training as Professional Social Scientists," *Items* (Social Science Research Council), V, No. 3 (September, 1951), 26.

study of culture—and discuss my topic in relation to it, so that the problems become at once concrete and particular. I am not to be understood as meaning that all that I write here about social-science research is true of all of it. I do think that it is true of a good deal of it and not only true of the comparative study of culture.

In his recent paper, Sibley remarks that in the natural science field "it is considered fundamentally important to learn *how* knowledge is created, while [social-science programs in general education] are not yet designed to make the average student aware that any peculiarly scientific methods, however primitive they are, can be applied to the investigation of social phenomena."[2]

Is this true? Does the student who learns about social science in his general education become aware that peculiarly scientific methods can be applied to the investigation of social phenomena? What are the procedures, peculiarly scientific or not, that can be so applied? In making students aware of these procedures, is it not first necessary that those who teach social science be themselves aware of them? Might it be that the social scientists themselves are not fully aware of how new knowledge, leading to general propositions related to special knowledge, is obtained in their field? I think about these questions and, seeking light, turn to a personal experience which I now venture to relate.

Last winter, while staying in Mexico, my son, a student in the College of the University of Chicago, carried on the work of certain courses of that program of general education, and I worked with him, learning as he did. Two of the courses presented an interesting contrast. In the second of the three year-long courses in the natural sciences ("Natural Sciences 2"), we found ourselves reading the original texts of a series of scientific papers having to do with diabetes, anatomy, and physiology. The series recorded the development of knowledge as to the causes of diabetes and, more generally, knowledge of those metabolic functions of which diabetes is one pathological disturbance. As we read these papers, we saw how one piece of new knowledge led to the making of another experiment, a new discovery. One saw the influence of research in anatomy upon the interpretations of the clinician, of experiment in physiology upon biochemistry, etc. The story went something like this: In 1840 a medical man sums up what observation of diabetes has shown as to the symptoms and course of the disease. This physician speculates as to causes. He sees that the failure of the body to dispose of sugar is somehow involved and asserts that it is a function of the kidneys to break down sugar. In 1877 Claude Bernard, a physiologist, reviews a series of brilliant experiments which make it plain that Prout was wrong: it is the

2 *Ibid.*, p. 27.

liver that is the source of the sugar found in the blood. Reading, we see
the ingenuity and technical originality of the experiments on dogs by
which Bernard was able to measure accurately the amount of blood sugar
in the portal vein as compared with that in the arteries. Bernard has
proved to us that the secret of diabetes is to be found in some future understanding of the normal processes of carbohydrate metabolism. At this
time the pancreas is barely suspected of any part in the matter. Bernard
has found it impossible to extirpate the pancreas from experimental animals without killing them. But in 1890 two experimenters in Strasbourg
succeed in doing this and prove that total extirpation of the pancreas results invariably in diabetes, while partial destruction of the organ never
does. Moreover, they tie off the excretory ducts of the gland and show
that this does not result in diabetes. Evidently, whatever influence on
sugar metabolism is brought about by the pancreas occurs without reference to the ducts. There is some other passage of influence from the
gland to the digestive and excretory system. Three years later an anatomist reveals the connections of the Islands of Langerhans of the pancreas
with the blood stream. The hidden outlet has been discovered. And in
1903 Opie performs careful autopsies on patients who died of diabetes
and confirms the conclusion of the anatomist as to the connection of these
islets with diabetes. But what is it that passes from these islets to the
system, and how does this whatever-it-is affect the metabolism of carbo-
hydrates? At last, in 1922, Banting and Best publish their wonderfully
conceived and conducted experiments in which, having deprived dogs of
their pancreases, they prevent diabetes in the animals by administering
pancreatic juice. Insulin is discovered. This technique and its product not
only relieve human suffering; the pancreatic hormone, now being studied
by the biochemist, is an instrument of yet further experiment, enabling
the researcher to investigate a variety of effects. In 1930 two Belgian experimenters remove the anterior pituitary from animals from which the
pancreas has also been removed, and the animals do not get diabetes.
Thus is shown the intricate and complementary effect of at least two hormones in regulating, the one by pushing in one direction, the other by
pushing in the opposite direction, on the homeostasis of carbohydrate
metabolism.

I break off the story as it was told, in the readings of this course, to my
son and me; there is more of it, and of course it is today far from ended
as research goes on. What struck me forcibly was the impact on the general education of the two of us, of the understanding we got of the way
in which new knowledge is achieved in much of the natural sciences. True,
we learned something about human physiology and something about diabetes, but I venture to suppose that it was the intention of those who

made up this course in general education, as I am sure was the effect of it on us, to convey something of the progression of knowledge, by observation, hypothesis, and experiment. In much of the natural-sciences method, new learning goes on as in this instance. Observations lead to inferences; the inferences are tested by experiment and either retained or displaced to make way for new ones. Once it is learned that the kidneys do not break down sugar, the mistake is not repeated. And workers in many different fields constantly affect, correct, and stimulate each other. The autopsist reports the pancreas diseased in diabetics; the anatomist then explores more carefully the normal organ; the physiologist takes the clue these men have given him and devises experiments to make use of the new knowledge so as to yield yet more knowledge. It is this about natural science that belongs, whatever else does, in general education.

The other course for which my son and I did the readings during this same winter was the first of the three year-long College courses in social science ("Social Sciences 1"). Here, too, we read original documents, and here, too, the ordering was roughly chronological. But we were learning about a very different sort of thing, and the logical connection of the content of one document with another was of a different sort. This course is about the formation of American national policy, beginning before the Revolution and extending to recent times. The readings consist of passages from books by Englishmen who affected Americans or by thoughtful Americans, political speeches, decisions of the United States Supreme Court, important state papers, such as the Virginia Declaration of Rights and the Mississippi Black Code. I thought the course highly interesting and illuminating, but it was soon plain that there was very little in it that had to do with social science, in the strict sense. The course showed the minds of men working in relation to events, and events working upon the minds of men, in society and history, not in the laboratory or the library. When we read the Court's opinion in *McCulloch* v. *Maryland,* Henry Clay's Cincinnati speech on the American System, the congressional report on the Second Bank of the United States, and Jackson's veto message of the Bank Renewal Bill, we had before us sources on the interplay of men and mind, of happenings and opinion, of theory and practice, interest and policy, in the intricate interrelationships which are man acting and thinking in society. We certainly did not have anything about scientific method. Nor did the researches of historians appear to us. We learned very little as to how new knowledge is obtained.

At once it is to be replied that this course was designed as history, not as science. It was designed to give understanding as to the development of some ideas and ideals fundamental to American life and as to their manifestation in events and in institutions. We are reminded that history also is included in what must be taught about man in society in programs of general education.

Let us turn to the second of the three social-science courses given in the College at Chicago. This is the course that includes readings that are more apparently scientific; and this is the course, recently described in this *Journal*,[3] that has to do with culture: it is referred to as a course in Culture and Personality. Does this course give an awareness of how new knowledge is obtained? In it we do find some presentation of the collecting and analysis of particular fact in relation to general idea. Elton Mayo's account of the Hawthorne experiments[4] is read. In this reading, and in others, the student may get understanding of social-science method—if by that phrase we mean the collecting of particular fact as guided by hypothesis. But I think it truly fair to this excellent course to say that such readings constitute a very small part of the whole and that discussion of matters of special experimental procedure, or procedure closely similar to experiment in natural science, plays no large part in the course.

Certainly this course in Culture and Personality is sharply different from "Natural Sciences 2" in one important respect. In the social-science course the learner gets no account of science making progress from point to point, moving from observation to hypothesis, confirming or rejecting the hypothesis, and moving on from the new base to make some new observation, hypothesis, or discovery. Not at all. The readings begin with a very recent work, Myrdal's *The American Dilemma*. This account of Negro-white relations, partly in terms of contemporary institutions and motives, partly in terms of history, is discussed at the beginning of the course. It is followed by readings from Freud and from Ruth Benedict. These readings do not show, with any sharpness, the design and conduct of experiment or of precisely controlled observation. They certainly do not show that social science has moved from Freud to Benedict or from Benedict to Freud. Rather, as Mr. Riesman writes,[5] the staff of the course stage a kind of dialectical argument between these two writers, these two points of view. Freud takes one view of culture, of any culture, as a sort of painful restraint upon a universal, instinctively defined human nature. Benedict regards the many different cultures as alternative provisions of motivation to people who need motives. She thinks of culture as creative influence upon highly plastic original nature. I do not stop to qualify these characterizations; the point I wish to make is that Freud and Benedict are not related to each other as are the physiological experiments of

[3] David Riesman, "Some Problems of a Course in 'Culture and Personality,' " *Journal of General Education*, V (January, 1951), 122.

[4] Elton Mayo, *Human Problems of an Industrial Civilization* (Cambridge, 1933).

[5] Riesman, *op. cit.*, p. 125.

Claude Bernard to the discovery of insulin by Banting and Best. It really would not have mattered much which came first, Freud or Benedict. They present contrasting views of man in culture. It is the understanding of these contrasting views, the examination of particular fact as lighted first by the one view and then by the other, and the exploration of the ways in which the two views are necessarily inconsistent, or in which they may be made consistent, which is, I come to feel, a part of the way in which social science moves forward into new knowledge.

Probably this course does not communicate the nature of the getting of new knowledge in social science as well as it might be communicated. But I am convinced that the course does communicate something of how the effort for new knowledge, controlled so far as it can be controlled by specially sought-out fact, does in truth go forward in this part of social science. It does not show the collecting of special fact, the arranging of experiment or of strictly controlled series of observations, as the only procedure for getting new knowledge here. It is right in not doing so, for such procedures play, at this stage of development, only a limited part in social science. And, it seems to me, there is much more to the getting of new knowledge than quantification and the design of experiment. The course does show something of this "more." Indeed, I should say that the utilization of such contrasting views as those of Freud and Benedict is not only teaching; it is also a part of the operations by which trained minds, attentive to particular facts, make the effort to remove a gradually growing body of knowledge from the realm of speculation and subjective opinion to the realm of demonstrated facts and principles about which it is no longer necessary to argue. The very argument is a part of the effort. In the comparative study of culture, the argument, the dialectic, between Freud and Benedict is itself an essential operation in moving from speculation to accepted principles. This, too, is a part of what needs to be learned as to how new knowledge is obtained in social science.

This brings me to an enlarged view of what is involved if we are to include in general education understanding of how new knowledge is obtained in our field. It is to include understanding of the use of quantification, the design of experiment, and the making of a series of controlled observations. But it is to include these things only in so far as they are actually useful in social science. And it is to include understanding of such ways of advancing knowledge in social science as are actually employed whether or not they conform to the model of the precise design and the quantitative expression of result. We are not, then, to adopt a view of social-science procedure which conforms to the model of the natural sciences (or, possibly, to the model of how natural sciences are imagined to be). We are to represent the getting of new, dependable knowledge in social science as it actually is. We might contrast the former view of social science with the latter and speak of social science in the natural-science image and of social science in its own image. Then we might see that two kinds of things, interweaving with each other, could go into the understanding we seek to communicate as to how social science advances. It is the interweaving that matters: quantification and precise design are to be represented as they actually and fruitfully occur in the context of discussion and exploration of illuminating ideas.

Therefore, we do not best teach about procedure by making demonstrations of experiment and design of controlled observation, as if the value of these lay in their own inner perfection. These procedures are effective only in so far as they are attached to ideas that are clear and significant. The Hawthorne experiments point to the conclusion that something about personal relations motivates workers to produce more. Two things about these experiments are at least as important as the design of the experiments themselves: the history of the shifting of "hunches"—hardly hypotheses—as to why workers produce more or less; and the great limitations, arising from ignorance of many factors, as to the inferences to be drawn from the experiments. To understand these things is to begin to understand about how social science advances. It is also, I say, to begin to learn about how to be a social scientist. We might teach about quantification by including formal instruction in statistics. But in general education we can better teach about quantification by, say, considering Murdock's way[6] of trying to prove that the nuclear family is universal: then we shall find ourselves considering the nature of correlations and of sampling by looking at Murdock's samples of human families and his correlations of certain institutions with others. Method and subject matter are best taught about by not separating them. What is needed is chiefly a little effort to look, realistically, at a particular method used in a particular context of inquiry. Malinowski's book, *Sex and Repression in Savage Society,* is regarded as a designed experiment, a "crucial instance."[7] It apparently shows that in matrilinear societies the Oedipus complex, as seen by Freud in Vienna, appears as, or is replaced by, a complex in which there is desire for the sister and hatred of the mother's brother. If this were a critical experiment, like the experiments of Banting and Best, the whole history and thought in regard to basic psychic complexes would be changed. But Malinowski's book has not wrought that change. In discussing the book as an example of designed series of observations, it is

[6] George Peter Murdock, *Social Structure* (New York, 1949).

[7] Harold Lasswell, "A Hypothesis Rooted in the Preconceptions of a Single Civilization Tested by Bronislaw Malinowski," *Methods in Social Sciences* (Committee on Scientific Method in the Social Sciences, Social Science Research Council, No. 34 [Chicago, 1931]), pp. 480–88.

necessary to consider the limitations of the design, the shortcomings of the proof. On the other hand, it would be a misrepresentation to throw out what Malinowski did because of the imperfections of the method. The book has had influence: it has shifted emphases, suggested possibilities. It is this shifting emphasis, this suggestion of new possibilities, which plays so important a part in social science as it really is, while it falls so far short of realizing the model of social science seen in the image of the natural sciences.

I lay stress especially on one respect in which adoption of the model of the natural sciences might result in misrepresentation of social science. Social science, being more loosely connected to precise observation and well-defined concept than is much of the natural sciences, does not make progress in quite the same way. Progress is not so clearly a chain, a stairway, a wall being laid. It is not so evident just what observation confirmed a hypothesis, what controlled experiments made knowledge leap forward, leaving mistakes now forever behind. It would be hard to find, in the development of knowledge as to the comparative study of culture, a sequence of observation, hypothesis, experiment, and inference as is provided by the history of our knowledge of diabetes and carbohydrate metabolism. I think there are instances of progression that are roughly comparable, but I think it is important to recognize the "roughly" and to know that instances are scarce.

The development of knowledge as to inherent mental differences between races illustrates, in comparison with the story of knowledge about diabetes, resemblances and differences. Otto Klineberg, who has been working on this subject for many years, has recently reviewed concisely the history of scientific knowledge in this field. As we read his paper,[8] we see that here is a place in which hypothesis and conclusion are revised by improvement of observation and refinement of technique. Between 1910 and 1926 two American psychologists and a sociologist (Brigham, Goodenough, and Odum) published opinions to the effect that Negroes were inferior in intelligence to white people; the psychologists gave as proof the differential results of intelligence tests. In 1929, however, Peterson and Lanier showed the apparent inferiority of Negro boys to whites in three cities varied directly with the degree of inequality of social opportunities. In 1931 Brigham made a statistical examination of the methods of testing he himself had used in the Army study, concluded that the method was not sound in that it did not eliminate errors due to differences in environment, and repudiated his own earlier conclusion. In 1935 Klineberg published his studies showing that the improvement in test

[8] Otto Klineberg, "Race Differences: The Present Position of the Problem," *International Social Science Bulletin*, II, No. 4 (Winter, 1950), 460–66.

scores made by Negroes who migrated to New York is proportionate to the length of time the Negroes have lived in New York, and in the same year Garth showed that, as samples of Indian and white children tested are made more and more nearly equivalent as to environment and experience, the difference in the success on the tests is reduced. In 1942 Rohrer showed that prosperous Osage Indians did better on the tests than did less prosperous whites. In 1946 Gesell and Pasamanick showed a correspondence between success on the tests and nutrition and general economic level, no matter what the race. In 1950 Goodenough reviewed her work and concluded that the test she had used concealed some expression of environmental influence; accordingly she reversed her earlier conclusion (and so did Odum in 1936).

Although these events do show science advancing, the history of intelligence testing with respect to racial differences is not quite the same as the history of new knowledge about carbohydrate metabolism. One notices that the reversal of opinion did not come as the result of a crucial experiment, or as the end of a series of progressive steps, but rather from the cumulative effect of a good many observations and tests that worked together to produce an impact. And the possibility remains that changes in the general view of the Negro current in American society may have influenced the change as no such changing popular view of carbohydrate metabolism influenced science in that field. Moreover, the new knowledge in the case reviewed by Klineberg is, in a sense, merely negative knowledge. We have learned that an instrument—the intelligence test—which we thought was useful to determine the relative inherent intelligence of racial groups, does not in fact do what we thought it did. Deprived of this instrument for that purpose, we now find that other facts about Negroes and white people make better sense if it is assumed that there are no such differences. No one has yet proved that there are no such differences.

I find it necessary to consider such facts as these about the way knowledge advances in the study of cultures in order to begin to think about the potential impact of frontier research in that study upon general education. What frontier research here has to say to general education is not for the most part a report of positive new knowledge that leaves old knowledge behind. Frontier research in the study of cultures consists chiefly of viewpoints and interpretations as to how cultures come to be, how they change, what their relationships are to human nature and to the personalities of men and women, and how, by or with or in spite of a culture, children grow to be adults. These viewpoints are partly but not entirely inconsistent with one another. On the whole, they have come into existence through some one or few original minds that conceived an explanation or interpretation of man's actions in relation to some body of material that happened to be under observation. Veblen sees the phenomena of consumption in the light of the cultural conventions of a status-conscious people. Sumner looks at the scraps of descriptive ethnology and reduces man to a mechanical creation of a cultural life that grows in its own way apart from anything man can do about it. Freud looks at the dreams and free associations of troubled Viennese middle-class patients and creates a vast and powerful scheme for the understanding of sick souls. Each of these views then undergoes modification as more and different data are reviewed, and certain of these views are entertained simultaneously by workers who now strive to bring them into some harmony. Thought moves from Sumner's position toward that expressed by Benedict and Margaret Mead in which the culture is seen, not as a die for stamping robots, but as a provision for human dispositions to think and feel: culture is still the maker of men, but the making is seen now as creative and liberative rather than as repressive. Malinowski strives to connect culture—any culture—with a simple list of primary needs shared with the animals and of secondary needs, such as a need for religion and esthetic expression—which are derived from the universal conditions of human living. Murdock, comparing one society with another in a wide sample of primitive societies, endeavors to state some of these universal conditions, and their chief variants, in terms of forms of family life. Meanwhile Freudian thought, now much modified by other healers of the sick and by psychological students of normal people, has profoundly affected the students of the world's cultures—especially the American students—and some of these try to develop a system of ideas that will combine psychoanalytic thought and cultural relativism. We find ourselves reading Kardiner and Linton or the analyses of national character offered by Mead, Bateson, Gorer, and others.

But I say again that these views remain as alternative and partly complementary instruments of understanding. The educated mind is not compelled to adopt one advanced position as correct, regarding the others as merely superseded hypotheses. The educated mind is one that has some understanding of some of the viewpoints as to the place of culture in the understanding of human behavior and is able to see some of the consequences and some of the difficulties of entertaining the one and of entertaining the other. Even on limited sectors of the frontier of research it is not possible to learn what is *the* position of the research workers. There is no such one position. I cite the following facts. In 1949 an anthropologist published a paper in which he announced that, simply by adopting a procedure for toilet training of our children appropriate to the kind of human beings we want to produce, "we are potentially able to shape almost any kind of human personality."[9] This certainly implies a high degree of precise knowledge, including power to predict and control, with regard to the making of personalities. In the same year an experimental psychologist, reviewing the evidence, concluded that the kind of care given the infant does not determine the personality; that several other factors are involved in ways not at all clearly understood.[10] Both of these judgments of knowledge at this frontier cannot be true. These positions are, of course, extreme. But look at the middle position. In a recent publication Mead tells us that it is not claimed that infant care *causes* the kind of personality that prevails; rather we are to recognize "a circular system . . . so that the method of child rearing, the presence of a particular literary tradition, the nature of the domestic and public architecture, the religious beliefs, the political system, are all conditions within which a given kind of personality develops. Attention is focused upon the child's learning processes simply because this is a convenient place to interrupt the circle for purposes of study."[11] If architecture, toilet training, and the political system are a circular system, then, while we may come to understand the circularity of any one cultural system, we are not going to be able to tell parents what will happen to their children if they change the toilet training.

Now I may return to the double answer to the question we are discussing. A program of general education in the field of social science that will continuously express the influence of research upon knowledge is one in which the teachers are themselves carrying knowledge forward and in which the true nature of social-science progress is made clear. In making known to young people, some of whom will become social scientists, how knowledge is created, we are to make it known how it is in fact created in social science. This we may do by presenting particular works of investigation and conclusion in their true historic and argumentative contexts. We are to present them as they really affect the next investigator, the next thoughtful and trained mind. Designed experiment and observation, and method conceived as whatever is quantitative or whatever is precise, are not, alone, social science as social science really is. These things lie within a much larger thing, a thing which teachers of social science are themselves in part carrying on. Social-science procedure includes the definition and application of basic concepts. In this a good teacher takes part. It includes the construction of explanatory theo-

[9] Weston La Barre, "The Age Period of Cultural Fixation," *Mental Hygiene*, XXXIII (1949), 209–21.

[10] Harold Orlansky, "Infant Care and Personality," *Psychological Bulletin*, XLVI, No. 1 (1949), 1–42.

[11] Margaret Mead, "The Study of National Character," in Daniel Lerner and Harold D. Lasswell (eds.), *The Policy Sciences* (Stanford, Calif., 1951), p. 74.

ries organizing concepts into a systematic body of propositions, the evaluation of such interpretive systems in terms of clarity, internal consistency, adequacy to known facts, and fruitfulness—the stimulation of new ideas and of new investigations. All this can be contributed by social-science teachers in the course of their teaching. Included also are analysis of underlying ethical assumptions involved in social-science knowledge, both theoretical and practical, and analysis of the process of rational deliberation as applied to arguments about public affairs.

Research, as a part of general education, occupies in programs representing social science a place of peculiar difficulty, delicacy, and opportunity. The difficulty and the delicacy arise in part because general education in this area is directed toward communicating several notably *different* things: (1) something about the historical development of our society; (2) something about the social problems of our society and of how specialized knowledge and the scientific spirit may help us to deal with them; and (3) the description, or analysis, of man in society, as a widespread phenomenon, by the use of concepts and generalizations. All this—and method too! General education about man in society, in a degree much greater than is true of general education as to stars or organisms, is to make man ready to act, to form judgments as to the right and the possible, with regard to a great many matters as to which the procedures of science, in the image of some part of natural science, are not ready to offer answers, whether or not they ever will be ready. Part of the subject matter of general education in the social sphere is opinion—intelligent and informed opinion—even in the absence of scientific proof.

So Sibley is right in saying that in general education courses now given there is discussion of "problems of terrific complexity."[12] Such problems have to be discussed, because educated man has to face such problems and cannot wait for science, in the strictest sense of the word, to catch up with them. When Sibley goes on to deplore that these problems in general education courses "are either treated dogmatically or [are] freely discussed as matters on which any intelligent person has an equal right to his opinions," we join him in deploring such dogma as we may have been guilty of. But we insist that these are questions on which every intelligent person has not only a right but a duty to have an opinion: and part of the duty is to become as intelligent about them as he can. It is the difficult task of the social-science teacher to show how to bring special knowledge to bear upon even the most difficult questions. He must do this even if the result is, as it often is, to leave the issue one on which reasonable men may still differ. We cannot wait for

[12] Sibley, *op. cit.*, p. 28.

precision and quantification before taking up in our courses discussion of personality formation, Point Four programs, or world government. In developing in future citizens the capacity to know when one opinion carries more weight than another, the teacher of social science cannot restrict himself, and should not, to the patterns of advancing knowledge which depend upon quantification and linked hypotheses and proofs from series of controlled experiments and observations. In so many fields these things will be lacking. But the important thing to add is that, in helping to make future social scientists, the general-education teacher should not limit himself to these things either. By teaching how valid knowledge of man in society really goes forward, we do what we ought to do both for general education and for making social scientists.

The difficulties are matched by unusual opportunities. Just because social-science knowledge advances in part through influence of the consideration of alternative viewpoints on the same or similar facts, the connection between teaching and what I would here call research, were it not for the sensitivenesses of which I have spoken, is peculiarly close. The social-science general-education teacher, as he joins with his colleagues representing different training and different influential viewpoints, àdvances knowledge as he teaches. To develop this aspect of his work, it is only necessary to formalize the staff discussions which underlie the teaching. There results a seminar: a forum for the development and testing of those viewpoints as to central questions about man in society which, in a looser way, correspond with hypotheses in physics or physiology. The social-science teaching staff can make contributions to the gaining of new knowledge which departmentally organized staffs find it hard to make. The variety of teaching and viewpoint and the coming-together to plan a program of teaching involve just those operations of the mind upon fact which make for new knowledge in our field.

On the other hand, it is probably true that social science teachers would be better teachers, as well as better contributors to new knowledge, if they were more closely connected with the precise and limited investigations than they are. In order to create a general education in place of a number of competitive preparations for specialized life, we have in a number of institutions established independent courses in general education and given their teachers autonomy. These necessary conditions for general education are, of course, to be firmly retained. But I think that in making a program of general education we have produced teachers who have little direct part in the specialized and more precise aspect of the pursuit of knowledge. It becomes necessary now to provide some of these teachers with opportunities to carry on such work and to participate in the communities of specialized investigators while they retain their membership in communities of the less specialized. They are the link between social science conceived as physics or physiology and social science as it really is. To take this remedy, which I named first, we have to solve problems of the organization of teaching and research faculties, problems of relationships between people who are primarily teachers and people who are primarily devoted to advancing knowledge, and problems of time, money, morale, and motivation. The more specialized research that some teachers might well be doing is not, necessarily or at all, research into education. It is research as to something about man in society.

The teacher of social science in general education has peculiar advantages in bringing, into his teaching, experience with the design and conduct of observations to some degree controlled. The materials of social science—some of them—are right at hand in the community, in the schoolroom, in the day-to-day experiences of members of his class. No difficult experimental setup is required to put students to observing their corner store. Interviewing can be done anywhere. The recording and graphing of the temporal distribution of students entering the classroom before or after the bell rings will produce a skewed curve. The scientific method, in its simplest and most basic character, as objective observation with regard to a defined question, can be practiced more easily in connection with man in society than it can be practiced in astronomy or geology or comparative anatomy. Some of these things can be done by the teacher before the student or be done by the student. Man is the most interesting and the most immediately present of all that surrounds the learner. How to find out something about man can be, in the limited sense of precise observation and limited inference, a part of general education. But it would be a wrong to both general education and the training of social scientists to show this finding-out in this limited sense only. If the word "method" is to be reserved for the precise and limited procedures, then let us say that both general education and social science require much more than method. It is so much more that, if we choose these terms, "method" becomes much the smaller part of what the social scientist must know, and a very small part indeed of all that an educated man must know. To make the specialized work fruitful in the larger context of thought and discussion, to be a link between "method," on the one hand, and learning and full preparation of social scientist, on the other, can be a principal function of the general education teacher.

PART III

RACE

THE NEGRO AFTER THE WAR

Robert E. Park used to say that the American Negro became successively a population, a folk, and a race. Imported from Africa with native traditions interrupted, the Negro arrived here as so many human beings, as so many laborers. Without common language or customs, these men and women were at first a mere population. Thereupon, in the relative isolation of the plantations but with the raw materials of living provided by white men and with whatever vestiges of African life remained, the Negro developed the only important American folk life. Later, as education and sophistication gave him awareness of his position and the will to change it, he became conscious of the cause for which he would, and must, struggle. And so he became a race, not in the anthropological sense, but in the sociological sense of an ethnic group conscious of its distinct nature and common interests.

This remark was probably first made by Park more than a score of years ago. When he first made it, the problem of the American Negro was thought of as a problem of the United States. It was recognized as the outstanding social problem of this country. The important change that has occurred since that time is the conversion of this local and national problem into an international, a world-wide problem. So perhaps now it may be said that the American Negro has undergone yet another change. Perhaps it may now be said that the Negro has become an international responsibility. He is a responsibility to all men of all racial origins who want a peaceful and a just world. And he is a new responsibility to himself. For his conduct and the solutions reached as to his problem now stand as symbols for all men who are denied justice and equality in all parts of the world. We might almost say that whereas a generation ago the Negro had become—in the sense explained—a race, he will be, after this war, *the* race. He will be, at least, the most critical and symbolically significant case of a people denied full participation in human civil and political rights because of race.

In this world two plans of human living contend, as never before, for supremacy. One plan denies human rights, adopts expediency as its rule, and makes the individual a mere means to the strength of the state or an imagined dominant "race." The other plan extols human rights, adopts moral principle as its rule, and places the human individual above state or imagined "race." The end of the war will not see the end

Unpublished paper, 1944.

of the struggle between these two ways of living. It will rather bring about a redefinition of the struggle between them. During the war the totalitarian states fight for the first plan, and the United Nations, on the whole, represent the other plan. But everybody knows that within the United Nations there is internal struggle between these two plans of living. The end of the war will remove the immediate and obvious adversary of the democratic and liberal way of life. As another result, it will make plain to view the internal struggle. The struggle between the two plans for living will be seen for what, more lastingly, it is: a struggle that goes on within every nation, every community, every heart. It will be seen to be both local and international, both personal and global.

The American Negro will lie across the battleground between these two plans for human living. No other group anywhere in the world presents so sharp a conflict between the ideal of democracy, the proposition that all men are created equal, and the great qualifying fact of injustice and prejudice. This country, great in power and paramount in democratic leadership, is the same country that cannot solve the problems of its own persisting racially directed injustices. The American Negro will receive the anxious gaze of struggling minorities in every land, and the American white man will have upon his conscience a wrong that works against not only himself but against his fellow men who stand in other communities for the democratic and liberal way of life. As Paul Robeson said, the cause of the American Negro has become part of the struggle against fascism.

It will not be seen to be so by most men, white or Negro. As the white man will seek to preserve social arrangements which are easy and comfortable and convenient to him, so the Negro will seek to change them, not in the interests of all men, white and Negro, but in order to get some immediate advantage for himself. The Negro, too, will see the short-run interests, will cry out with the immediate pain. He will follow the political leader who promises him a better job even if the leader be corrupt. He will see the white returned soldier take the job which he, the Negro, held during the war, and he will nurse his natural anger or vent it in mere expressions of bitterness. So too, the white man will seek to restore the Negro to the position of social and economic subordination which he occupied in the local communities before the war. "The laws of biology will reassert themselves after the war," writes a southern editor. The conflict will be felt, on the whole, as many local struggles, as so many little unconnected attempts of a subjected minority to wrest an increment of material security from a dominating group. It will be in part blind, in part clouded with fear or resentment. In part it will go on as it has always gone on.

And yet, in ever increasing part, it will be understood by those of both races who are thoughtful and who read and reflect that this is no longer a matter of who gets what somebody else has and hasn't enough of himself. It will be more and more seen to be a conflict, not between white and Negro, but between free and slave, between men of good will of all races and men of power of all races. It will be recognized as a part of the great effort toward a decision as to whether the world will be ruled by expediency or by principles of justice, by what serves me or by what serves all men. In so far as Americans—Negroes and whites— see the problem of the American Negro in these terms, we shall go forward toward the right.

RACE AND HUMAN NATURE: AN ANTHROPOLOGIST'S VIEW

In the troubled affairs of men race is of consequence because of what men think and feel about it and not because of anything that race is of itself. This is the cardinal fact. There are physical differences, great and small, among men, and these differences enable the scientist to make a classification of mankind according to these differences. But we do not know that there are corresponding mental differences. We do not know that the physical differences, of themselves and without regard to notice paid to them, place limits on the powers of the human beings who exhibit them to reason, feel, learn, create, or enjoy. The anatomical and physiological differences that make human taxonomy possible are not known to make any action impossible to any racial group that is possible to the others. We do not know that the shape of the lip, as such shape differs racially, places any limits on the powers of men to speak well or wisely. We do not know that the differences in proportions of the long bones of the arms and legs, of themselves, have any consequences for good or bad government. If the small differences in brain anatomy as between Negroes and whites which some investigators have reported are in fact there, it does not follow that such differences represent inherent differences in intelligence. There may be such differences. We do not know that there are. There are reasons for doubting that there are. For it has been certainly established that in all such anatomical and physiological features there is much overlapping as any population is compared with another. The biological composition of all populations is so varied that all kinds of personalities and abilities are

Reproduced from *Half a Century Onward,* Fiftieth Annual Report of the Foreign Missions Conference of North America (New York, 1944) with permission from the Division of Foreign Missions of the National Council of Churches of Christ in the U.S.A.

found among them, and the statistically demonstrable physical differences that do exist are not known to constitute inherent limits on behavior. If there are important biologically determined differences in temperament or intelligence among racial groups, that fact is still to be established; in the meantime it is clearly important to take account of race as a social, a cultural, phenomenon.

A leading student of race declares that race "is purely a biological grouping. The term has its origin in biology and never should be used in any other sense. Racial characters are carried by the germ plasm, but language, religion, and nationality are individually acquired." Let us not misunderstand these statements. They are true. They say what has to be said about race as seen by the biologist. They do not say what has to be said about race by the sociologist. It would indeed make for clarity if race should never be used except in a biological sense. But the term is popularly used to describe cultural and political and linguistic groups. This use is a fact too. The prejudices and other attitudes that attach to race are facts also. They are facts in the realm of culture. They are the facts of which account must be taken in understanding the place of race in human affairs. The people known as Jews differ so much in physical features from one another and resemble so much in physical features people who are not known as Jews that the anthropologist and the biologist tell us that the Jews are not a race. They are not. That is one fact. It is also a fact that people have conventional collective judgments about people known as Jews and associate their beliefs about Jews with real or imagined physical characteristics of Jews. This is a fact too. It is a fact of such immense importance that it would be impossible justly to write the history of our Western world without frequent reference to it. The Jews are not a race, but they constitute a group believed to be a race, and no amount of repetition of statements of the first fact will do away with the second and vastly more important fact.

Therefore I say that understanding of the importance of race is to be found not in man's physical nature but in his human and social nature. What are the characteristics of that nature which give rise to the social consequences of race? In the first place it is human nature to feel oneself a member of a valued group set off from other groups of less value. In the clans of primitive society, in boys' gangs, social classes, and modern nations we see the disposition of mankind to classify in accordance with the sentiments of loyalty to one's own kind and of disapproval or hatred of other kinds. We note further that the disposition to depreciate groups not one's own is in most cases selective in that one or a few other groups become social objects of depreciation or aggression. One such specification of the out-group sentiments is directed toward the people near one but who differ from one's own group only in small degree. Referring to the feuding and ridicule between Spaniards and Portuguese, between English and Scotch, Freud[1] observes that such sentiments represent "a convenient and relatively harmless form of satisfaction for aggressive tendencies through which cohesion amongst the members of a group is made easier." Freud then goes on to remark with fine irony that the Jewish people, scattered as they are, have rendered services which deserve recognition to the development of culture in the countries where they settled, but that it is unfortunate that not even all the pogroms and massacres of history have been sufficient to give a peaceful integration to Christian societies. For while upon certain groups fall only the aggressions of their neighbors, others become scapegoats to all the world. At least this has been the historic role of the Jew. We assure ourselves of the worthiness of our own people by declaring the unworthiness of other people. In aggression against others there is a basis for solidarity among ourselves. And when that solidarity or security is threatened there is in the need of the group to restore its security a special cause for the casting of blame upon some convenient group. If the group is already defined by tradition as a proper object of aggression, as in the case of the Jew, it is so much the easier to commit new aggression against them.

For men take the paths of least resistance in thinking and feeling, as they do in walking through a wood, and these paths are those trodden by men who went before them. We do not, on the whole, make the effort to form our own independent judgments. We take over the judgments arrived at by others. We attach our sentiments to the customary objects of attachment. The extent to which this is true escapes us, attentive as we are to those few cases—our wives, children, and chosen intimates—in which our own special and personal experiences play a large part in the organization of our sentiments. The truth is that to a great extent we rely, for the placing of our feelings and judgments, on the convenience of categories. It is an aspect of our nature that we see experiences, including people, as divided into classes. We think and feel not as to each individual of the class, one by one, as we might come to know the individual; we think and feel to the class as a class, and to the individual simply as known to be a member of the class. This way of behaving is useful, as any energy-saving device is useful. It saves effort to respond to categories rather than to individuals; there are far fewer of them. To have prejudices saves thought, and thought costs effort. Moreover, an established prejudice is motivated by the sentiments; it is ready to authorize action; it exhibits none of the hesitating which dis-

[1] *Civilization and Its Discontents.*

tinguishes reflective and critical thinking. The Nazis make a virtue of prejudice; they think, as they put it, "with their blood."

I have spoken of two characteristics of human and societal nature: the social utility of dispraising or despising a group different from one's own group, and the personal and social utility of attaching judgments and sentiments to categories rather than to individuals. Put together, these two characteristics provide the matrix within which is formed much of the social importance of race. For race offers human nature a plain and commanding definition in terms of which to know the out-group. Before speaking of the plainness of race and its special authority, it is well to remark that race is not the only convenient basis upon which to classify mankind into our people, who are good, and other people, who aren't. Custom and culture are more nearly universal criteria for distinguishing the undervalued outsider from the overvalued insider. It is an anthropological commonplace that most tribes refer to other tribes by contemptuous epithets, and that each people tends to regard itself as the only really civilized group on earth. Since the development of the world religions, religious differences have motivated as much cruelty and bloodshed as has race. Indeed, in many cases it is not possible always to declare the extent to which the out-group is defined in racial terms. Race, culture, and religion enter into the definition of the Jew in varying and perplexing ways. Between the anti-Semite who thinks that Jews are born to be a slave-race and the anti-Semite who thinks the Jews smart but no smarter than others, have built up a dangerous international conspiracy and should be suppressed for that reason, there are differences; but they are not greatly important differences. It is today urged that Americans of Japanese ancestry should be locked up, or deprived of their citizenship, or sent to Japan, sometimes upon a racial argument and sometimes upon a cultural argument. "Show me a man with one drop of Japanese blood and I will show you a traitor," one United States Senator declared recently, but others content themselves with declaring that no person of Japanese origin can be a good American because all Japanese worship the mikado and presumably anybody born here of Japanese parents has taken over the custom, to his eternal perdition. The racial element in group prejudice is often unclear and mixed with other elements.

Nevertheless, in the prejudging of men by other men, race has a special and a double importance. In the first place, race—this obvious color of the skin, this unmistakable contour of the eylid, this unchangeable thinness or thickness of the lip—makes easy and often certain the classifying of individuals in the accepted categories. The distinction between the faithful believer and the heretic or the infidel has been in some societies and at some times a social classification of prime importance, but then it has not been easy to tell the heretic from the non-heretic at a glance. One can, on the other hand, tell a Negro from a white person at a glance. At least it is true that you can tell the one from the other in such a large majority of the cases that the assigning individuals to accepted categories goes on easily and swiftly. The doubtful cases do make difficulty, as in the occasional individual who is socially a Negro although in appearance a white man, and in the small rural minorities in Delaware and elsewhere who—descended from a mixture of Indian, Negro and white—resist classification as either Negro or white. But these doubtful cases prove the strength of the categories, for other men and women in communities where such doubtful individuals or groups occur seem to demand a solution of the problem in the assignment of the doubtful case to the one racial category or the other. The school system, the Jim Crow practices, the very customary logic of the American's mind, call for a resolution of such ambiguities. They should not be there; they upset the system; in this country every man must be either a white man or a Negro. In some societies the problem is met by the development of intermediate categories defining marginal groups. In our own society, so far as the Negro is concerned, the tendency has been to adhere to a simple system according to which the customary single drop of Negro blood is enough to make a man a member of the inferior category. Race, in the sense of a visible physical evidence of a biological difference, is here the single guide to the principal social category. In Bahia, Brazil, on the other hand, one drop of Negro blood is of no significance, and even a great many drops have only the effect of suggesting an inferior social position for that individual, a suggestion that can be overcome by education or personal success. The emphasis upon race, in the sense of real or supposed difference in blood, as the prime basis for setting off the best people from the less good or the worst, is probably a fairly recent development in the history of man's inhumanity to man. It lends itself well to this human tendency to separate the superior sheep from the inferior goats by virtue of the durable visibility which it gives to the members of the class. Race "works" as a mechanism of social categorization because the racial mark is there to stay. It can't be changed as can a Cockney accent or a pagan religion. The Nazis had a little trouble with the application of their racial doctrines to Jews and to Poles, the distinguishing visibility being low, so to speak; so they came to require these hunted Helots to wear labels of one kind or another on their costumes. We do the same thing, in effect, when we accept the racial stereotypes in cartoon or moving picture. We, too, have our second-class citizens with second-class rights, and although these fellow Americans are for the most part visibly brown in color, we reinforce the definition of their inferior position with a thousand practices and social gestures. A simple device is to label one door "For Negroes" and the other door "For Whites." Segregation, imposed by the dominant, amounts to the imposition of stigmata of inferiority. These symbols of our collective prejudices emphasize and amplify the meaning given to the racial mark.

The second respect in which race has special force as a criterion of difference between "my superior people" and "those inferior people" arises from the connection of the racial mark with beliefs as to biological differences between the races. I have remarked that white men do not wait for proof that black or brown or yellow men are inferior by nature to white men before believing that they are. For many years scientists have looked for conclusive evidence that black men or yellow men are born different in intelligence or ability from white men, and today they still lack proof of such difference. Yet white men believe that such differences exist. They believe that black men or yellow men are inherently different or inferior, in part because such a belief is an apparent justification for the prejudice they feel and the injustice they commit. To deceive our consciences we invert the truth. We say that we treat the Negro as inferior because he is inferior. The truth is that we think the Negro to be inferior because we treat him as inferior. It is the act that is the father of the thought. The Negro is a half-citizen because white men will not allow him to be a full-citizen. It is a rationalization to say that he is born incapable of being a full-citizen. White Americans justify the oppression they permit by believing that Negroes are less competent than are white men. What really lies in the social order, for which we are responsible, we push off into the biological order, for which we are not responsible. What is in the biological nature of men is there to stay and is none of our business. Science—a false science—becomes the mythology of the modern man. It must be true, so we think, that Negroes' skulls close early upon their brains, for we treat Negroes as if that were the case. It is not the case, and every competent student knows it to be untrue. Nor is it true that the Negro is necessarily handicapped by the fact that Africa is only a few generations behind him. If this were true, then it would be true that the descendents of Englishmen would be handicapped as compared with Greeks or Egyptians by the fact that barbarism is only a few generations behind them. A child of one skin color starts even with a child of any other skin color, if you let him. We don't let him, and we entertain a false biology which seems to justify us.

I say again that race is of consequence because of what men think and feel about it and not because of anything that race is of itself. So we must look to the ways in which conceptions of race enter into our personal and social lives. I will speak here of how the conceptions we entertain as to race, like the conceptions we entertain as to anything else, may work for integration and high morale or for disintegration and low morale. If our ideas as to race are the same as those shared with others of our group and are consistent with the other ideas of the group, then, for that group, ideas as to race will make for solidarity and confidence. I have spoken of the tendency of primitive tribes to regard themselves as true men and everybody else as something less than men. This works well enough in a state of society in which every people is more or less hostile to every other, in which each little group subsists on its own independent efforts, and in which no doctrine of universal brotherhood has appeared. In such a small society it is a source of strength to hate the enemy and to believe oneself superior to the enemy. The enemy is all outside, and all one's own people are inside.

That is not the case today. Although we fight a national war, some of the enemy are inside the nation; some of our friends are in enemy countries. Today we need the help of half the world, or more, to live in the manner to which we are accustomed. Today we send our brothers to die in the name of principles of living which apply, in theory, to all men. So today an in-group sentiment defined in racial terms works for disintegration. Race prejudice and discrimination provide a categoric principle in conflict with other major categories by which we live. It is a great divisive fracture across the life of today. It is a sword we turn against ourselves.

Today the great divisions among men are the divisions into nations. More than any others, these divisions play the role played in primitive society by tribal groupings; more than any others, these divisions make for war. Yet it is no help to a people fighting a national war to entertain principles or to carry out practices of racial inequality. For the races against which we discriminate are within our nation. Racial inequality is a denial of national solidarity. It is a waste of resources and an act of social disintegration. A ship must be built; welders are needed; an available welder is not hired because his skin is black. In this way we not only waste the welder's labor, but also impair the moral strength of Americans. We deny the welder full solidarity with us, who fight beside him, and we deny ourselves full solidarity with him, who fights beside us. The bitterness that today grows in American Negroes is matched by the growing shame of white men. A people do not fight well who have bitterness and shame.

It is not even true to say that racial prejudice directed against our present enemies is a contribution to the fighting strength of America. We cannot hate our enemies as racially apart from us without applying the same prejudice to those who are not our enemies. Our prejudice against the Japanese has run from one extreme to the other. When they defeated the Russians two score years ago the Japanese enjoyed our high favor as a wonderful little people. Today they are the grinning ape-men, beastlike, and treacherous. In so far as we now think of them as bad because racially different from us we find ourselves, by the same prejudice, condemning our fellow citizens of Japanese ancestry—the Oakland and Seattle high-school boys and girls whose fathers and mothers were born in Japan—and denying them the right to enter our communities, to room in our lodging houses, to study in our schools. And on the other hand, our long-standing prejudices against the Oriental kept us, until a few weeks ago, from granting the right of naturalization to our Chinese allies. Men fight as nations, and our nation is made up of all races. Therefore we cannot define our enemies in racial terms without injuring ourselves.

But the essential weakness that follows from racial inequality follows from the inconsistency between the ideals we profess and the racial discrimination we practice. A people that profess one way of life and act another is a people without integrity, as such a man is a man without integrity. That is our case. We claim a leadership of the free peoples of the world, and we deny full freedom to some of our fellow citizens because of their race. We are the apostles of democracy, and public affairs are kept in the hands of a racial majority. We celebrate the Bill of Rights as a charter of liberty, and while we celebrate that document, we deny some of these rights to fellow citizens because of race. In a well-integrated society the goals for living are consistent with the institutions and practices of the people. In our society, in large part because of the social consequences of race, we speak one way and act another.

On whose side are we fighting in this war? Do we propose to help in enforcing justice for disadvantaged racial minorities in other lands? If we cannot give justice to such minorities in our land, shall we then be able to do so abroad? On Christmas Eve the President told us that the doctrine that the strong shall oppress the weak is the doctrine of our enemies. It is the doctrine and the practice of our enemies, but it is, to a significant extent, also the practice of ourselves. What becomes of the integrity of a people who deny, yet practice, a doctrine of their enemies? Can we assume responsibility for the enforcement of justice in Asia when we do not enforce it in Atlanta or Detroit? Shall we continue to send missionaries abroad to acquaint distant people with a religious and ethical doctrine in large measure belied by the missionaries' fellow citizens in the homeland?

Racial inequality contradicts major principles that we have embraced. The disintegrating effects of the social consequences of race go far beyond the effect on the fighting strength of the nation. Even in a time of war when men fight by nations and plan the peace through alliances of nations, there is a tendency to modify the national alignments by alignments that are individual and moral. A German national is on our side if he hates naziism and shares our principles. We know that many Italians do not share Mussolini's views, and we treat Italians accordingly. We search for the signs of political democracy in Russia, and we look into the face of China for the reflection of our own ideals. Though nationalism may long divide us, though wars may continue for many generations, nevertheless we continue to grope for a moral order that will embrace the world. And across all these persistent, resurgent, ecumenical conceptions, across the idea of the Kingdom of Heaven on earth and the conception of a democratic world-order, lies racial inequality.

To the anthropologist the rising acuteness of the conflict between world-embracing principles and racial discrimination is an aspect of a society in process of reorganization. It is the nature of human society for its conceptions and institutions to adjust themselves to one another. Over long periods of time consistency rather than inconsistency is the rule. Cultures and civilizations are such in so far as the ways of life which make them up form a coherent way of life. As Sumner said, there is a strain to consistency among the folkways. Two immediate circumstances make the present inconsistencies difficult to maintain. One is the making explicit of our ideals forced upon us by the war. We find ourselves declaring, very loudly, many faiths we aren't living up to. The other is the increasingly apparent interdependence of racial and minority problems throughout the world. When the Tokyo radio takes up our race riots and makes propaganda weapons out of them within a few hours after their occurrence, when a Marine in the Solomons writes home to California his indignation that his fellow Californians are organizing to keep all persons of Japanese origin forever away from the Pacific Coast, only to stimulate a demand by the organizers that the distributors of the letter be investigated as subversive, when State Department—invited visitors to the United States from a Latin American republic are Jim Crowed in a Southern state, when a thousand such occurrences take place and are made widely known—then it becomes clear that unless it adopts a stringent isolationism and a reactionary ethics, this country cannot reach an adjustment between its ideals and its practices without reference to the rest of the world. To achieve a new integrity, we must work out a race policy and practice that will make coherent sense to ourselves when we state it and that will command the confidence of other free peoples everywhere.

RACE: FACT AND BELIEF

INTRODUCTION

This is the first time that I have ever spoken to the police, although police, on occasion, have spoken to me. I want to say something about beliefs and facts as to race, especially in situations in which the police have to deal.

We think of the beliefs that people have about race as factors in the situation, just as traffic difficulties, bad weather, or a blow on the head are factors in the situation. These beliefs are matters that we need to understand if we are to comprehend more completely all the things that enter into a situation of disorder or that might contribute to a situation of greater order. Violence, bitterness, the law, bad housing, and beliefs about race are all on the same level—they are things you have to think about and to understand. We are not considering beliefs about race, then, as the moralist would think it. It is not the function of the police to bring about heaven on earth. But I take it that it is the business of the police to keep things running as decently as police can, and the *beliefs* about race are a part of the circumstances of which they have to take account.

My plan is to set forth, on the one hand, what science knows about the nature of race and, on the other hand, to make some suggestions as to how the difference between what is known to be true by science and what is believed to be true by people contributes to our problem. The main point is one that you could announce as well as I. It is that what matters in race relations are the beliefs, not the facts. We could put it this way: if people did not notice that other people differed from them conspicuously, if people ignored the obvious differences between Negro and white, the fact of race, as the scientist knows about it, would have probably no consequence for the police. But it is the fact that people think things about other people in racial terms that contributes to the problem. In trying to understand this—to make it understandable to myself—I have conceived of an imaginary example. I would like to put this imaginary case before you, because I hope it will guide your thinking as I find it has guided my own.

This is the case: Let us imagine that everywhere we went in this country we found that nearly everybody believed that automobiles of a red color were more mechanically defective than automobiles of any other color. Never mind how people got to think so; let us just assume that they did. Let us suppose, then, it was believed that every time we

An address to the Chicago Police Force, University of Chicago Law School, July, 1952.

saw a red automobile we felt—I mean ordinary people—that that automobile was more likely to run into a traffic island than would a blue automobile or a black one; that there was something wrong with it as compared to automobiles of other colors; and, moreover, that the supposed weakness of the red automobile made you regard that automobile as less desirable, less praiseworthy than automobiles of any other color.

We might even extend our imaginary case and suppose that it was believed that red automobiles gave off a bad odor as compared to automobiles of any other color—although actually that might not be true. Now, let us imagine further, in order to make this parallel a little nearer to our case of race, that no man could choose the color of the automobile he owned but had to take an automobile of the same color as his father drove before him.

Supposing these things were believed, what would be the necessary responsibility of the officer who was trying to keep traffic running smoothly? He would have to know that every time he saw a red automobile in a traffic difficulty he could anticipate a greater chance of accident than if the automobiles present were not of that color—if they were blue or brown. It wouldn't matter that people's beliefs were wrong; what would matter is that trouble would be likely to occur. So we have a situation. The problem is not in terms of the real mechanical comparison between the red automobile and the black, but in terms of what people thought.

I want to add one more consequence which I think we can deduce from this situation. What would be the effect of these beliefs upon the drivers of red automobiles? I think you can see that if it were widely believed in the community that red automobiles were necessarily more inclined to accidents than automobiles of other colors, the drivers of red automobiles would not drive quite as steadily as other drivers. Some of them might even think it might be so, even though they might be a little ashamed to say so because they were stuck with their red automobiles. But the mere fact that everybody told them that they were likely to run into accidents would make them more dangerous drivers.

Imagine, for example, what would happen: There would be arguments as to whether red automobiles are really more inclined to accidents because of mechanical difficulties than other automobiles. And people would come up with statistics; they would say, "Look, other things being equal, there are 28 per cent more accidents with red automobiles involved than automobiles of a black color." And it would be so. But the statistical proof would, of course, not really be proof that the cause of the accident lay in the color. It would lie in something else; it would lie in the way people thought about the situation.

Well, this, it seems to me then, is where we are in regard to race and trying to deal with it in the human community. We cannot deny that these beliefs really exist; they exist in the sense that some of the things that are thought to be true about racial behavior are true in some degree. But they are not true for the reason which people think them to be true. It would be just as much a mistake to pretend that the presence of the Negro or the white man in the community is irrelevant to public order as to believe, as most people do believe, that the cause of public disorder lies in the inherent "carburetors" of the Negro and the white. Now this is all really that I have to say; the remainder of my remarks will take up a few cases and try to contrast what is known by science and what is believed by ordinary people.

FACTS ABOUT RACE

We might make two short lists—one list of the principal things science knows to be true about Negro-white differences and the other, things people think to be true about Negro-white differences. I use the case of the Negro and the white man for the obvious reason that it is the most important in our culture, but everything I say applies as well if we were dealing with Orientals or other racial groups. Ignoring his beliefs and preconceptions, the scientist examines the Negro and the white man as he would examine any two animals discovered in the jungle, and this is about what he is able to say about one as compared to the other. I can state it in either terms: the white or the Negro, but I happen to state it now in terms of the Negro.

The Negro's head is slightly longer and slightly narrower, *on the average*, of course, than is that of the white man. The cranial capacity is slightly less. The distance between the pupils is slightly greater. The nose is significantly broader and the lips significantly thicker. The external ear is slightly shorter. The pelvis is narrower and smaller. The stature is shorter. The skin, of course, has more dark pigment. In many cases, the hair tends to be wavy, woolly, or curly. The distribution of the hair on the body is wider and much less dense.

There are more sweat glands in the skin of the Negro, and this is connected with the pigmentation. The tendency of the upper dental arch to project forward, which has the name of prognathism, is the result of the fact that in the case of the Negro the face continues to grow after the period in which it does characteristically in the white man. And, of course, brown eyes and dark hair are common. Now all these differences are statistical, or differences in averages, that is, there is a great deal of overlapping among the racial groups. Another way of saying this is that the differences among the individuals in either the white or the Negro race are greater than is the difference in the averages of the two races.

With regard to some of these features, as the pigmentation of the skin, the overlapping is slight; that is, relatively few "white" people are darker than many Negroes. With regard to others, as the shortness of the ears, the overlapping is great. The difference with regard to the presence of antibodies in the blood, which are important in producing clotting and, therefore, have to be taken account of in blood transfusions, has been found to be statistically different between Negroes and whites, but there is a very great degree of overlapping. So it is impossible to predict with any assurance what type of blood you will often find in individual Negroes or white men. This is certainly plenty for what science really knows. The discussion could, of course, be extended a great deal, but it would only be with regard to refinement of details.

BELIEFS ABOUT RACE

Whether or not there is such a thing as race does not obviate the fact that people believe that there is. Moreover, people have many beliefs about race. Let us first consider some popularly held beliefs which the scientist has shown to be false. The cranial suture, which is the division between the bones of the skull, is believed to close earlier in the case of the Negro. This is not true. It is often said that the difference in speech between the Negro and the white man is due to a different anatomy of the vocal cords. This is also not true. It is often said that there is something in the nature of the foot, the heel, or the shin bone of the Negro that makes him a better athlete in certain fields. Examinations of the anatomy show no such things. And so the story goes. These are familiar examples of the kinds of things that are believed in regard to purely anatomical differences which don't happen to be true.

It is also believed that some of the supposed anatomical differences or some of the real anatomical differences have consequences for conduct; that is, it is believed that certain differences which the scientist can confirm contribute to human behavior. For example, the scientist has shown that the Negro has, on the average, a slightly smaller brain case and brain size as compared to the white man. This is taken by many of us to mean that the Negro's intelligence is less than that of the white man. All the information that scientists have been able to gather shows no correlation between the size of the brain and intelligence, except at the very greatest extremes—that is, brains of a cranial size over 1500 cubic centimeters capacity, which are monster brains, or brains under 1000 centimeters capacity tend to be in individuals with defective intelligence. But these are such extremes of range of human differences, and the cases are so few that one cannot make out differences between Negro and white in terms of these extreme cases. The difference between the average size of the Negro brain and the average size of the white man's brain is not known to have any effect on behavior; nor has any difference in the anatomy of the brain itself been firmly established.

Similarly, it is generally believed that the dark skin has something to do with the susceptibility of the Negro to disease. Now here is a case in which the belief may be true. All that can be said is that the scientists are not quite sure. It is true that abundant sunlight is favorable in preventing a person from getting rickets and probably also tuberculosis; and it is true that pigmentation in the skin reduces the amount of ultraviolet light which is absorbed by the system, being the fraction of the light which is useful in preventing diseases. However, there are certain other anatomical features in Negro skin—the multiplication and development of a great number of sweat glands and the production of sebum in the sweat glands —which apparently contribute to prevent deficiency diseases. Actually, we do not understand this matter thoroughly as yet. It may be possible that the Negro's sweat glands operate to offset the effect of pigmentation in retarding the effect of ultraviolet rays. But more important than these purely biological questions in regard to the relation of pigmentation to rickets is the fact that the Negro is generally subjected to environmental conditions favorable to the development of rickets and tuberculosis. The Negro generally lives in more crowded conditions; his diet and his hygiene are not too good, and it may be that the differences in disease are determined by these environmental differences and not by anatomical differences at all.

Let us now consider some special beliefs. First we shall deal with them as the scientist would and then as the popular man would and see what sense we can make out of it. In advance, the conclusion that will emerge is that the differences between Negro and white may be significant with regard to human behavior, but we are not in a position to say that they are. Now this is not the same thing as to say we know there are no differences. We cannot say as scientists that we know there are no differences that are significant. But what we can say is that we do not know that there are any differences.

Take the case of body odors, which is a very good example because popular feelings are very strong on both sides. Many white people report that the Negroes have an objectional body odor. Negroes say the same thing about white men. In fact, the objectional odor of the white man has been reported in primitive communities often enough. I have had the experience myself with some of my Indian friends. But this is a very hard matter to study. Some attempts have been made in the use of sweat. All the results are negative. Testing in this way, we were unable to see that people could really distinguish, by nose, a representative of one race from another. And again we have this question of environmental differences.

The amount of washing and use of soap probably have something to do with body odor. At any rate, body odor is a good case because the belief about it makes a fairly significant contribution to this general context of behavior. Body odor is easily associated with prejudice and dislikes of one sort or another, and I think the belief would probably occur even if there weren't these environmental differences which might produce, in an indirect way, a real difference.

Another case of such a belief is that of the black baby born to white parents. This is a very old one and is reported, I believe, in some classical sources. The belief seems to recur perennially. The fact, however, is that children are rarely darker than the darker of the parents; and if the child is, it is only a little darker. There isn't a case known of a notably dark child born of conspicuously white-looking parents. While I am on the subject, let me say that we have the experience at the University of Chicago several times a year of receiving in our office some infant whose parents, guardian, or legal advisor are interested in the possibility that the child may have Negro blood. The question is raised for some legal question or as a matter of family arrangements. My colleague, Professor Washburne, who is about as good a physical anthropologist as they come, refuses to judge in many of these cases. In fact, he will not see them any more because he always tends to mislead them. He will not see them because he just can't tell.

Let us go now to the special problem of mental traits. This is a central issue. The popular beliefs with regard to this can be summarized as follows: First, that Negroes are inherently less intelligent either always or most often than are white people. This is the belief held by the white part of the community. Or it is especially believed that the intelligence of Negro children is equal to that of children of other races but that the Negro slows down or comes to a stop at an earlier age in his intellectual development. Or there may be special beliefs to the effect that the Negro may be superior to the white man in some kinds of abilities.

Superiority of the Negro in musical ability is a common belief. This is interesting because here we encounter beliefs that appreciate rather than depreciate the Negro. The question is: Under what social contacts do white people think good things of the Negro or do Negroes think good things about the white man? Returning to the question of intelligence and special capacities between the races, science does not know the answer. I regret the fact that some of my anthropological brethren, in their enthusiasms to set the record straight, have overstated their case. But most are cautious. Some have tended to say that the Negro is equal to the white man or the white man is equal to the Negro—it doesn't matter how you state it. We cannot say that the white man is equal to the Negro in all respects because we haven't found any way to find out. But what we can say is that the popular beliefs with regard to the equalities or inequalities of inherent capacity between whites and Negroes are unsupported by any scientific proof.

Personally, I think it is not out of the question that the scientific method may be sufficiently developed so that scientists may be convinced at some future time of a statistical difference with regard to certain kinds of characteristics. But though I cannot foresee what these differences will be, I see no reason to suppose that the popular belief about the superior musical ability of the Negro or the superior managerial ability of the white man will be the ones. Actually, we know little about the genetic differences between races of men. The point about blood-clotting agents is one of the few examples which the geneticists know about with some degree of certainty; but we can't see how this gene trait has any relevance to behavior.

The students of genetics estimate very roughly that if you put together all of the characteristics of the Negro and of the white man that one sees and uses in distinguishing the one group from the other, either according to popular belief or scientifically, we are taking account of less than 4 per cent of all the genetic factors that are present. And of this 4 per cent we know the mechanisms of heredity with regard to only a few. This suggests, then, the state of real scientific ignorance as compared with what is popularly supposed to be so.

But most scientists would predict that if such differences ever come to be established they would be so small and the degree of overlapping would be so great (in the order of 80 to 90 per cent) that no intelligent policy of managing human relations in the city or any intelligent policy of education or legislation could ever be based upon those differences. In fact, the differences will not be great enough to make it worthwhile to take them into consideration in planning police training or in planning how police should treat people in a traffic jam. What will continue to be important is what people think and that is what we have to deal with.

WHY DO PEOPLE BELIEVE WHAT THEY DO ABOUT RACE?

The principal point about the examples of beliefs already discussed is that they are adjustive or adaptive; that is to say, we can understand why it is that people believe these things—these beliefs aren't just capricious. People don't believe just anything about other races. They believe things that make the believers feel more comfortable. This idea is so simple that it is almost silly to say it. But it helps us to understand the true nature of the beliefs. One will not find many white people believing that Negroes are inherently great statesmen or that they have great capacities for leadership as compared to white people. You don't find these beliefs because they wouldn't fit with the way white people think of themselves in our society as compared to what they think about the Negro. People believe the things that make the habits they have set well with them.

This point helps us understand how beliefs work. If the white man curses the Negro, or breaks his window, or breaks his head, the white man can find ready-made justification. This is so because the beliefs are already in the back of his mind. I suppose corresponding things can be said about the Negro in his disadvantageous position. He is likely to develop beliefs that will give him some consolation, though his head will be broken anyway. To believe that the other fellow deserves what is done to him makes it easy for one to go to sleep easily at night. And if the white man who believes that the Negro is not as good as he can then look around and find that the Negro lives in more disagreeable houses, pays a little more for what he gets, and gets paid less for the same kind of work, he feels better. All this is all right, he figures, because, after all, it is not the same kind of work because the Negro is not as good as the white man.

In the rural South the well-to-do whites often hold a more condescending and almost affectionate attitude toward the Negro than do whites in the Northern cities. The reason for this is that in the North the white man is compelled by changing circumstances to look *across* at rather than *down* at them because the Negro is more nearly on the same level in regard to the work or trade that he is carrying on. In the South, on the other hand, where there is separateness—though not as great as in the old South—the Negro is in occupations generally below that of a white man; and, accordingly, the whites can afford to be kindlier, while also more convinced that there are great natural inherent differences between whites and Negroes. If you combine these beliefs with the beliefs that the Negro is lazy or immoral, you don't have to work quite so hard to justify Negro slums.

But if you combine certain favorable beliefs about the Negro, such as his musical ability or his easy way with children, you can believe all the favorable things that fit in with the general position you accord the Negro. But you can't believe that the Negro is a great statesman simply because you don't accord him that position. And the supposed lack of virtue in the Negro women—one of the popular beliefs—may, therefore, be connected with the same line of persuasive argument, with the record of miscegenation. Some white men can say that the unfavorable living conditions for Negroes ought not to be. Many other white people can merely answer by pointing to the record.

KNOWLEDGE FOR WHAT?

The final point comes back to the way the drivers of the red automobiles would drive if everybody believed that red cars were defective. The

Negro, like the red car, has, to a certain extent, been made into the image of the beliefs which white men have about them. That is to say, to some extent, the behavior of the Negro is what actually corresponds to what white people come to believe the Negro is. Now this is maybe a little difficult for whites to accept, but it is so. Of course, one can say that the "Negro makes the slum." The reasonable and thoughtful way, however, of considering this idea outside of popular belief is to say that the "slum makes the Negro" what he is. The slum makes the man who lives in it in some way inferior; anybody who lives in the slum would be made inferior in some respects. They would, for example, be more inclined to get sick—that is an inferiority. They would work fewer days in the year. They would be crowded, frustrated, prevented from achieving the aspirations that other humans have, be less well educated, have fewer and less desirable parks; and as a consequence of this would tend to get them more easily into certain kinds of crime. All this, too, is an inferiority in the sense that we think it is worse to have criminal behavior than to have law-abiding behavior.

But this, from the viewpoint of the scientist, is a product of the social circumstances in which the Negro finds himself. Simply stated, the Negro has been made into what the white man has thought the Negro to be.

If we return to the world of music, we find an example which is easy to discuss without stirring up much feeling. On the whole, you can look around and find Negroes doing very well in many musical lines. I don't think the scientist has any way of telling you whether Negro babies are born more musical than white babies. It may be that this is just one of the activities in which the Negro is allowed to develop. Even under slavery, music was one field that Negroes could enter. Negroes were given some leadership by white people in connection with religious exercise—hymns and the like. Furthermore, as American history went on, popular musicians and other entertainers were more tolerant—racially tolerant—than many other groups in our modern society. Entertainers are not concerned much about skin differences. When we try to understand the success of the Negro in recent years in certain sports, notably pugilism, we find that his success is explained in the same way—by circumstances in society which tended to bring about a gradual displacement by successful Negro fighters of fighters of other racial origin.

I could make this point this way: One of the beliefs with regard to the difference between the two groups is that the Negro is inclined to tuberculosis, and we know that they die more often of tuberculosis than do whites. But two generations ago the white people had, proportionately, more often tuberculosis than the Negro. Why? The answer is that at that time the Negroes weren't urban. But as the Negro came to live in the city, these diseases caught up with him. In the meantime, the white man was getting the benefits of the improved medical treatment and better housing more rapidly than was the Negro. Much in the same way, such a matter as the success of the Negro in pugilism will some day come to be understood. So, I am inclined to think that we have made Negroes an inferior people. Negroes die oftener; they get into certain crimes oftener; they are less well trained; they are worse paid; they are less well educated, and all of these conditions will develop the inferiority attributed to him.

So my point is that these examples may help us to slightly improve our understanding. It is not claimed that this line of thought will give us the means to change the attitudes and beliefs that Negroes are inferior. These things are harder to change than the weather, and I'm not joking when I say that maybe the scientist will get around to altering the weather before he gets around to altering these beliefs. The beliefs serve, therefore, as factors which make for the trouble with which the policemen have to deal.

There is a real difference between what people believe to be true of the Negro and what the Negroes actually do. The reason for this difference lies in the social situations—in the beliefs—and not in anything that is in the Negro's "carburetor" or in the white man's "carburetor." To understand this fact is, I think, to be able to foresee and understand how this factor of race contributes to the situation of disorder as other factors contribute to it. At least we get this much difference: By acquiring this degree of understanding we free ourselves, to some degree, from the passion and the prejudices which attach to the ordinary citizen who is not thus freed; and if we can think about it with a degree of dispassion and understanding of why the thing is as it is, I suppose we are the wiser operators of the situation.

ETHNIC RELATIONS: PRIMITIVE AND CIVILIZED

It will be remembered that Robert E. Park began one of his best-known papers[1] with a suggestion that prejudice ought to be defended. It is, he reminded us, a human characteristic that supports our most admirable sentiments of love and loyalty and friendship. He began his discussion in this way because he wanted us to accept the kind of prejudice we do not like as an instance of a class containing other instances that we do

Reproduced with permission from Jitsuichi Masuoka and Preston Valien (eds.), *Race Relations, Problems and Theory* (Chapel Hill: University of North Carolina Press, 1961).

[1] Robert E. Park, "The Bases of Race Prejudice," in *Race and Culture* (Glencoe, Ill.: Free Press, 1950), pp. 230–43.

like and so see the class itself as a natural species—to see it with an eye free of the jaundice of our personal involvements. So seen, prejudice is that classification with corresponding attitudes that tends to support the existing organization of people according to status. It may or may not involve antagonism and is more likely to do so when the prejudice is failing to maintain the organization.

In the same spirit, in presenting to us "The Nature of Race Relations,"[2] he made us see that those relations between different ethnic and genetic groups which do involve race consciousness and race conflict are but special cases of the larger class of situations in which two or more groups distinguishable genetically and ethnically are in some characteristic adjustment to one another. In this wider sense the Carthaginians and the natives of the West African coast who, according to Herodotus, exchanged goods without seeing or talking with each other were a case of race relations, although what each group thought of the other was a matter private to each group and involved no conflict. Included also are the relations that have come about between people who are obviously of different racial and cultural origins but who maintain their ethnic integrity although in close association with each other; the ethnic enclave may give rise to "race problems," as with the East Indians in South Africa, or may not, as with the Gypsies in our cities. Park wanted us to understand that the relations between Negroes and whites do not constitute a type-form in the natural history of ethnic relations but are rather to be seen as an instance of a very variable class of human relationships between groups.

In further contribution to our understanding of ethnic relations in the perspectives of the widest comparisons made in a spirit of scientific detachment, Park showed us that the transformations of relationships between ethnic groups could be examined in historical perspectives short or long. They can be regarded in the short run of a few years or generations. Park's account of the race-relations cycle in Hawaii and his famous presentation of the shift of the line between Negro and white in the United States from a horizontal to a vertical position are examples of the study of the short-run change. A viewpoint in the middle distance of history is represented in his comparisons of race relations in India and in China, in which explanation is offered as to why caste resulted in the one case and not in the other. And in many places in his writings one finds Park taking the very long view of all of human history everywhere, looked upon as one great series of typical events. In more than one paper he discussed the world-wide transformation of ethnic relations that resulted from the rise of city-states and civilizations. In adopting this most inclusive and far-reaching viewpoint, he discussed the change in ethnic relationships

[2] *Ibid.*, pp. 81–116.

from territorial separation of insiders and outsiders into relationships of subordination and superordination within a state, the accompanying acceleration of ethnic amalgamation, and the development of such interstitial groups as commercial foreigners and marginal men.

Adopting this third and widest viewpoint, I may here pursue a little further the attempt to contrast the ethnic relations of primitive societies with those that came about with civilization, or, as Park sometimes called it, with "civic" society. What may be said about ethnic relations before the rise of civilization? The only knowledge we are likely to have of the matter is that provided by the state of things among the primitive peoples of the present time; we may suppose that such ethnic relations as appear among societies unaffected by civilization today are the kinds of ethnic relations which probably appeared, here or there, before cities and civilization.

For understanding of the primitive conditions, Park liked to make a beginning with Sumner's conception of primitive society as small groups scattered over a territory. However such small groups may be allied with one another, there is, Sumner said, a sharp distinction between a we-group of comradeship and peace and an out-group of hostility and war. His paragraphs on ethnocentrism stress the pride and vanity which the members of the in-group feel with regard to themselves and the scorn and contempt which they feel for those of the out-group.

Now this is a true but simplified and schematic description. A review of the actual situations in primitive societies of recent times would show many kinds of modification of this simple form of ethnic relations. The ideal and extreme form in fact appears to us in the cases of some very isolated small hunting groups. The Siriono band, about sixty people, rarely see any other human beings in their Bolivian forest and have no established ethnic relations. Of other Indian tribes the Siriono know of two, and these they fear and avoid; both are referred to by a term meaning a kind of monster.[3] Here in-group and out-group correspond with the human world within which one lives and everybody outside of it. (The slight modification of this situation brought about by white settlers I ignore.) But in more cases than not, the primitive peoples that we know directly have such established relationships with other kinds of people as at least to distinguish among the friendly and the unfriendly. The Maricopa Indians of the Gila River country felt friendly with the Pima and several other Yuman peoples and visited and traded with some of these. With other tribes there was traditionally warfare, and with yet others the relationships were equivocal, sometimes friendly and sometimes hostile.

[3] Allen R. Holmberg, *Nomads of the Long Bow: The Siriono of Eastern Bolivia* (Smithsonian Institution, Institute of Social Anthropology, Publication No. 10 [Washington, D.C.: Government Printing Office, 1950]), p. 63.

Further, the character of the relationships shifted over periods of time. Maricopa were most similar in customs to the Halchidhoma and intermarried with them, while they objected strenuously to having their girls marry into neighboring tribes that were without sibs (clans). Spier tells us that the Maricopa thought the Halchidhoma "a queer lot," looked toward them with "amused tolerance," and told pleasant stories of the latter's absurdities.[4] It is probable, I think, that such varying kinds of ethnic relations had come about before civilization in many parts of the world.

As local groups came into persisting relations of usefulness to one another, we may be sure that the distinction between an in-group and everybody else became complicated into a series of distinctions in which grades of nearness and farness came to be recognized. In the Ituri forest of West Africa the pygmies establish relationships, family by family, with some of the Negro peoples and exchange with them honey and meat for bananas and ax blades. There is affection and loyalty between the pygmy family and that Negro family with which it has become connected, and from what Putnam tells us we get the impression that the pygmies are aware of the Negro's view of ethnic relations. In this view "there are four orders of living beings: people, pygmies, chimpanzees and other animals. The pygmies are thus considered a species apart, neither human nor animal, but in between."[5] So even in very primitive conditions there may be a scale of ethnic prejudice.

The increase in size and density of local populations, looking now to the growth in numbers of the same people, also gives rise to graded distinctions. In areas of fairly dense settlement primitive peoples commonly recognize distinctions between those people closest to me whom I meet in friendliness and loyalty, those farther away but still my kind of people with whom I may be friendly, or may perhaps be hostile, and those still farther away who are not my kind of people at all and whom I either avoid or destroy. The Ifugao of Luzon might dispute with a member of another kindship group in his own settlement, but such disputes had to be composed in the interests of the common peace. In such disputes no heads were taken. If a dispute arose between two men of different districts, heads might or might not be taken, and a feud resulted, very difficult to terminate. And between two districts remote from each other there was simple and continual war, with heads always taken, even heads of women.[6] Evans-Pritchard shows us eleven concentric zones of nearness

[4] Leslie Spier, *Yuman Tribes of the Gila River* (Chicago: University of Chicago Press, 1933), pp. 44 ff.

[5] Patrick Putnam, "The Pygmies of the Ituri Forest," in Carleton S. Coon (ed.), *A Reader in General Anthropology* (New York: Henry Holt & Co., 1948), p. 324.

[6] R. F. Barton, "Ifugao Law," *University of California Publications in American Archaeology and Ethnology*, XV (1919–22), 75–78.

and farness within the large Nuer tribes of the Sudan, and the relations the African has with those of the most remote zones are hostile or predatory. Next outside lies another tribe, the Dinka, whom the Nuer regard as created just to provide Nuer with enemies. The point is that in such large and dispersed tribal peoples the out-group feeling is a change of sentiment away from those near at hand to those far away and yet quite like one's self, and becomes absolute as one leaves the land of one's own kind of people to meet a people with somewhat different language and culture.[7] We might say that familial and neighborhood relations are of one piece with ethnic relations, while yet distinguishable.

Returning to the relations of one ethnic group to another under primitive conditions, I recall the fact that, even where civilization has had nothing to do with it, one ethnic group occasionally establishes itself within the territory of another and shares its local life. The attachment of a band of North American Indians to a tribe of another speech and tradition was a not infrequent occurrence in early days. In some cases the enclaved people became a minority group, as is true today of the Tewa (Tano?) village on Third Mesa who have lived for two and a half centuries among their Hopi neighbors, intermarrying freely with them and yet maintaining their tribal and cultural distinctness. Whether or not the father or mother's father is Hopi, the children born into this subcommunity learn Tewa: No Hopi ever learns it. Tewa ceremonials are very different from those of the Hopi; their religious life is directed more to curing than to bringing rain, and the formal societies of the Hopi are lacking. The Tewa tell a myth of an ancient curse which helps maintain the separation of the two peoples. The Hopi view of their ethnic minority is mixed; they respect the practical success of the Tewa and seek their advice in matters of business and affairs with the outside, but they regard the Tewa as bold and barbaric and disrespectful.[8] One begins to imagine possible comparison with other successful, envied, and depreciated minorities. Students of the large African tribes have encountered many ethnic minority groups. The Lozi of Rhodesia somewhat despise certain recent immigrant peoples within their realm, and with one such tribe they refuse to intermarry.[9]

I am sure that one could assemble many instances of ethnic relations and ethnic prejudice in primitive societies. One would be struck by the

[7] E. E. Evans-Pritchard, *The Nuer* (Oxford: Clarendon Press, 1940; later editions; 1947, 1950), p. 114.

[8] Edward P. Dozier, "Resistance to Acculturation and Assimilation in an Indian Pueblo," *American Anthropologist,* LIII (January–March, 1951), 55–66.

[9] Max Gluckman, "The Lozi of Barotseland in North-Western Rhodesia," in Elizabeth Colson and Max Gluckman (eds.), *Seven Tribes of British Central Africa* (London: Oxford University Press, 1951), p. 6.

variety of these relationships. In trying to make order among the cases one would see, I think, that from Sumner's extreme case there could be demonstrated a range of situations in which a people of one ethnic character had come into established relationships with another people, being outside or partly inside or almost wholly assimilated within the culture and society of the other; and one would find that the relationships were in most cases supported by prejudices, these prejudices colored by sentiments of different kinds and degrees of feeling. The disposition to feel friendlier to those near me and like me and more hostile to those farther off and less like me would remain as very generally present, but one would become interested in the qualifications of this generalization and in the subtypes of ethnic relationship. One would probably see that the hostility is most intense with regard to people not very remote and resembling, while yet different from, the people who feel hostile. It is those people over there who are not my people but who live much my kind of life and perhaps crowd me a little against whom the most unfavorable prejudices run, in primitive societies if not also elsewhere. For another thing, a review of primitive ethnic relationships would turn up instances of neutral sentiments with regard to out-groups; some people look at other peoples as just different, neither bad nor good. I think that before European influence it was probably already true in the highlands of Western Guatemala, as it is today, that the Indians of one local community do not prejudge the Indians of many another local community as either bad people or good people; they think of them as having different ways, and that is their affair. Much travel and much commerce bring Indians of many communities together superficially; an Indian trader meets a people of another dialect, costume, and custom in almost every town to which he comes; and ethnic variety is a commonplace.

Looking now forward to comparisons with the ethnic relations characteristic of civilization, I find it possible to make at least two generalizations about the primitive conditions. First, each set of prejudices as to other peoples is local for the people who hold it. Each world of thought is small and ends with that band or tribe. In the next band or tribe one finds some other set of attitudes as to the ethnic groups known to that little people. Primitive life is a patchwork of cultures-and-societies, and ethnic prejudices are parts of the patches. No one great set of prejudices as to the goodness or badness of people who follow this god or have this custom or show this skin color breaks loose from the local cultures and establishes its influence over many of the patches, becoming a wide-running, prevailing tincture of the human scene.

The other generalization is even more negative. Ethnic prejudice in primitive life is—to use a word in an unusual sense—unprincipled. It is not grounded in a choice of principle for including some and excluding others, for exalting my people and degrading those others. A principle is such a reason for an attitude as compels action in accordance with it in unanticipated cases even against conflicting considerations. The relations between two primitive ethnic groups are not so governed. The Tewa, in the instance mentioned above, tell a myth to the effect that once they came in response to a Hopi request that they help the Hopi in war and that when they had done so and had settled among the Hopi, the latter broke their promise to share their food and women with them. Then the Tewa dug a pit and made the Hopi spit into it, the Tewa putting their spittle above; the pit closed, the separation of Tewa from Hopi was thereby sealed. Such a myth explains and justifies the relations between Hopi and Tewa. It bears no relation to relations between Tewa and other people, and it offers no principle for distinguishing good people from bad, or lower people from higher people. So it is with each set of ethnic relations in primitive life. This is why one cannot well speak of race relations in these societies; no prominence is given to skin color or the symbol of black or white blood or to any one emphasized characteristic of birth, appearance, religion, or custom. One must use such a phrase as "ethnic relations"—it is suitably vague. A tribesman may fix on some element of appearance or custom in the derogatory phrases he uses of other tribes, as Sumner's examples remind us, but the choice is accidental and unimportant and leads to no general rule for classifying or ranking peoples.

It is in these two respects, at least, that ethnic relations come to be different once there are civilizations. A civilization is regional, expansive, and purposeful. Among the thousands of little primitive societies the civilizations are the few giants: Toynbee counts twenty-one or twenty-three of them in all history. Each civilization is an extension of preponderating influence over less civilized and dependent peoples. The lesser peoples may be similar to one another as in China, or more various, as in India. A civilization includes so many people, and so large and complex a structure of relationships and specializations, that tradition becomes thoughtful or reflective, critical, and consciously systematic. In most civilizations this development is helped by the presence of writing and books. Whether or not we are to see in every civilization a universal church and a universal state, we may more simply observe that in a civilization men seek out and define principles for the ordering of life. Each principle or group of principles comes to have its own independence and dynamism. It tends to make order among groups of people in accordance with itself and even against countervailing ways of ordering them. "With the decline of tribal societies and the rise of cities . . . men's beliefs began to assume the form of creeds, and the myths which grew up to support traditional beliefs assumed under these circumstances a rational and an ideological character."[10]

I am thinking here of the civilized religions, governments, purposes, and policies. The religions of civilization—the "world religions"—get to have a certain separateness from local life and come to be taught and extended to many kinds of people. Hinduism, though a multitude of different things for the multitude of small communities, is one thing for all India. Christianity and Islam undertake, as their purpose, to include all people of whatever ethnic origin within them. Buddhism is inclusive and expansive. A great religion is a principle for ordering the relations of men. It emphasizes one difference—that between believer and unbeliever—and tends to deny or reject other kinds of differences among them.

The management of the secular affairs of a civilization leads to its own principles for ordering people. In a civilization, in contrast to a primitive tribe, people come to have a sense of their important place in human history. They think of themselves as they will be looked at by quite other men at some later time. Judging from Pericles' funeral oration and from the opening words of Thucydides' history, the Athenians had this conception. What is important is to be an Athenian. But Athens was but part of a developing civilization. When a people take the hegemony of an entire civilization, they commonly develop a principle—cultural or political—for the ordering of peoples other than themselves. I do not have the book here but seem to remember that John Wilson tells us that in a later period of its history there developed in Egypt a sense of manifest destiny to maintain Egypt's preponderating influence over lesser peoples. The Romans took the burden of managing civilization, and the principle for ordering the relations of people became that of Roman citizenship. The Greeks, the Chinese, and later the French emphasized a cultural principle of discrimination; in theory, and in considerable degree in practice, to become French in culture erases differences in birth or color.

Each principle—religious, political, or cultural—tends to develop its accompanying explanations and justifications. Theologies and political dogmas alike support the convictions and strengthen the dynamism of the civilization that employs that principle for arranging its relations with other people. The matter is thought out, ambiguities are clarified and the principle is intellectually connected with an appropriate source of authority: revelation, holy writ, moral responsibility, or "scientific" knowledge.

In a civilization there are always real differences between some people of one origin and way of life and other people of another origin and way of life. Even in the most homogeneous civilized communities such differences come about from the very rise of civilization. The civilized com-

[10] Robert E. Park, "Race Ideologies," *Race and Culture* (Glencoe, Ill.: Free Press, 1950), pp. 304–5.

munity includes different occupational communities and communities that differ according to rural and urban, sophisticated and unsophisticated. Herskovits tells us[11] that the people of Abomey, in that African kingdom of Dahomey which was nearly a civilization, treat the villager in an arrogant manner: he is an ignorant rustic. A student of the Book of Genesis tells me that much of it seems to have been written from the viewpoint of tent-dwelling shepherds who distrusted the townsman and did not think well of farmers. But the greatest differentiations of groups in civilizations are of course the results of expansion, migration, and conquest whereby peoples of different traditions and perhaps appearances are brought together. Then one or more of the principles of government, civilization, religion, or other rationalized prejudice decide how the exotics are to be ranked and treated.

The more explicit and formally managed principles for ordering the statuses of peoples ethnically different are supplemented by other principles not always connected with church or state. Toynbee reminds us[12] that as civilized peoples expand over less advanced peoples, the difference between us better and wiser people and Those Natives becomes a principle for ordering ethnic relations. The Islamic invaders of Africa offer religious brotherhood in Islam to the natives—but look down on them as natives. The American Negro found in Liberia natives on whom he could look down. Where the white European was the conqueror, "the white man's burden" appeared as a doctrine or principle in support of this emphasis on the difference between civilizing conqueror and native.

That principle for ranking people that looks to visible permanent signs on the person as evidence of inherent unchangeable difference and that often refers to "blood" as symbol of the essential distinction between Them and Us is the latest of the major principles for ranking peoples that have arisen with the civilizations. Its presence in the complexes of attitudes and principles that governed ethnic relations in the ancient world cannot be entirely denied, and the Oriental and Middle Eastern peoples are not wholly unaffected by it. Occasionally it has appeared with reversed spectrum: Arab conquerors looked down on the Persians as unpleasantly ruddy or fair in contrast to their own attractive swarthiness.[13] But we are all familiar with the strong association of race prejudice with the recent expansive phase of Western civilization carried by white men over much of the world. It is a principle almost peculiar to one civilization and to only the later part of that. The rapid conquest of other peo-

[11] Melville Herskovits, "Dahomey," *An Ancient West African Kingdom* (2 vols.; New York: J. J. Austine & Co., 1938), p. 55.

[12] Arnold Toynbee, A *Study of History* (London: Oxford University Press, 1954), VIII, 574.

[13] Arabic sources cited in Toynbee, *op. cit.*, VIII, 567, n. 1.

ples by white Europeans brought it about that several of the principles
for ranking peoples came to have a certain congruency. Where the man
of dark skin was also native, barbarian, heathen, and slave, at a time
when economic competition among ethnically different peoples was becoming intense, when many of these new rulers of the world were imbued with the Old Testament spirit of a people chosen by the Lord, when
a little later biology and applied genetics seemed to provide more secular justifications among people for whom "black" was already a word of
unfavorable connotations—in these and many other circumstances already
much discussed in our literature, the race principle reached great power.
As an explicit principle in politics, it is—since 1955—confined to a few
areas.

The feelings of utter inherent separation and horror which attend
the racial principle are by no means confined to that principle. The convicted heretic was horrible too. The caste-outcaste distinctions of India
include this element of untouchability, and for the conservative and or-
thodox there the feeling of uncleanness is real and deep, "in the soul."
Even as between social classes in the West something like it is approached. In Victorian England blue blood was spoken of much as black
and white blood are spoken of. If Trollope is an acceptable authority, I
refer to his Lady Alice, who, raised humbly with a tailor's son as play-
mate and made an earl's daughter by a court decision, then persisted in
determining to marry the tailor's son. Her new gentry friends regarded
the marriage as "monstrous and horrible," "so abominable that it is not to
be thought of."

Yet it is easy to join with Toynbee in regarding the racial principle as
the worst, the most dehumanizing, of them all. The reasons do not lie in
any greater cruelties accomplished by its application nor in any greater
irrationality of the principle. They lie in the fact, as in substance he says,
that the racial principle denies the excluded the full opportunity to join
the human race in its struggle upward. Principles for ranking people that
arise from the great religions, from differences in civilization or education or occupation, while they exclude or deny, also extend an invitation
to the excluded to become worthy of inclusion. And the grounds for
worthiness have something to do with humanity, with the improvements
of ourselves through education, religion, or culture. The racial principle
extends no such invitation. It is an apparently permanent relegation of
those unfit because of a supposed absolute difference in animal nature. It
is the native African's distinction between "people, pygmies, chimpanzees
and other animals."

But yet not like that, for the reason of the difference stressed in these
pages between the local and unprincipled ethnic relations of the primitive
man and the widely applied and principled, or ideological, ethnic rela-

tions of the civilized man. In a civilized society ethnic relations are matters for critical consideration and discussion. In primitive societies men have purposes and ambitions; they strive, as we do, to advance themselves and their communities. But only in a civilization do they have aspirations on behalf of the human race. The perfectibility of man is a civilized idea. So ethnic relations, along with other of the problems of moving along that perfectibility, come to be tested by the religious, ethical, and intellectual forms in which this perfectibility is expressed. Powerful as it is, this latest of comers among ethnic principles, race prejudice, finds itself in manifest conflict with most of the other ordering principles that are formulated. The religious and cultural principles come to be joined by others—radical political equalitarianism, the sense of brotherhood within the working class, that liberal humanism which defends and raises humanity in all men. In each of these considered purposes for the advancement of mankind race prejudice finds an adversary, a dynamic principle that demands that the racialist yield. The yielding is often slow. Caste, the central institution in India, has been denounced many times, and sects have striven to abolish it only in the end to demand their own rights as a caste. Yet today caste is on the wane. And some of the same countervailing principles that have caused racialism to wane also in this country are effective there, for the ideas, the principles, that rule events are now world-wide. The tribesman lives out his ethnic relations as tradition and immediate circumstance shape them. The civilized man also thinks them out. It is a more difficult way, perhaps a more painful way. But the examined life, as Socrates remarked, is, for civilized people, the only one worth living.

OUTLINE OF ARGUMENT TO THE EFFECT THAT SEGREGATED EDUCATION WORKS INJURIES AGAINST WHICH THE INDIVIDUAL IS PROTECTED BY THE EQUAL PROTECTION CLAUSE (AN ATTACK ON PLESSY VS. FERGUSON)

I. The Constitution forbids the legal enforcement of unequal treatment resulting in injury.

II. Segregated education is such legal enforcement of unequal treatment resulting in injury.

Unpublished notes, n.d. [The Supreme Court decision in *Plessy vs. Ferguson* in 1896 affirmed that the equal protection clause of the Fourteenth Amendment could be satisfied by offering equal but separate facilities to the different races, in this case in common carriers.—EDITOR.]

A. It cannot be saved from the constitutional prohibition by the argument that the segregation is required to accomplish the ends of education because the principle of classification (racial) bears no reasonable relation to the end (Klineberg evidence).

B. It cannot be saved from the constitutional prohibition by the argument that the segregation is required to accomplish the ends of education because in bi-racial communities public sentiment is such that education cannot be effectively carried on unsegregated; the evidence is that the abolition of segregation brings about no increase of tension or other difficulty.

   1. The evidence points to the conclusion that the closer white people have the actual experience of association with Negroes in common enterprises, the more willing they are to work with them in these enterprises.

      a) Army and housing: summarized in *To Secure These Rights,* pp. 84–86.

      b) Army, housing, retail buying: summarized in Will Maslow, "Prejudice, Discrimination and the Law," *Annals American Academy of Political and Social Science,* Vol. 275 (May, 1951), 9–17.

      c) Experience as to removal of segregation in education: R. M. Hutchins, R. Redfield—testimony in Sweatt case.

III. The nature of the injury.

A. The injury that results from segregated education is to:

   1. the individual who is segregated against his will (Negroes and some whites);

   2. the individual who wishes the segregation (many whites);

   3. the general community, through these injuries to its individual members.

B. The injury is of several kinds:

   1. The segregated individuals receive an inferior education; segregated education is never equal.

      a) The inferiority consists in part of poorer teaching and poorer material facilities—books, buildings, etc.—than are received by the white children (the whole history of segregated education; abundant testimony in particular legal cases).

      b) The inferiority consists in part of a stigma of the undesirable which attaches to one segregated against his will. (This may be expanded to include argument made in

Pekelis' brief in the Westminster School District Case, *Law and Social Action*, pp. 159 ff.: the value of a facility depends in part upon its association with persons enjoying a certain reputation; official assignment of a group based on a conviction of the group's inferiority is an assignment of facilities inferior per se; the law may not adopt or sanction social classification based on feelings of inferiority inherent in and inseparable from those classifications; the official adoption of such a classification deepens the inequality; therefore official segregation of a group considered as "inferior" is a discriminatory denial of equality to that group and a violation of the Constitution of the United States.)

2. Segregated education is more costly than unsegregated education.

3. Segregated children and young people suffer injuries to the personality which, like injuries to the body, are recognized in science and medicine as definite and serious. These injuries are:

  a) injurious feelings of frustration brought about by the mere fact of enforced separation from others in the community;

  b) distortions of the sense of reality by withholding the child from the real world: the segregated child is taught symbols from American history and idealism which do not truly represent his situation (personal experience of a teacher in a segregated school in this respect reported by Esther S. Cumby in "Teaching in a Segregated School," *Journal of Education*, Vol. 133, No. 1 (January, 1950);

  c) neurotic, or at least personality-crippling, feelings of "not being wanted," feelings of persecution, tendencies to withdrawal, etc., resulting from:

  (1) the fact that segregation is not enforced against the white to the same degree. Segregation never works equally both ways (this argument, I suppose, cannot be made because the attack is not upon the way the law is enforced, still less against the general customs of the community as to the association of the races, but against law and constitution requiring that each race be educated apart from the other);

  (2) the fact that segregated education is required and enforced by the white against the Negro and contrary to the will of the Negro;

(3) the fact that segregated education always assumes the inferiority of the Negro and is a symbol of that assumed inferiority (dictum in *Plessy vs. Ferguson,* contra).

(*a*) Argument summarized in A. D. Beittel, "Some Effects of the 'Separate but Equal' Doctrine of Education," *The Journal of Negro Education,* Vol. XX, No. 2 (Spring, 1951), and in Myrdal, Chap. 28.

(*b*) That these injuries are in fact produced in the personalities of the segregated is supported by the evidence given in the South Carolina case, and in the survey made by Deutscher and Schein on "The Psychological Effects of Enforced Segregation," *Journal of Psychology,* Vol. 26 (1948), 259–87, wherein ninety per cent of the social scientists replying to the question (517 scientists) expressed the opinion that enforced segregation has detrimental psychological effects.

(*c*) At the time of *Plessy vs. Ferguson,* these psychic injuries were not clearly recognized by science, as they are today.

4. Segregation in education prevents the development in the segregated child of those understandings and capacities which are required of every citizen, by reason of:

a) the formal and institutional separation of the child from a part of the community with which he must carry on his affairs and those of the community (the argument recognized, as to professional education, in the court's opinion in the Oklahoma case);

b) the emphasis given by formal and institutional separation to the discrepancy between American ideals and practices, thus making it more difficult to learn American ideals of democracy and equality;

c) the limitation of opportunity and encouragement to act toward the member of the other race according to basic human and humane inclinations. (This is argued, *passim,* in Myrdal, and is presumably confirmed by much experience of those who have taught in segregated schools.)

5. Segregation produces in the white person psychic injuries, chiefly suppressed guilt feeling. (This is, I suppose, about the last argument that the Court might accept.)

PART IV

THE UNIVERSITY
AND SOCIETY

RACE AND RELIGION IN SELECTIVE ADMISSION

The Institutions of higher learning of this country practice racial or religious discrimination in violation of a major principle of our national life. The truth of this general fact will not be seriously contested, although in any particular institution the discrimination there practiced may be denied, ignored, or justified. I am today concerned with the justifications offered in defense of the practice of these discriminations in enrolling students. With those who deny or ignore that discrimination exists one cannot usefully discuss the principles of conduct involved. In large part, however, the practices are defended as wise or as necessary. It is these defenses that have my attention today. I bring them before you for examination, in the hope that discussion of them may help to clarify the duty and the opportunity of colleges and universities in meeting a common problem.

That the problem is common may not at once appear. Jews and Negroes are the two groups that notoriously experience discrimination, and the situations of the two may appear more different than similar. The relative difficulties of the Negro in obtaining a higher education form only a small part of his disadvantages and arise from a great system of institutions and attitudes rooted particularly in the history of our country, which relegate him to a position as a sort of half-citizen, or citizen with only secondary rights. The discriminations from which the Jew suffers are derived from prejudices ancient and world-wide; his social and educational advancement is as great as is that of the white gentile; and the obstacles to his enrollment or employment created by colleges and universities constitute one of the chief injustices of which he is conscious.

The Jew and the Negro are perhaps not always aware that each is engaged in the other's cause. Indeed, the different attitudes occasionally taken by Jew and Negro as to the application of a quota suggest viewpoints diametrically opposed. The Jew regards the quota as an unjust limitation on his right to compete in education and in the professions with non-Jews. On the other hand, some Negro leaders ask that Negroes be included in this association, in that committee or agency or other group, in proportion to their numbers in the national or local community. For the Negro, often denied any admission at all to a public

Reproduced with permission from the *Journal of the American Association of Collegiate Registrars,* July, 1946, 1–16.

group, the argument of proportionate representation offers an opening toward the improvement of his situation. For the Jew, the application of a quota prevents him from bettering his position in free competition. Whether or not the quota is defensible in either case is something to be considered later in this paper.

The differences as between North and South also obscure the common character of the problem. In the North the Negro is excluded, or his admission is made difficult, without the support of the law. But in seventeen states the denial of admission of Negro citizens to the principal institutions of higher learning is obedient to law as well as to custom. How can the colleges and universities take any single position with regard to racial discrimination in education when a great sub-community of the nation has made segregation, in a multitude of details of community life, a legal requirement? Do the colleges of the South then share with those of the North any common responsibility in the matter?

One may point out that one of the differences between North and South in regard to racial and religious discrimination makes each region the victim of discrimination practiced in the other. On the whole the Negro finds it less difficult to get a good higher education in the North than in the South, especially education in some of the professions, and therefore southern Negroes who have the means to do so go North for higher education. In some southern institutions, on the other hand, discrimination against the Jew, especially in medical schools, is less severe than it is in many northern institutions, and therefore some northern Jews go south for such higher education. In this way each major American region bears a burden of higher education which is thrust upon it by the greater discrimination practiced by institutions in the other region. Perhaps this fact alone provides a basis for consideration of the problem as common and national.

With regard to another ethnic group of students, the adventures in discrimination experienced by our colleges and universities in recent years did not divide into patterns along the Mason and Dixon line. I refer to United States citizens of Japanese parentage. Here, during the war, the obstacles to enrollment differed greatly from one institution to another, but not according to the location of the institution in the North or in the South. Some colleges and universities showed more courage than others in admitting such students at a time when the Japanese-Americans were unjustly excluded as a group from participation in the national life. Some small colleges, especially some with church leadership, were bold in admitting Japanese-Americans against opposition in their local communities. Others—and some of the largest and most independent universities were included in this number—seemed positively eager to use the ambiguous and changing pronouncements of the War Department as to enrollment of Nisei students as a cover for their own disposition to discriminate. The large institution with war contracts to carry out and military officers close at hand often offered little resistance to advices that Nisei be excluded from its campus. Certain results were absurd. An administrative officer found himself denying admission as a student to some young Americans with Japanese parents and perhaps on the same day signing a form appointing to the teaching faculty some Japanese alien hired to teach the Japanese language to soldiers of our army. The point in mind here is that the problems of discrimination in education raised by the removal and dispersion of Americans of Japanese origin were nation-wide and presented to all of us in common terms the basic issues of ethnic discrimination in American education.

That the problem is in fact the same problem in all parts of the country and with regard to all minority groups appears from a mere statement of the principle of our national life and from recognition of discrimination as discrimination, no matter how explained locally.

The principle is simply that nothing granted one citizen is to be denied another by reason solely of his membership in a racial or religious group. Every fundamental American document has stated this principle, and no judicial decision, no great public pronouncement, has denied it. The inherent equality of all men with respect to the fundamental human rights declared in 1776 makes no exception against men of any particular racial or religious group. The Constitution contains no provision which would authorize racial or religious discrimination, and the Fourteenth and Fifteenth Amendments were enacted in order to preserve this equality, as against discriminatory legislation of the States, for Negro citizens. Moreover, the principle of equality of all individuals, no matter what their religious or racial character, has in recent years become explicit and fundamental in the nascent international community. If any one document today approximates expression of the conscience of mankind, it is the Charter of the United Nations Organization. In signing this document, our own country has pledged itself to promote respect for human rights and for the fundamental freedoms without distinction of race. Article Thirteen, defining the powers of the General Assembly, provides that the Assembly shall make studies and recommendations to promote "international co-operation in the . . . educational . . . field(s)" and to assist "in the realization of human rights and fundamental freedoms for all without distinction as to race. . . ." Thus the right to education is recognized as a fundamental human right which is to be enjoyed by all without distinction as to race. A principle early enunciated in the United States of America has become a principle of international co-operation; the failure of the United States to realize its own principle within its own borders can then hardly be a matter for Americans to ignore.

It will be pointed out, however, that in many States of the union separate education for Negroes and for whites is provided by law and that it is the duty of the college or university to obey the law. That, of course, is true. But it does not follow that it is the duty of the college or university to stand silent before educational discrimination. It is notorious that educational facilities offered Negroes are inferior to those provided for whites. The Gaines decision is now eight years old, but it will not be claimed that Negroes find ready for them everywhere state institutions of higher learning and professional training equal to those open to whites. The law of the State may require an institution to segregate Negroes from whites; it does not require it to do nothing about bringing about equality of educational opportunity. Decisions of the Supreme Court have given legal recognition to local practices of segregation, but they have not made racial or religious discrimination lawful. It is the duty of every citizen to work to overcome such discrimination.

Moreover, the law does not require that citizens do not change the law. Let it be remembered that there is no national pronouncement adopting racial segregation as a national measure. Let it be recalled that Congress once adopted a federal civil rights statute and is free to do so again. Let it also be admitted that the decisions of the Supreme Court which make racial segregation legal rest on arguments of questionable validity, that the constitutionality of segregation has never been fully argued in terms of the broad social consequences to the nation of these practices, and finally that, with the growing dependence for survival of all of us on the rapid development of a world community in which the principle of racial and religious equality has already found vigorous expression—then will it not follow that any citizen whose conscience so directs has an obligation to examine the bases and consequences of segregation in education and to call for a reversal of local practice and legislation? And if a world community is really required for survival, is it proper that the interests and traditions of one part of the country, when in conflict with a fundamental national principle, should stand in the way of the paramount interests of the whole?

To these questions someone may reply that whatever may be the conviction and the duty of the individual citizen, it is not the business of a college or university to question race discrimination or racial segregation in education. It will be said that education is the sole business of the college, and education and research the sole businesses of the university, and that neither education nor research includes questioning the accepted decisions of the community as to the relations between the races, let alone trying to change them. It will further be said that single acts that fly in the face of the prevailing attitudes of the community do not change the attitudes of the community and therefore are not to be attempted. The first argument says that the college or university has no responsibility, or no right, to change the prevailing attitudes of its community; the second, that it is helpless to do so. Both arguments involve assumptions as to the relation of single acts to community attitudes. Both involve assumptions as to the role and responsibility of institutions of higher learning in the national life. Conclusions as to these assumptions lead to conclusions on the questions at issue.

I take the second argument first. Is it true that the institution of higher learning is helpless to act to reduce discrimination if the attitudes of the community approve of the discrimination? I say it is not helpless. The assumption may be questioned that law and administration are no more than expressions of the mores. It may rather be asserted that the relation between law and administration on the one hand and the mores on the other is a reciprocal relation. Legislation and administration express the mores, but it is also true that they make the mores. A courageous act by a legislature or by an administrator, whether in a public or a private institution, that is consistent with the national principle of equality as among men changes the mores to make them by some degree more nearly consistent with the principle. The mores are not extra-human pressures, like the weight of the atmosphere or the pull of gravity. They are not something external to the wishes and the sentiments of men. They *are* the wishes and the sentiments of men (so far as imbued by a sense of rightness), and men change their wishes and their sentiments in response to what other men do and in response to what they themselves do. If one man or one institution takes a public position against racial prejudice so as to make effective an equality as among racial groups that was before denied, that act gives encouragement to all others whose attitudes inclined toward equality and justice but who were held from acting in accordance with their inclination by uncertainty or timidity or other causes. As a result, some of these will now act on their convictions; others will then be in their turn encouraged and commit themselves to justice rather than injustice by performing just acts. And, as men tend to believe in the rightness of what they do, having done what is just, attitudes of these men will have changed toward racial and religious equality and away from prejudice and injustice, and so the center of gravity of the attitudes of the whole community will have shifted. On the other hand, an administrative decision to exclude citizens from a college, or from some facility of that college, or to limit the opportunity of students to enrol in the college because of racial or religious origin, results in moving the mores of the community in the opposite direction. An unjust act makes men complacent about their own unjust attitudes. We have seen the operation of this principle in the case of the Japanese-Americans in the recent war years. There is, I think, little doubt that the act of the national government in removing all persons from the Pacific Coast whose ancestry was Japanese, on that sole basis of selection, hardened the attitudes of a part of our people against their fellow citizens of Japanese ancestry. The important act of their own government, in seizing and so stigmatizing as possibly disloyal all persons of a certain ancestry, seemed to give a formal and general approval to the prejudices of many Americans. Perhaps the act was made possible, not only by the war, but also by pre-existing anti-Oriental prejudice in some quarters; but, on the other hand, the act increased and widened the prejudice.

The point has been recently well argued with respect to legislation by Carey McWilliams.[1] He has assembled impressive evidence to show that in California prejudice against the Chinese and later against the Japanese was a creation of the agitation of small groups with special interests. Some special groups with a special interest, perhaps in a vested economic advantage, perhaps merely in professional super-Americanism, would agitate for passage of a law restricting the freedom of the Oriental. Once enacted, its existence helped deepen and generalize the prejudice. Similarly, it was not the mores of the whole community but the special interests of the railway unions that excluded Negroes from jobs as trainmen and foremen—jobs custom had permitted them to fill for fifty years before the exclusion policy was adopted. In part, then, the mores follow legislative and administrative acts. McWilliams also argues that the legalization of segregation between Negro and white in the South has intensified racial prejudice and quotes the prediction of that eminent Kentuckian, Justice Harlan, who dissented in the important *Plessy* case in which the segregation of the races in common carriers was upheld: "What can more certainly arouse race hatred, what more certainly create and perpetuate a feeling of distrust between these races than state enactments, which, in fact, proceed upon the grounds that colored citizens are so inferior and degraded that they cannot be allowed to sit in public coaches occupied by white citizens."

What can more certainly arouse race hatred, what more certainly create a feeling of distrust between racial or religious groups than rules of schools or colleges which proceed upon the grounds that citizens of

[1] "Race Discrimination and the Law," *Science and Society*, Vol. IX, No. 1 (Winter, 1945).

one racial or religious origin are so inferior—or so dangerously competent in free competition—that they cannot be allowed to attend, or to attend in numbers proportionate to their scholastic competence, institutions of higher learning controlled by white gentiles? It seems to me that the reasoning offered by Justice Harlan has great force for those of us who make or administer the rules of admission of colleges and universities. The responsibility for the general consequences to our national community of acts of discrimination in schools and colleges cannot be escaped by a claim that what we do is necessarily a reflection of public attitudes and cannot itself make the public attitudes. The acts of colleges and universities have that same effect upon the mores which have the decisions of national and State governments. Indeed, within the field of education they have much more effect. Colleges and universities are the principal organs of society that function as to education; they are the laboratories and the forums and the assemblies in which those of the community most concerned with education experiment and make decisions, and the people respond to these decisions, changing their own attitudes in accordance. Whether we like it or not, our every act of discrimination or of equal treatment as between ethnic groups is an influence upon the general attitudes of the community. If we act so as to bring about just treatment of all citizens, the people of our community will, on the whole, tend to uphold that justice; if we act unjustly, then men will be helped to excuse their unjust attitudes. We are not helpless to reduce discrimination in the community.

If the policies and practices of the college or university inevitably tend to influence the community toward justice or away from it, the responsibility of the college or the university is clear. It is to lead toward justice. The colleges and universities must discharge a responsibility they cannot escape. The university especially, in this view, is an institution of moral leadership in the community. The university is not a mere agency of the general public opinion. I reject the view that it is the simple duty of a university to bring together teachers and scholars concerned, each separately, with teaching and studying what each wishes to study or is hired to teach. A university is put there by society, not that each of its professors shall pursue his own interests, but that there shall be a better society. The freedom of academic people does not have its final end in the relative freedom from interference enjoyed by the professors. Knowledge is to be sought and to be taught for the common good. The very privileges of academic people and the special opportunities to study and to reflect which they enjoy give the university a role of leadership in the common effort which it would be stupid to ignore and cowardly to refuse. What the college or university does within matters

subject to its control is presumably what, on the basis of the special opportunities of its members to think about the matter, it believes to be
right. If it excludes students whom the law permits it to admit, because
of the racial or religious origin of the students, presumably that is what it
believes to be right. If it puts any limitation on the free association of
citizens to meet under its auspices or on their freedom to discuss public
questions, including the question of segregation itself, then presumably it
regards this action as a right action. But our national society has not as a
whole said that either of these actions is right. If the university does either
of these things it leads away from, not toward, the direction of the common effort.

The society we have said we want to be is a society in which the dignity and worth of the individual is a central good and in which every individual is judged only by qualities which are personal to him and is
denied no opportunity because of his race or religion. The many prevailing exceptions to the realization of such a society are admitted to be exceptions, even when they are justified. In the opinion of most Americans
they should disappear. The university, more than any other institution, is
the transmitter and refiner of our heritage. Freedom and equality are
parts of that heritage, and in the university, itself a community in which
what is thought is inevitably interdependent with what is done, the clarification of the problems of achieving freedom and equality cannot be carried on apart from action within that community that will tend to achieve
freedom and equality. To argue that the university, or the college, must
take no step toward racial and religious equality until the attitudes of the
people outside have caught up with the spirit of the action is to deny the
function of education. For who is to work to change these attitudes in
the direction of the declared common ideal if it be not educators? If an
institution of higher learning, within matters in its power, does not take
every measure to make our society more nearly what it has declared it
wishes to be, it has failed a responsibility. The rest of society has a right
to ask if it has a good excuse for its failure.

To exclude citizens from opportunities to education legally open to
them because of the applicants' race or religion is such a failure. To limit
the number or proportion of students of any race, nationality, or religion
in the total enrollment, is failure also. The consequences of excluding all
Negroes or all Jews or all Catholics are bad, but at least the action is
clear, and raises without confusion the issue of racial or religious discrimination. The application of a racial or religious quota is in two respects
more serious in its consequences than is total exclusion. In most cases the
quota (or the informal procedures whereby the number of Jews, Negroes,
Catholics, or Italians is restricted without the fixing of a definite numeri-

cal limit) is invisible; its operations occur in private offices and in informal discussions, and the practice is not admitted or perhaps even recognized. In other cases the limited restriction of students of some minority group is defended by arguments which have specious plausibility. It is said, in effect, that the limitation of educational opportunity on a racial or national or religious basis is done in order to realize good ends. The ends which it is said to serve are three. In this last part of my remarks I will consider if these ends are indeed good, if they are served by application of a quota, and if they conflict with even greater ends.

The educational quota is sometimes defended on the grounds that to have a good society there must be such a limitation. This justification is commonly heard in professional schools. It is argued that there should be no more Jewish doctors or, maybe, Catholic lawyers in a community than would correspond with the proportion of Jewish or Catholic citizens in the community. This argument assumes that Jewish doctors should take only Jewish patients or that Catholic clients should look only to Catholic lawyers for legal aid. The United States of America was not founded on such a principle. It has never been assumed that this country should be composed of self-sufficient ethnic or religious groups, each providing all the services required of that subcommunity from among its own members. Only in the case of the Negro has such a semi-separate ethnic group developed, and the result there is the plainest of all inconsistencies with our national ideal. (Even in this case, where segregation is most strongly established, there are communities in the North where Negro teachers teach white pupils and communities in the South where Negro doctors treat white patients.) The quota, or *numerus clausus,* is no characteristically American device; it is well known in Europe; and we have lately seen to what horrors it leads. To apply the quota on the ground that the specialists in the nation should have ethnic origins corresponding to the numbers of such groups in the population is to deny the American assumption that men of all religious and all ethnic origins may come to acquire the capacities for carrying on the common life. That men of all religions have this capacity is not often denied today. That men of certain racial origins lack the capacity is asserted often enough, but no anthropologist of any repute reaches that conclusion. The capacities to carry on the activities and responsibilities of the citizen, the doctor, the lawyer, or the educated man are as common and as general among the representatives of one ethnic group as of any other. To insist that specialists shall be limited by ethnic quotas is to deny the truth that human nature and intelligence are present in all ethnic groups.

A second justification for the quota is based on consideration of, not the general community, but the college or the university itself. Restriction of

enrollment on an ethnic basis is defended as necessary to preserve a quality of the college community: the college must remain "Christian" or
"non-urban" or must, still more vaguely and generally, "remain the kind
of college it has always been." This argument is defective in at least two
respects. In the first place it is not to be accepted without question that
every college and every university ought to remain what it has always
been. Institutions must change as society changes; our society has, on the
whole, tended to realize, in a series of slow steps, the inclusive and democratic principles on which it was established. Even educational institutions that are accustomed to the preservation of one particular strain out
of the manifold cultural heritage of America may find, on thinking it over,
that it is to the interests of the learning and education they serve to widen
their ethnic and cultural representation. They may, simply, do a better
job by so doing. In the second place, even assuming the end a good end,
the application of a quota in racial or religious terms, as a means to preserve the face and habits of the institution itself, is inappropriate because
it is not adapted to the end sought and improper because it violates a
more important principle. To limit the number of Jews, because they are
Jews, is to assume that certain qualities of mind, character, or manners
are present in every Jew. This is not far from the principle of collective
responsibility for crime. And besides, it isn't so. If we assume that proper
qualifications for admission to a college or university include more than
evidence of sufficient ability to learn, all additional qualifications, like the
qualifications of educational preparation and intelligence, can and should
be tested for each individual applicant, as an individual. It denies the
principle of responsibility of the individual for his own acts only to seek
to realize those qualifications in a student body by attributing them to a
student because of his ethnic origin.

No, the arguments for the educational quota are shown to be unworthy
of respect by incontrovertible facts. It is never applied consistently, and
it is never applied against the ethnic or religious group of the people who
apply it. The administrator of the dental college who restricts the number
of Jews admitted to ten per cent of the students never insists that another
ten per cent of the students be Negroes. Never do we hear a demand that
"Germans be limited in breweries, Catholics in municipal administration,
Poles in symphony orchestras, Irishmen in fire departments and police
forces, and whites in well-paying jobs of all sorts." These words are those
of Yves Simon,[2] who goes on to declare that he will believe, "with Pascal,
in the sincerity of witnesses who allow themselves to be martyred; . . . in
the sincerity of the partisans of the *numerus clausus* when they demand

2 "Secret Sources of the Success of the Racist Ideology," *The Review of Politics*, VII,
No. 1 (January, 1945), 84.

that their principle be applied with a rigor fatal to their own interests. Until we see white workers demanding a limit on the number of white workers in well-paid positions, we shall refuse to believe that the advocates of the *numerus clausus* are really interested in the common good and in the harmonious distribution of the various parts of the community." The real reasons behind the application of ethnic quotas lie in the motive to preserve, for a privileged group, the competitive advantages its members enjoy, with respect to both jobs and prestige. When the competition gets hard, we hear a demand for the quota. Race or religion provides a criterion, for excluding people of a group to which, one may be sure, the excluder does not belong.

There is yet a third argument offered in justification of limitation of enrollment on a religious or racial basis. With a comment on this third justification I will conclude. This third argument justifies restriction as a measure conducive to the welfare not of the general community and not of the college community but of the minority group itself. It is the argument stressed by President Hopkins in his famous letter written a year ago to Herman Shumlin about the limitation of enrollment of Jews in Dartmouth College. It is argued that the number of Jews admitted should be limited in order to prevent an increase in anti-Semitism. It is argued that it is not safe to admit Jews and non-Jews merely according to the capacities of the applicants as individuals, but that even competent Jews should be excluded after there are already so many Jews in the college that to admit more would result in more anti-Jewish sentiment than existed before. From this point of view the non-Jewish applier of ethnic discrimination does the Jew a service, for he prevents a "concentration" which would be "ill-advised."

This argument is often buttressed with reference to the concentration of the Jews in Germany before the rise of naziism and statements that it was this concentration which laid a foundation for Hitler's work. Therefore, this argument runs, let the non-Jew, by excluding the Jew, protect him from the results of his efforts to find his place in society in equal competition with non-Jews.

What is to be said about this argument? It may be said that the concentration of Jews in Germany was not as it has been represented by Nazis or by those who have uncritically accepted Nazi representations. It may be asked if the greater association of Jews with non-Jews, or of members of any ethnic group with another, always results in an increase of prejudice between them, or if it even usually has this result. But these are not the principal weaknesses in the argument for educational quotas which I am now considering. The trouble with the argument is not so much that it is false in fact but that it is in some part true in fact. It is in considerable part true that increase in success achieved by members of a group that has for long been the object of discrimination brings an increase of prejudice or even hatred against that group. The real weakness of the argument is that it is made by the wrong people. It might be open to the Jew to ask that fewer of his kind be caused to appear in areas where the Jew fears that an increase in his numbers might do him harm. But is it proper that members of the majority group should compel an unjust limitation of the numbers of members of the minority group, against the will of the minority, on the ground that the majority group is thereby protecting the minority from injustices or even violence that would be committed by the majority? Is there not something disingenuous in one, not a Jew, who contends that the Jew is his own worst enemy and that to keep him from injuring himself by pushing his case too far, he, the non-Jew, should limit the enrollment of Jews, when it is remembered that it will be the self-appointed protector's own group that will do the threatened damage to the Jew? There are occasions when we are compelled to take measures of this sort. If a man, innocent or guilty, is pursued by a mob bent on his destruction, the sheriff may rightly put into the safety of the jail the man who is pursued. But it is understood that this is a remedy of desperation. We know that it is the mob that should be jailed, and we jail the man only because we cannot jail the mob. But all such cases of protective custody are confessions of wrong done by the jailer, and all such cases carry the danger that the power exercised by the majority may be used against the minority in the real but hidden interest of the majority. To limit admission to the schools or the professions against the will of a minority is to admit one's own group to be the doer of the wrong which one claims to prevent, and the measure chosen therefore cannot be a measure that goes to the heart of the difficulty. In every such case, whatever be the nationality, the religion or the color of the group thus compelled to accept an injustice in what the dominant group says to be the interest of the group so treated—in every such case we may look into the underlying circumstances with some care. For, by limiting the minority one gives an unjust advantage, in the getting of jobs or the getting of an education, to himself, to his own group, and the honesty as well as the effectiveness of the measures one employs are open to challenge.

DISCUSSION

MR. HOY TAYLOR: I want to direct a question to Dean Redfield. Assuming the mores as they exist in seventeen states, I believe, and the statutes as they exist in that number of states in regard to racial segregation, and assuming, as Dr. Redfield does, that that is not the ideal, I wonder if

Dr. Redfield would like to step out of the academic role just a minute and talk about what probably an administrator of a college ought to do in one of those states in regard to this.

DR. REDFIELD: I arise to disclaim any power to make such a statement. I don't think I am wise enough to tell anyone what he should do in any particular institution, least of all one of the institutions of the South. I have had my troubles in trying to define general principles of action in terms of which a policy could be formulated. It was only my hope that a common agreement upon those principles could be reached, so that the general character of the policy might become to a degree uniform and consistent throughout the national community. Beyond that point, I will not venture to go.

I am willing to add that if we had clear agreement that the general direction of effort was to be that which I have suggested in my remarks, if we had a sincere commitment on the part of those of us who have responsibilities to pursue that effort in a common direction, I am sure that every man who has a particular situation to face will take whatever step it is within his power to take that will help in moving toward that common end.

MR. R. B. THOMPSON: It occurs to me that the reason that we have these elective admission procedures is that in the various racial, religious, and geographic groups, those people do not adequately take care of their own college and university students. Now, what hope may we hold out that those various racial, religious, and geographic groups will more adequately take care of their own students, so that the burden will not rest on the other groups?

DR. REDFIELD: I can only return to the question. The question is whether it is not an assumption of American life that every minority in this country is to take care of its educational needs, or perhaps of all its other needs. To put the matter otherwise, has it not been assumed in this country that there is a common responsibility to develop to the fullest the capacities of citizenship by all citizens? If we carried the principle as suggested to its ultimate end, we would expect members of every sectarian and every national group to provide the educational and perhaps social-service facilities for its own kind. I cannot contemplate such a situation.

FATHER J. J. HIGGINS: I would like to address a question to Dr. Redfield. It is just for clarification, not exactly a question. Dr. Rosenlof mentioned at the beginning that every admissions officer should clarify his own ideas on the functions, the objectives, and the philosophy of his own institution. I am wondering whether Dr. Redfield's paper started with the assumption that all colleges and all universities start with the same philosophy and the same objectives and the same functions. For instance, if a good Baptist college here in Atlanta has as its philosophy and objective to train good Christians in the Baptist religion, I wonder how they would feel about accepting me in that institution, when my philosophy may be quite different from that of that institution.

DR. REDFIELD: That is of course a very good question. It helps me to clarify a confusion I may have created. I do not assume that every institution and every educational institution in this country should perform the same function. I do not assume that there should not be educational institutions which should be directed to the performance of special functions; some institutions in this country will train rabbinical students or students of other kinds of religious specialization. I also assume that institutions of education in this country will continue to exist which will be confined in their clientele to members of particular religious groups. I do, however, hope that all educational institutions in this country will join in a common assumption that it is the responsibility of all of them, along with other institutions in the country, to make our way of life far more democratic and that they will do that, each of them in the ways appropriate to themselves. Where we have an institution that is not devoted to the training of particular people, people for particular kinds of priesthoods or the like, where we have an institution that offers itself as an institution of general education or education for the professions, where, by definition in this country, the religious and racial qualifications are irrelevant, there what I have said applies.

EDUCATION: FOR ARISTOCRACY OR EQUALITY?

The problem of democracy in higher education is a compound problem. It requires that we give everyone a liberal education that carries us all forward toward excellence. Nothing will be said here about that part of the problem which has to do with constructing and administering a liberal education of which every young person can take advantage up to the limit of his capacities. We do not yet know how to do this; but it is a part of the problem which is much discussed and on which much work is being done.

The second and third aspects of the problem are the subject now. Even if we knew how to construct a universal liberal education, we should still have to bring it about that all young people had equivalent opportuni-

Excerpt from an article in *Common Cause,* IV (December, 1950), 248–53.

ties to get it. Exact equivalence of educational opportunity is neither possible nor desirable, for to attempt to bring it about would require an intolerable interference with private life and would result in uniformities of men and minds we would not want. Our second task is, rather, to remove those unjust discriminations with respect to educational opportunity which now waste our human resources and prevent us from according to each human being the respect he merits.

The third aspect of the problem is the problem of raising our people's standards of excellence. If by democracy we mean equality of opportunity, then democracy provides a necessary and favorable condition for the improvement of standards but does not assure that we move toward excellence. It provides the condition by opening the competition to all men and to all ideas. In a democratic system there is a chance for the best to get to the top. But the best will get there only if we judge each competitor by the standards of excellence which each of us has, appropriate to his knowledge and training. The best will not get to the top if we allow the most popular to prevail over the inherently better, or if we do not listen to a good idea because somebody we don't like, a Communist perhaps, takes a favorable view of that idea. The third aspect of the problem is how to create models of excellence and to make them influential. It is the problem of clarifying the hierarchy of values. It is the problem of leadership in truth, morals, and taste—it is the question of how to make the college and the university no mere reflection of what the people are but rather a guide toward what they ought to be. . . .

What are the inequalities of educational opportunity in our country? Three kinds of such inequalities arise respectively from differences of wealth, of class, and of race. One boy's opportunity to get a liberal education may be greater than that of another, because the father of the first is a rich man and the father of the second is poor. Or the son of a plumber may meet such treatment in the schools as to discourage him from the college education toward which the same school helps the banker's son and the professor's son. Or, in the third case, the Negro or the Jew is denied a chance to get education equal to that which is granted the white man and the gentile. All these denials of equal opportunity occur in America. All are contradictions of democracy.

What is notable about educational discrimination based on class is that it is ordinarily not noted. It is almost a discovery of certain anthropologists and sociologists. While school teachers and administrators are sometimes aware of the fact that it occurs in their schools, the subject takes no large place on the programs of public discussion. Americans conceive America, on the whole, as a classless society, and the subtle ways in which children of manual workers are directed into vocational training while the children of professional people are directed toward the college and university go unnoticed and undeclared. But Warner and Havighurst, and Allison Davis, among others, have shown that this quiet little shunting of the youth of America into one of two dividing channels of separated preparation for what ought to be common citizenship does occur. While in Germany we are insisting that the Germans give up or modify their explicit and formal separation of young people into those technically trained and those to be culturally educated, it might contribute a softening humility to our efforts at reform in that country if we looked back to see that we accomplish something of the same result with our own young people by informal means.

Nevertheless, the inequalities that result from our unexpressed class system are not too severe. Nor are they rigid. The children of parents of all walks in life are represented in our colleges and universities. Many young people from the wrong side of the tracks are encouraged to get a liberal education and a professional education. Most of the undemocratic class discrimination that does take place occurs in some of our secondary schools. By the time the young people reach the college or the university the difference in treatment given the plumber's son and the doctor's son is probably insignificant. The fact of this kind of discrimination is avoided and denied. It seems that we are a little pretentious about it. We like to think that of all nations we alone do not make the ancient confusion: the identification of people of property or of inherited status with the intellectual elite. Warner, Havighurst, and Davis show that some of us do fall into this confusion.

The inequalities of educational opportunity that follow from the fact that one young person has more money than another are, on the contrary, well recognized and widespread. There are many young people who do not have enough money to permit them to get all the education of which they are capable. And the differences in the quality of education offered in different states and communities of our nation are notable. They have been often reviewed. The differences between the educational opportunities offered a youth in South Carolina and a youth in New York are no less than the differences between what is offered a Negro in South Carolina and what is available to a white youth in South Carolina. If a young man wants a Harvard education he may get one, but it will certainly improve his chances if he first provides himself with a wealthy father. In the competition for education, the poor are handicapped, the rich advantaged. The inequalities here are far-reaching and important.

But in the case of undemocratic discrimination as to educational opportunity based on differences in wealth, the oligarchic tendency is recognized and something important is done to restrain it. The system of general primary and secondary education at the public expense prevents the wealthy from monopolizing educational opportunity. The system is extended upward to provide at least some of the elements of higher education to most people. The selection of young people to enjoy the blessings of private education according to their fathers' abilities to pay is modified by the provision of scholarships and by aid given to veterans. And the great differences in the economic power of states and communities to provide education are lessened by means of contributions to the poorer communities from the central treasury.

It has been said that the inequalities of educational opportunity arising from differences in wealth are more important than those arising from racial differences. It is perhaps true that differences in wealth affect more people than do those which discriminate against members of ethnic groups. But when we deny the Negro or the Jew the opportunity to get an education that is given some other kind of youth, we fail in democracy in two respects more serious than attend the inequalities of opportunity arising from differences in wealth. For one thing, the American who is a Negro is almost sure to remain one all his life. A poor boy may get the money for an education, but the black boy will not turn white. And if the Jew finds it harder to get into medical school than the gentile, because he is a Jew, this is a handicap which he cannot hope to overcome except by denying or concealing that ethnic origin of which he has the same right to take pride as has one who is a Swedish Lutheran or an Irish Catholic. For the worse failure of democracy in the cases of racial or religious discrimination is the stigma of inferiority which attaches to the discrimination. According to the American social theory, a poor boy is encouraged to make money and so to rise, but the Negro is required to stay down. He may rise only within his own society, which white people insist be separate and define as inferior. And if the Jew is excluded, or his admission to college or professional school is limited, it is not by a judgment in which he has participated, and the decision to exclude him implies a condemnation of his worth. These are all cases of Americans stigmatizing other Americans as inferior or dangerous in competition. And they are all cases of oligarchic privilege. In every case of exclusion, segregation, or application of an ethnic quota, a group that has power denies a boy or girl access to education because the boy or girl is one of a racial or religious group. According to our democratic theory, each boy or girl who applies for a higher education, every applicant for a job as teacher has a right to be considered for acceptance solely by virtue of the qualities he has as that one unique human being. If it were true—which it is not—that Negroes or Chinese were twice as intelligent, on the average, as white people or that they were half as intelligent, on the average, our democratic principle would still require us to judge the intelligence or capacity for education of the next Negro or Chinese or white boy who asked for the education in terms only of his intelligence and capacities and his alone.

We do not meet this requirement. We exclude Americans from opportunities to study or to teach which they are competent to accept, and give the opportunity to someone no more competent, because the one excluded belongs to a particular religious or racial group.

This is not substantially denied. The replies we hear ourselves make when these facts are asserted are pleas of extenuation, or pleas that some other consideration justifies or makes necessary these failures of democracy. The replies take the form, "Yes, but—."

There is the reply made in those seventeen states where segregated education is required by law. This reply runs: "Yes, but we provide separate but equal facilities." Today the consistency of this reply with American democratic principle has been found wanting by the justices of our Supreme Court. Segregated education is discrimination because the facilities almost never turn out to be equal when they are separate, and never does the racial group in power get the worse school building or the draftier school bus. But segregated education would be discrimination even if Negroes and whites were given equally good buildings and equally competent teachers. For education for common citizenship is not equal when Americans with the power to do so insist that other Americans accept the separation of facilities as a sign of their inferiority. And the inferiority is inevitably implied when the separation is imposed on the one group by the other in public education, a common enterprise to make young people ready for a common life. When, in Austin, Texas, I took a small part in one of the cases recently before the Supreme Court,[1] I sat in the witness box and looked at a courtroom in which whites sat on one side and Negroes on the other. The seats on both sides were equally hard. But the seats were not and could not be equal facilities, for it was a white marshal who moved Negroes into the seats set aside for them, and it was white men who had made the rule of separation.

Some of us find ourselves deciding among applicants for a chance to get educated or to teach partly by reference to the proportion of Negroes, Jews, or other kinds of people already in our student body or our faculty.

---

[1] [The case referred to is that of *Sweatt v. Painter,* reported in the *United States Law Week,* 18 L.W. 4405 (1946). Herman Sweatt in 1946 was denied admission to the University of Texas Law School simply because he was a Negro. The University of Texas attempted to meet the equal protection clause by setting up a law school for Negroes only. The Supreme Court, though it did not at this time affirm the inequality *inherent* in segregation to which Redfield's testimony was directed, did reverse the judgments of the lower courts. Mr. Sweatt was then admitted, with a minimum of disturbance, to the established Law School of the University of Texas.—EDITOR.]

I think now not so much of a quota in the sense of a strict *numerus clausus* such as fixed the number of Jews to be admitted to this or that European university, but rather in the more flexible and subtle form in which ethnic discrimination is practiced in colleges and professional schools of our northern states. Then the questions, irrelevant to democracy, which we raise to our own confusion are often asked inexplicitly, even unconsciously: How Jewish is this young man? How many Jews are already practicing medicine in our state? Doesn't the Department of History have several Jews in it already?

To this particular variety of failure of democracy in higher education we hear ourselves make several replies of justification. Elsewhere I have tried to make plain how invalid are these replies. . . .

How are our colleges and universities to do their part in the common effort toward excellence? How are they to help clarify the hierarchy of values? How are they to hold fast to that principle of equality underlying democracy by which men and ideas are equal in opportunity but unequal in virtue?

As we turn the problem around, the answer discloses itself as made up of several related aspects. We may do our part in the effort toward excellence in so far as we find out how to frame and put into effect a liberal education for a society in which all men rule and are ruled. We may do our part in so far as we live democratically within our own academic societies. And we may do our part in so far as we hold to and hold up the standards of excellence which our special opportunity to study and to consider has disclosed to us.

The example of democratic living, the joining with us those students and colleagues who are best fitted, as men each judged for his own qualities, to join in our work, no matter what their race, class, or religion, is only one of many examples and practices of excellence appropriate to colleges and universities. To realize perfect democracy of opportunity is alone not enough to realize a democracy that moves toward excellence. A college which admits anyone to student body and to staff without regard to race or religion can yet be a very bad college. Equality of educational opportunity is a model of excellence for other kinds of equality of opportunity, and it provides a condition favorable to education. But it does not assure it. Furthermore, the very emphasis on equality of educational opportunity exposes us to the common American confusion as to equality: the confusion of equality of opportunity with equality of worth. One thinks of the American disposition to regard as good that which everybody does or that which is recommended by someone of whom everybody has heard. One thinks of the ease with which popularity is confused with excellence, and current approval with lasting value. One thinks of the rapid development in American colleges of that planless education by which any thirty-six units of hours spent or courses taken were supposed to be equal to any other thirty-six units or courses—a degradation of the democratic principle which we now strive to correct in our efforts again to construct a unified and universal program of liberal education. One thinks of the colleges and universities occasionally yielding to the demands of the general public that to study typing be regarded as important for education as to study history, or that embalming be included in what is taught. One thinks of the general feebleness of the leadership in taste and intellectual excellence which our colleges and universities offer people without firm guidance from a cultural tradition, a people exposed to the debasement of good taste through the examples provided by mass media of entertainment.

So it seems that the problem of achieving democracy in higher education is really a problem of achieving aristocracy—not, of course, an aristocracy of hereditary privilege, but an aristocracy of the excellent, in ideas, in men, in values of all sorts. The democracy goes to the opportunities: each youth to be educated, each applicant for a teaching job, to be judged, equally with all others, by what he is, himself, alone. Each idea that offers itself to be judged by what that idea declares and implies, not by its popularity, or the popularity of him who promotes it. The entries are open to all. But the judging is to be done not to make all equal in value; it is done to raise the good on high. Equality of opportunity is not to level; it is to exalt. As we wish it to be, democracy is a way and a spirit by which the aristocracy of the intrinsically good is to be made, and to be continuously tested and remade. And so I think that our task as educators is not done when we open the doors of our schools to all young people and the doors of our minds to all ideas. At this point, in America, we hesitate, listen to our own applause, and feel satisfied. We want the many; that is right. But it is not right to judge good that which the many want. Our responsibility is not discharged when we have established fair rules for winning the race. We have also to judge the victors; we must form our judgments as to the men who are wiser, the ideas that are better, the conduct that is more virtuous, the book, the music, the political action that is superior, and this superior man or idea or act we must put in the earned position, high in the hierarchy of good things. Against the judgment of the general community, if need be, we assert the worth of that which has earned its high place. So does democracy lead us away from oligarchy, and toward an aristocracy, an aristocracy brought out of the people by equality.

THE SOCIAL USES OF SOCIAL SCIENCE

The subject of my remarks today might be expressed as a question for which three different forms of words suggest themselves: What beneficial functions may social science hope to perform in our society? What is the task of social science? Why have a social science?

Institutions are good, not only for what they are, but also by reason of what we strive to make them. I think, then, not only of what social science is, but also of what it might be. I think of social science as one of many institutions that contribute toward the making of the life we want and that could do it better than they do. I would review the functions and the goals of social science as I would review the functions and the goals of medicine, the fine arts, or the press.

The social uses of medicine are to reduce human suffering and to prolong life; this is well understood, and it is clear that to great degree medicine performs these functions. The social uses of the press are to tell people, truthfully and comprehensively, what happens around them, to provide forums for public discussion, and to reflect and clarify the ideals of our society. It is more or less well known that this is what our press is expected to do, whether or not it does it as well as it should. But the social uses of social science are not, I think, so generally recognized. People do not know, at once, why there should be social science or even what social science is. Therefore there is a special duty, in the case of social science, upon you and me who have thought more about that subject, to make clear its nature and its usefulness.

In our own company today it will not be necessary for me to say much about the nature of social science. It is a group of disciplines that provide descriptions of human nature, human activity, and human institutions. These disciplines are scientific, first in that they are concerned with telling us What Is, not What Ought to Be; and second, in that they exercise objectivity, pursue special knowledge, and move toward systematic formulation of this knowledge. So they strive for descriptions that are more illuminating, valid, and comprehensive than are the corresponding descriptions of common sense.

You will readily understand that I have in mind the social sciences that one meets in the catalogues of graduate schools and in the membership of the Social Science Research Council. Just which of them are to be included in any roster of the social sciences does not concern us here; the existing division of labor as among the special social sciences is not

An address delivered April 24, 1947, at the Honors Convocation, University of Colorado, Boulder, Colorado, and reproduced with permission from the *University of Colorado Bulletin*, Vol. XLVII (May 24, 1947).

wholly defensible and may not endure. I am not thinking of ethics, which is the criticism and organization of principles of right conduct. I am not thinking of the social arts and professions, such as law or social-service administration, which are ways of acting on people to get certain results. I am thinking of the application of the scientific spirit toward the description and explanation of man in society. I am asking how its application there serves the common good.

A further limitation of my subject is required. History is not in my mind today. The social uses of history have a special and important character which I shall not discuss. History, being a content of preserved and considered experience, has those social uses which memory and tradition have. From history, as from memory, we expect "a knowledge of our own identities," "orientation in our environment, a knowledge of its usual uniformities, including . . . some knowledge of the characters with whom we must deal, their strengths and weaknesses, and what they are likely to do under given circumstances." Further, ". . . we all hope to draw from past experience help in choosing successfully between the alternatives offered by present events." These social uses of history have been recently summarized by Garrett Mattingly,[1] from whom I quote these phrases. Today I am thinking of that social science which is analytical rather than historical, which seeks to understand a social problem or which describes the general characteristics of some class of social phenomena. How does such social science serve the common good?

The familiar answer is that social science tells us how to do what we want to do. The reply is that the understanding that social science gives can be applied to the purposes of society. The descriptions of social science lead to more effective practical action than would be possible without social science. Social science is, from this point of view, like physics or biology. Just as those sciences reach understanding and explanation of the physical and the organic worlds which lead to practical applications in engineering and in medicine, so social science reaches understanding of man in society which leads to practical applications in social action.

Surely it is true that social science does this. It does tell us how to do what we want to do. It tells us some things that common sense does not tell us or does not tell us nearly so well about how to select people to pilot airplanes or to perform other special tasks, how to predict the consequences of a given tax policy, or how quickly to discover fluctuations in the opinions of over a hundred million people on current issues. The competence of social science to guide useful social action has grown greatly in a few years. The contributions of social science to the national effort at

---

[1] "A Sample Discipline—the Teaching of History," address delivered February 20, 1947, at the Princeton University Bicentennial Conference.

the time of World War I were almost limited to certain studies of prices, to the work of historians in war information, and to developments in mental testing. The contributions of social science in connection with World War II were so numerous and varied that a mere list of them would fill many pages. In the army and in the navy, and in scores of civilian agencies, social scientists were employed for the reason that their efforts as social scientists were recognized as helping to win the war or the peace. This direct service to the community, through the application of their special knowledge, continues in the efforts of social scientists after the war. Of the many fields of research which have already found practical justification I mention three: the understanding of problems of morale and of human relations in industry; the prediction of human behavior in regard to the stability of marriage, criminal recidivism, and certain other kinds of behavior where dependable prediction is useful; and the analysis and control of communication made to mass audiences through print, radio, or screen. Social science had indeed so well established its usefulness in certain fields that specialized technicians are recognized in those fields —professional appliers of social-science knowledge. I mention clinical psychiatrists and city planners.

The question I asked appears at once to be answered. Why have a social science? Have it because it is useful. Have a social science because it gets things done that society wants done. According to this answer social science has the same nature and the same justification that physics and chemistry have. It is supported by society as physics and chemistry are supported by society: because what is learned can be directly applied to the service of mankind. Society less and less can take care of itself; more and more is it true that conscious decisions are required in the management of human affairs, and social science provides guidance in the making of these decisions, just as biological science provides guidance for decisions as to health and hygiene. This is the simple answer that is often made.

I will state my own position at once. I think that this is a true answer but that it is far from a complete answer. I think social science is notably different from physics and chemistry, and that its social uses are not exhausted when one has recognized the practical applications of social science. I think that social science has other important social uses in the testing and in the development of social values.

What has social science to do with the proving and making of values? What is its role in regard not merely to the valuation of a means to reach an end sought, but also to the more ultimate values of society?

The plainest values with which social science is concerned are those necessary to science: objectivity, honesty, accuracy, and humility before the facts. To the preservation and cultivation of these the social sciences are devoted. In the course of carrying out research the social scientists invent and promote means to realize them. In doing so the social scientist shares with the physicist and the biologist the effort to maintain and extend the common morality of the scientific mind. It is, moreover, a morality quite consistent with the morality which the citizen who is not a scientist may embrace. Honesty, accuracy, humility before the facts, and faith in the power of truth to prevail in Milton's free encounter are virtues in their own right. Science is one of the institutions that contribute to the cultivation of these virtues.

In the work of cultivation of these values the position of social science is critical because it is by no means sure that even our free and liberal society will allow the extension of the scientific spirit to the study of social problems. Many people do not understand that it is useful to society to extend it there. While the usefulness of physics and biology is generally acknowledged, the scientific study of many social problems is popularly regarded as either futile or dangerous. This is because many of the subjects studied by the social sciences are protected from rational examination, for the general population, by tradition, sentiment, and inviolable attitude.

In short, the subject matter of social science is not morally indifferent. It is morally significant. The social scientist himself, and his neighbors and fellow citizens, are also concerned with that subject matter. They have convictions, prejudices, sentiments, and judgments about the tariff, party politics, relation between the sexes, and race relations. All of these things the social scientist studies, and what he has to say about them in the course of his trying to improve our understanding of them encounters these convictions, prejudices, sentiments, and judgments. They are all "tender" subjects. People feel a sense of distress if their convictions or assumptions on these matters are challenged or controverted. Often they are distressed at the mere looking at these subjects objectively. Some social scientists study such subjects as the relations between husband and wife or the attitudes people have toward racial or religious minorities or the profit motive in economic activity. It makes some people uncomfortable to hear that these subjects are being studied with critical impersonality. The social scientist is then resented or distrusted. If, furthermore, his descriptions or conclusions appear inconsistent with the more sacred values of the community, a cry may go up that the social scientist be restrained or that his publication be suppressed or that he lose his job.

Therefore social science is the test case of the vitality of those ideals I have mentioned which are common to all science and which play so large a part in the freedom of the modern mind. The scientists as a whole understand this. In discussions which are now going on as to the drafting of a bill for a national science foundation, it appears that almost all the scientists, natural scientists as well as social scientists, think that if government money is to be provided for the support of science, social science should be included. On the other hand, with similar unanimity the scientists understand that Congressmen are much less likely to provide such support for social science than for natural science. The scientists see that science is one way of looking at the world around us, a way applicable to men and society as it is applicable to molecules and cells. They feel this common morality of the scientific mind and respect the usefulness of social science in not only making useful social inventions but also in developing this morality throughout society. But they also know that people who are not scientists do not see it that way and imagine social science to be political propaganda or doctrine, or speculative futility. These scientists perhaps realize what I believe to be true: that that freedom of the mind to inquire, propose, test, and create which is so central and precious a part of the more ultimate values of our manner of life may, in a military or reactionary trend of events, be first tested and won or lost in our country in the freedom of social science.

In effect, social science is a new instrument, not only for the getting of certain specific things done in the management of society, but for the clarification and development of our more ultimate values. The social uses of social science are not exhausted when we have said that social science can improve the efficiency of industrial production or test the aptitudes of young people for one kind of occupation rather than another. Social science is one of the ways to form our convictions as to the good life. This it does not as preaching does it, by telling us what the good is and what our duty is. It does not do it as ethics does it, by examining central questions as to the nature of conduct and by criticizing and formulating systematic rules of conduct. It does it by remaining science. It does it by making clear to us where our choices lead us and what means must be employed to reach what ends. It does it by extending our understanding of where our ideals are in conflict with our practices and where our ideals are in conflict with each other. And it does this through those intensive studies of particular societies and particular men which are not ordinarily carried on in ethics and which are outside the powers and the responsibilities of the preacher.

An example may make this clear. Recently a study of the Negro in the United States was made by Gunnar Myrdal, a Swedish social scientist. The resulting work is not a sermon, nor is it an analysis of the principles of conduct. It is a description of the Negro in American business, government, and social life. It is also a description of the white man in his positions toward the Negro in American life. Myrdal's book does not tell us didactically what we ought to do. The propositions that make up the books are Is-propositions not Ought-propositions. Nevertheless the book can hardly be read carefully by anyone without some effect upon the reader's system of values, his conceptions of duty, justice, and the good life. The effect is enhanced, in this particular case of social-science research, because the author and his collaborators took for their problem the relation of the Negro's place in our society to the ideals of freedom, liberty, and democracy which are genuinely held in our nation. They were interested in finding out what effect, on the white man especially, results from the presence of practices and institutions inconsistent with these ideals. The book does not argue for any norm of conduct. It just tells about norms in relation to customs and institutions. But any American reader at all thoughtful finds himself understanding better than he did the choices that are open to him: less democracy, liberty, and equality, and race relations as they are; or more democracy, liberty, and equality, and a change in race relations. Or, as a third possibility, he learns something of the effects on his state of mind if the inconsistency persists. And this increased understanding is a leaven in those workings of the spirit which lead to the remaking of our system of ideals.

I think it is self-delusion for a social scientist to say that what he does has no concern with social values. I think that people are right when they express their feelings that social science does something to the values they hold with regard to such particular institutions as restrictive covenants or the tariff. For one thing social science tests those special values, by showing what they cost. It hears the people say, We want freedom. Social science listens, studies our society, and replies, Very well, if you want freedom, this is what you will pay in one kind of freedom for enjoying so much of another. To every partisan the social scientist appears an enemy. The social scientist addresses himself to the question, How much security from idleness and want is compatible with developed capitalism? and equally to the question, How much political and civil freedom is compatible with socialism? To partisans on both sides he appears unsympathetic and dangerous.

For social science, along with other science, philosophy, and the general spirit of intellectual liberty, is asserting the more general and comprehensive values of our society against the more limited and special interests and values. It hears society say, We believe in the right of the human mind to examine freely, to criticize openly, to reach conclusions from tested evidence. Very well, replies social science, if this is your desire then you must endure the pain of the examination and the testing of the particular customs and institutions which you hold dear. Social science says to all of us: Except where your special interests are involved, you recognize that mankind have passed the period in which they took their ethical convictions from their grandfathers without doubt and reflection. Now we have to think, investigate, and consider about both the means and the ends of life. Social science is that science, which in other fields you so readily admire, directed to human nature and the ways of living of man in society. By your own more general convictions you have authorized and validated its development.

It follows that the successful functioning of social science is peculiarly dependent upon education. The realization of the social uses of social science depends closely upon the dissemination of the findings of social science and of the understanding of the very nature of social science among all the people. So a responsibility falls upon you and me, who have thought something of the matter, to make social science known to all. It is for us to make it clear to our fellow citizens what social science is, and why its development is so needed today.

Social science does not need to be sold to the people. It needs only to be explained. There never was a time when social science was more needed than it is today. The extreme peril in which we live arises from the small political and social wisdom we have in the face of our immensely dangerous material strength. We should have more control over the physical world, yes, surely; but it is far more necessary that we learn to control the relations among men. We know now that we can destroy one another and the fruits of civilization, and we are far from sure that we can prevent ourselves from doing so. If social science could effect an improvement of our chances of preventing it of no more than 1 per cent, a great expenditure in social science would be justified.

In explaining social science it needs to be said that social science is not only a box of tools. It is also a light. The social scientist is not only a sort of plumber to the circulatory and other ills of society; he is also, at his best, a source of understanding and enrichment. It should be pointed out that the test of good social science is not only: Will it work? There is another test: Does it make sense? For social science also justifies itself to the extent to which it makes life comprehensible and significant. That social science, also, has worth which, though it solves no problem of unemployment or of selection of competent administrators, shows men the order and the pattern of their own lives. Good social science provides categories in terms of which we come to understand ourselves. Our buying and selling, our praying, our hopes, prejudices, and fears, as well as the institutions which embody all these, turn out—under the light of sound social science—to have form, perspective, rule. Shown the general, we are liberated from the tyranny of the particular. I am not merely I; I am an instance of a natural law.

To say this is not to say that social science should be speculative or philosophical. The significant generalization may first appear in a flash of insight. Or illuminating generalizations may be built up out of many detailed observations. Out of the innumerable painstaking studies of particular facts, in biology, anthropology, and sociology, emerges now a broad conception of society, inclusive of ants, apes, and men, and the notion that the mechanisms of evolution operate through not merely individuals but the social groups themselves. This but illustrates the fact that comprehensive general understanding of society is often the work of many men over much time.

So we will praise social science both as a practical servant of mankind, useful as biology and physics are made useful, and also as a handmaiden of the spirit. It has on the other side some of the social uses of the humanities. It makes a knowledge which helps to define the world of human relations in which we live, which makes clear to ourselves our place in a social cosmos. Social science is not essentially a series of inventions to be applied. The inventions come, and they are useful. But primarily social science is a chain of understandings to be communicated.

And we will make it clear that in this work of increasing understanding, there is a moral commitment and a moral purpose. Social science is objective in that it cultivates deliberate consideration of alternative explanations, demands proof, and submits to the conviction which facts compel. But it is not indifferent. It will not tolerate cynicism. It expects responsibility from its followers, responsibility to use special knowledge for the common good and to act on convictions reached by reason and through special knowledge. It demands that the values that are implied in the conduct of its work be declared. It commits itself to the use of man's rational nature and the methods of modern empirical investigation to the service of society. The service is one not only to the strength of the social body. It is also a contribution to its soul. Social science is a proving ground of values. It is a means to wisdom. Let us, who are social scientists, so conduct our work as to make it yield more of the wisdom the world so sorely needs. Let all of us, who know something of social science, explain that this is its purpose, its highest ideal.

WORLD GOVERNMENT AS SEEN BY A SOCIAL SCIENTIST

I have accepted the responsibility of speaking on this subject with appreciation of the compliment but with certain misgivings. To these

A lecture delivered March 5, 1951, at Stanford University and March 6, 1951, at the University of California at Berkeley and reproduced from *Federalist Opinion*, I (1951), 9–20.

I should like at once to confess. There are two of them. Both of them cast doubt on the possibility, which the title of the lecture may admit, that I—or, indeed, that anyone—can speak about federal world government as seen, in a strict sense, by one who speaks as a social scientist and not at all as a private citizen.

The first misgiving is the doubt that anyone who would claim so to speak as a perfectly disinterested scientist can truthfully make the claim. It seems to me that the social scientist is at the same time a man who commonly cares about the outcome of what he studies. The sociologist who studies old age knows that he too will grow old, and the economist who studies business cycles knows he may get caught in the crash. I talk about world government knowing that war or peace, tyranny or freedom, are of intense and central interest to me, and I cannot be sure that what my tongue will utter will represent only the scientific aspect of my nature.

Like many another at the time when I was young, I was told by my teachers that the business of the social scientist, like that of other scientists, is to describe, not to evaluate. I was persuaded to believe in the moral antisepsis of science. I wonder if then I really did believe in it. I wonder if, as a young anthropologist, I imagined myself a student of the early Iroquois, studying Iroquois methods of torturing prisoners. Did I conceive of the cool purity of my notebook, myself dispassionately reporting?

I think the conception of the moral antisepsis of science has for all of us suffered somewhat in recent experience. For one thing, we have met civilized Iroquois. Speaking for myself, I say that the evil and the good in human affairs do not seem to separate themselves off from the scientific data as my teachers told me they would. I do not find, at any rate, that I am a scientist in my office, and then, when I put on my hat and coat and leave the office, at once I assume the human sympathies, the passionate concern with the well or the ill of my own and my neighbor's affairs. These things are mixed up together during all the hours of my day.

No, the title which I have accepted does not ask of me such moral sterilization. It asks only that I make the effort becoming a scientist to look at world government with a degree of detachment and in relation to such special knowledge as I can bring to it. I am still free to do what I cannot help doing: present the subject as it is guided by my special experience, but warmed and colored by a deep personal concern with it. When the topic offered me is so conceived, my first misgiving abates.

The second misgiving may be stated in the form of a question. Can a social scientist be said to see anything which does not exist? For world government certainly does not exist. We may have The English Parliamentary System as Seen by a Social Scientist, or The International Postal Union as Seen by a Social Scientist. The social scientist may study Indian tribes, the Australian ballot, the street-corner gang, and even the United Nations. For all these things exist. But world government is only something which somebody imagines might exist. And what business has a social scientist to stand upon a platform and profess to discern something which is a reality only of the imagination?

At once I recall that utopias do not exist, by definition, and that social scientists of respectability have studied utopias. I have seen an interesting book on utopias by a professor of social science. Perhaps world government is a utopia, a fanciful projection of a possible state of affairs? Does world government belong, then, with *Erewhon* and *The Republic* of Plato?

But then I remember that world government has been put forward, not by some single philosopher or ironic critic of the social world in which the critic happens to find himself, but by a great many people who have proposed to make it an actuality, something at once to be constructed and put in operation. The idea of world government cannot be connected with one Plato or one Samuel Butler. It is not only an idea; it is a plan, and a plan on which thousands of people have been working for a long time. We may find something about it in an article by Immanuel Kant and a great deal more about it in the writings of hundreds of Americans and Europeans who are living today. The papers that were contributed to the thought developed by one small group of less than a dozen men, who worked on the problem on occasions when I myself participated, fill five large albums on my shelves. The pages of half a dozen periodicals are today devoted to world government. There are national organizations to promote world government and also international organizations and assemblies. The people who contribute to this effort are not writing utopias. They are deadly serious about world government; they think it is something that should happen and that can happen. These people are of all sorts, and for what it may be worth let me say that according to my impression they are as realistic as are most people and more than ordinarily concerned with achievement in practical action. I do not see them as impractical visionaries. Among those who have asserted that we must have world government are such impractical visionaries as Mr. Winston Churchill and Mr. Justice Douglas of the United States Supreme Court.

So world government is not a utopia, because it is not conceived as an imaginary model in terms of which to develop social criticism or philosophical ideas of justice or of education. It is a plan, "a proposal to history," as Norman Cousins called it.

Moreover, I recall how close we came to having, actually in operation, some kind of elementary world government. The Baruch plan for control of atomic weapons included provision for an international authority to inspect installations in all countries and with power to punish individual violators of the proposed new world-wide law. When a political power representing the world's people is empowered to act to enforce world law, not on or through national states, but directly upon individuals of whatever national state, then there is already world government. This much world government was at one time a central objective of American policy, and I suppose that if we thought we could get this much now it would at once become national policy again.

So it will not do to regard world government as a utopia, and no more. It looks rather like a social invention in process. It looks like the beginning of an attempt to construct a social device that might meet problems of which many people are intensely conscious. Would it not have been possible and proper for a social scientist to say something about the juvenile court at the time that Judge Lindsay and other people were imagining the juvenile court? It is the business of the social scientist to describe, we say, and we say he may describe even when he cannot predict. He may describe world government in becoming even when he cannot predict whether or not it will ever come to be. He may describe not only what men do but also what they set out to do, for to set out to do something is also to do something.

I am beginning to persuade myself that there is something here which a social scientist may examine. It has some kind of reality. Indeed, it has many kinds. It is in part a projection of some part of human wishes. So considered, the programs for world government are documents about the hopes and fears of these times. Second, world government is an enactive institution, an institution in the process of becoming, whether or not it comes into actuality. And third, world government is a social movement. People organize to bring it about. These people are often quite passionate about it. They see doom in the sky. They come great distances; they give up money, time, and all sorts of practical advantages in an effort to bring it about. Though they are but a handful of the world's people, they do not despair. They remember other handfuls that have shaken the world, and they are convinced that the solution for which *they* strive will steady a shaking world.

In this third aspect we see world government as something more than an intellectual interest in solving a practical problem. It is more than architecture for a new institution. It appears to me as an expression of something more far-reaching, something stronger to stir the imaginations and the efforts of men, than are movements to bring about some local reform or some limited institution. This is a movement to make over the world. I almost say that this movement belongs with the great revolutionary movements.

And yet I do not quite say this, or if I say it I make at once an important qualification. World government, as a movement, is not utterly revolutionary. It does not, like radical pacifism or the tremendous ethic preached by the Nazarene, ask that human nature be fundamentally changed. It assumes that men will act next year about as they act this year. It supposes that evil will be everywhere, after world government as before. The movement recognizes that power is often used for evil. The advocates of world government propose to control this evil by means of institutions. They are not trying to make men over, one by one. The revolution they propose is a kind of institutional evolution. They would extend to all peoples the effectiveness of such political instruments as have been found effective in our own country. So they sit down and compose universal bills of rights, conceive of an international court of compulsory jurisdiction, and plan the delegation of certain powers from national states to an international federal state.

Now to my observation the striking fact about this movement is that it goes forward on the level of practical action and in the hands of practically minded men and women in the face of powerful arguments against it. It does not fly off into a vague hope for the millennium, nor does it become a sectarian movement to preserve an enlightened minority facing catastrophe, nor does it change itself into an effort at spiritual salvation when the Day of Judgment is at hand. It remains a practical effort of sober people in all walks of life to use human experience and reason to invent an institutional solution to the most pressing and terrible problems. The activities of these people are political. They try to persuade congressmen to pass resolutions; they act as a lobby in Washington; they support the United Nations Organization and strive to bring about its development into a federal government of the world.

And this remains the nature of the movement, although the arguments against it have immense power and although these arguments are brought forward by other sober and practical men and women no less intelligent and devoted to the rescue of civilization than are those who are striving for world government.

The arguments against world government are only two in number. There is, first, the argument that world government is impossible, and there is, second, the argument that it is undesirable.

One critic disposes of the whole movement for world government by merely pointing out the intense hold which nationalism has upon almost all the world's people. The fact is undeniable. Nations multiply in number, and nationalism intensifies. How could it be supposed that the peoples of the world, or any considerable part of them, would relinquish any substantial part of their national loyalty or any substantial part of national sovereignty to an entity yet to be created? Other critics dispose of the whole movement for world government by pointing out that the military and economic power upon which a world government, admittedly, would have to rest, is approximately divided between a Russian Communist half-world and that other world called "the West" and that in the face of this equally undeniable fact the concept of One World and of world government is a romantic dream. To the immensely powerful argument from this side the advocates of world government listen but are not convinced. Why are they not convinced?

On the other hand, the advocates of world government meet the argument that world government would be universal tyranny. When Dr. Bevan writes to Professor Toynbee that the danger before the Western world is not anarchy but despotism, universal world totalitarian state, the advocates of world government whom I know admit the risk but nevertheless go forward with their plan. They do not deny that great power in government can become tyranny. Yet they do not cease their effort in the face of this danger. Why do they continue nevertheless?

The immediate answer to these questions is of course expressed in the arguments put forward in reply by those who work for world government. To those who say that the nations will not give up their claim on political loyalty nor their uncompromising sovereignty, they reply first that we do not know that they will not until the advantages of the prevention of war and the promise of solution of great problems of human welfare through world government have been offered to the world's peoples. Second, they point out that several nations and many political leaders have already declared their readiness to give up so much of national independence as is necessary for world government. To those who tell them that world government might be universal tyranny, they reply, first, that the danger that this may occur arises out of the possibility of a totalitarian state through war and conquest and arises acutely if the world's peoples do not first succeed in instituting a world government that protects human liberty by constitutional means. As a second reply they set to work to devise the universal bill of rights, the constitutional provisions for division of powers and for control of an elected government by the people of the world, which might afford that protection. And, third, they point to the dangers to human liberty and to civilization itself from the continuing anarchy of warring national states.

The advocates of world government whom I know recognize the risk of tyranny in world government. But they grasp this nettle and come forth with a proposed political invention, a device of human reason, resting upon experience with constitutions, and conceived as a rational choice among courses of which all are perilous.

It seems to me that these are good answers, in the sense that they provide some basis for going forward with the effort toward world government in the face of powerful argument that world government is either impossible, undesirable, or both. Yet I think that these are only the apparent reasons why the movement for world government goes on. There seems to me a more underlying explanation for the vitality of the movement. I am disposed to look for the explanation in some general circumstance of man's nature or history. What is it that gives strength to this effort against such great and obvious obstacles? Why do reasonable men persist in striving to create something which relatively few people are willing to say is attainable and which many people say, with good reason, is highly dangerous?

We might distinguish between the immediate and the more remote settings in which the effort for federal world government finds its vitality. The immediate setting is, of course, the sudden terribleness of war. This immediate setting, this doom against the sky, has given new power to the conception of a rule of law for all peoples. Under a most urgent necessity there is a stronger will to invent. Though man now lives in a desperate danger of his own making, it is also true that, through the experience of civilization, he lives in the conviction, or half-conviction, that he can to a degree shape his own world, make his institutions, establish his own salvation.

The more remote setting is to be seen, I suggest, in certain great trends of history of which people are only partly conscious. It seems to me that the less apparent explanations for the vitality of the movement for world government in the face of fact and argument that stand in its way are to be found in certain changes that began long ago, that will probably go on for a long time in the future, and that maintain, through ups and downs, the same general direction of change. I seek the explanations in long-run trends of human affairs.

With all diffidence, I will try to name two such long-run trends that seem to me to give strength to the effort for world government. They are probably not two really separate trends, but rather aspects of the same long historical tendency. They are two ways of stating the same trend, or, perhaps better, the second is the great underlying change in human ethic, while the first is the consciousness that people begin to have that their human world is, in certain ways, different from what it was.

The first aspect is named by a familiar phrase. It is the developing world community. The second, the underlying ethic, I will call the developing idea of universal common responsibility.

The idea of universal common responsibility is, of the two, the conception which I have the greater trouble in trying to define, although it is the aspect of the matter to which I should like to give the greater attention here. What I have to say about the world community is not much.

The world community is a matter of the relationships among men. To put the question whether there is a world community is to ask how people in various parts of the world feel about people in other parts. We then ask if the people of the world share common understandings. We ask if they feel themselves to inhabit the same world of ideas. We wonder if they feel a common danger, if they are ready to put aside their conflicts with one another to realize a larger sense of world-wide common cause.

You will at once say, to those who advocate world government, that there is not yet a world community. And you will be right. There is as yet no sense of universal, all-inclusive community in which all the world's peoples might participate. In the United Nations, which is the principal current expression of such world community as there is or might be, we are now accustomed not to the voice of common human conscience, but to the struggles of power blocs with one another.

Yet on the other hand, there is more of a world community than there was before. The world society (*Gesellschaft*) is almost complete; the economic interdependence of peoples is a fact pressed upon us every day by a dozen news stories in every newspaper. And the world community (*Gemeinschaft*), while unrealized, is nevertheless nearer reality than ever it was before. Millions of people at least now know that the affairs of other remote millions of people affect their own lives. And it is almost respectable to admit the sense of participation in a world community. The public recognition of the idea attempted by the movement once led by Gerry Davis was a fragile effort, ineptly pursued, yet it represented an important, consequential event. Years before Gerry Davis, a Wall Street lawyer, who might have been our President, expressed the idea also. The title of his book, *One World*, may not describe the present-day world, but it does correctly name a trend of history.

What are the relations between world community and federal world government? Those who work to bring about world government can have only one answer: there is already enough world community to provide a basis for a universal rule of law, and the rest will come later. On the other hand, many men who think that world government is desirable conclude that it is impossible because there is as yet not enough world community to permit a world government to come into being and thereafter to persist effectively. Those who take this view of the matter feel strongly, perhaps because they cannot accept the possibility of a viable world government, the obligation to do something toward bringing about world community. And they find much to do. UNESCO exists explicitly to advance the effort to bring world community into being. If wars begin in the minds of men, then, without now attempting to make universal law to prevent war and control the occasions for war, let us—say those who work in this area of the field—change the minds of men. So the effort goes forward to provide all people with at least so much education as would enable them to know something about one another. Schoolbooks are purified of such untruth as might incline youthful minds toward war. The places in local communities where arise those tensions that keep men apart are studied and reported on. And deliberate effort is made to teach, in school and out, a sympathetic and friendly attitude toward peoples of different traditions and customs.

How long is this road to world community? Who can say? The road is interrupted by an immense chasm, that which we see between the Russian states and the West. It is impeded, too, by the fact that there is a third world, a group of peoples who feel themselves to be identified with neither Russia nor the West, and especially by the fact that the West, at least, does not really understand that this third world does not see the chasm at all or at most sees it as no more than a ravine which can be crossed.

For the development of the world community is confused by the fact that there is not only misunderstanding about our differences but also misunderstanding about our likenesses. The nascent world community exists in part in resemblances between the two great powers themselves, Russia and the United States, although the conflict between the two conceals such resemblances as there are. To some Asiatics, and probably to some Frenchmen, there is a developing world community—possibly one they do not like—which includes Russia and the United States, a community based upon confidence in increased production as a means to peace and welfare, upon the extension of economic security to the common man, and upon emphasis, generally, on material wealth. To some Asiatics, at least, the very great difference between Russia and the West with regard to the importance of the dignity and freedom of the human individual does not seem so great a difference, because outside of the West there has been less experience with the dignity and freedom of the human individual. This is one view of the world community. On the other hand, such contrasting Westerners as Herbert Finer and James Burnham have expressed the conclusion that the differences between Russia and the West are utterly irreconcilable. So the developing world community is not so simple a thing as all people everywhere coming to have the same ideas. It is a crossing and countercrossing of incomplete views of human likenesses and differences, as seen from a multitude of experiences and vantage points.

With regard to the possibility of a world government in an incomplete world community, we see these two opinions in opposition: the view that before it is possible to get world government, it is necessary to bring about a world community; and the view that in spite of the absence of a world community, a world government may be and should be established. If the social scientist is to say anything as to the validity or invalidity of these two opinions, it is probably to point out that institutions and attitude, structure and concept, are best regarded as the creatures of each other. I speak now of the general nature of causal relationship between institution and the way people feel, as social science tends to see that relationship today. The social scientists I know do not find adequate the viewpoint of this relationship that was so powerfully expressed by William Graham Sumner two generations ago. To Sumner, institutions were only the precipitation of unreflective attitudes, of the mores, as the mores were ethically justified outgrowths of the folkways. To him, reform was an illusion or an impossibility, and men did not change attitudes by acting toward their ends. They just found themselves doing what the mores told them to do. This viewpoint is of doubtful worth as an adequate account of the relationship of attitudes and institutions in primitive or precivilized society, and is surely inadequate as an account of that relationship today. Rather we see that men, by acting formally through social invention, legislation and judicial decision, so affect in turn the attitudes upon which were based the prior formal actions. So, just to mention a single instance, we do not find ourselves describing the relationship between race prejudice and law as one in which the law comes about only when the attitudes of the community are solidly behind the law. Nor do we seem to see that the passage of the law or the decision of the Supreme Court is effect only, a mere precipitate of the folkways or of public opinion. Rather we see that many a decision is reached in court or legislature when the state of the attitudes of the community is in an uncertain balance of indecision beween those attitudes which would support the law and those which would oppose it. And, still more importantly, do we begin to realize that once the law is passed or the decision is reached, so then may and often do the attitudes of the community relating thereto gain something of firmness and coherence in the direction which the law or decision goes. When men act collectively, they not only express their attitudes; they also shape them.

This is the line of thought which appears helpful in seeking to interpret the difference between those who say that world community must come first and those who say that world government may come although the world community is yet far from complete. Both are right, or both are partly right. The effort toward one world is a single effort, whether one seeks to change the minds of men or to build the institutions of the world community. Building the institutions, planning the government, taking part in the first beginnings of government—these are acts that shape the attitudes which in turn will provide a foundation of collective will for further acts.

Now I come to what I have called the underlying ethic. I turn to the second of the long-run conditions of mankind which seems to me to explain the strength which the movement for world government continues to have in the face of arguments and of political conditions which stand in its way.

I find this underlying ethic in what A. N. Whitehead has written about ideas in history. In his book, *Adventures of Ideas,* he has shown us how, at least since the ancient Greeks in our Western world, ideas move events. To him, and to many another, it is not possible to represent history solely as the impact of material changes on men's minds and institutions. It is not denied that changes in technology bring about changes in the way men live and also in how they feel about one another. But Whitehead, among others, shows that whatever may have been the case before the rise of civilization, after that at least, and most plainly in the case of ancient Greece, something else happens in history. An idea, a conception that there is a necessary or desirable condition of humanity, comes into existence, is developed, grows into power, and shapes the acts of men. An idea in history is a power in history. It is something that exerts its influence in spite of everything that is contrary to it in current institutions, in spite of all self-interest, fear, or other human passion. Such an idea in history is the creation, the largely unwitting creation, of men. But in turn it is the creator of men. It makes them do things in spite of themselves.

The great creative idea in history about which Whitehead writes is the idea of the dignity and worth of the human individual. "The growth of the idea of the essential rights of human beings, arising from their sheer humanity, affords a striking example of the history of ideas." This idea is far stronger now than it was three thousand years ago, two thousand, one thousand. In spite of the terror of our times, in spite of the return of torture and forced labor, the idea itself is clearer, more generally announced, and even obeyed than it was in earlier times. In Whitehead's book one sees how that idea found one simple expression in the realization of personal physical freedom. In ancient times it was apparent that a civilized community had to have a large slave population. "Slavery was the presupposition of political theorists then; freedom is the presupposition of political theorists now." Yet men who had slaves grasped the idea which seems to us now so inevitable, the idea of freedom, and went forward to develop the idea and give it strength. "Between them, the Hebrews and the Greeks provided a program for discontent." In the long run the program was successful. The idea of the worth of the human soul, of the right to be free, became irresistible. As conditions made it possible for civilized men to live without slavery, slavery was abolished. But the abolition did not come simply because the conditions permitted it. It came because the idea, the creative, long-run, convincing idea, had told men that it must.

As Whitehead says, such creative ideas start "as speculative suggestions in the minds of a small, gifted group." A literature arises "which explains how inspiring is the general idea, and how slight need be its effect in disturbing a comfortable society." At this stage the effect on institutions of the times is slight. "On the whole the social system has been inoculated against the full injection of the new principle. It takes its place among the interesting notions which have a restricted application."

But the idea finds embodiment in special programs of reform. Slavery should be abolished. Human rights should be recognized everywhere. Men should sit down together and shape a government to serve them all. "At any moment the smouldering unhappiness of mankind may seize on some such program and initiate a period of rapid change guided by the light of its doctrines." So the conception of the dignity of human nature produced better government, and was "nerving men, like Marcus Aurelius to rise to the height of their appointed task." And Whitehead likens such ethical ideas as "at once gadflies irritating, and beacons luring, the victims among whom they dwell." He contrasts them with "senseless forces, floods, barbarians, and mechanical devices": "The great transitions are due to a coincidence of forces derived from both sides of the world, its physical and its spiritual natures. Mere physical nature lets loose a flood, but it requires intelligence to provide a system of irrigation."

So it has been with the idea of universal human rights and human dignity. This idea has been nerving men to act, to act against the institutions and special interests of their time. It has produced the revolutions in which we all most fully rejoice, for in the long run all men are benefited by freedom, the freers as well as the freed. This idea still works among us, still insists that it be realized, finds new expressions in the productions of committees of the United Nations and even in the language of freedom in which, whatever the fact, both great opposing national powers clothe their demands and their aspirations. The idea of universal human dignity and freedom will continue to work among us, when, if it ever happens, all of us here are in slavery.

What I want most to emphasize here is my conviction that it is the all-inclusive ideas in history that have the longest life, the greatest power. The idea that all men are worthy of respect began in a small community in which most men were slaves or half-citizens. Yet the idea grew until there were no slaves, and it may be expected to grow until there are no more half-citizens. We all know how the sense of loyalty to a community has grown from the primitive band or tribe to the city-state, to the limited imperium, to the national state. I do not see anything that social science can tell us that requires us to believe that it must stop with the national state. On the contrary, such evidence as we have suggests that common humanity is the society to which loyalties move, through the years of human events. So, too, it was when religious ideas came to include all mankind that they acquired enduring power. When the Hebrews extended their idea of God from something local to something universal, an idea had appeared which could only move forward. All the great world religions have comprehended all mankind within their view; that is why they are great.

The hidden strength of the movement for world government seems to me to rest on its acceptance of these all-inclusive, powerful, and enduring ideas in history. The proponents of world government make an assumption which is unrealized in fact: that all men are brothers. Yet it is an assumption which is true in the long-run trends of history. Therefore the idea of world government will go forward in spite of the obstinacy of contemporary political fact.

Earlier in my remarks I said that I thought that the strength of the movement for world government lay in part in the underlying ethic of universal common responsibility. I have not yet said what I mean by this. The great idea in history of which Whitehead writes is the idea of universal human rights. In this idea the emphasis is upon freedom. It is the growing sense that dignity and opportunity to develop one's nature to good ends are owed to every man.

This idea, still working among us, is, I think, part of the underlying ethic of the world-government movement. It is apparent in so far as the advocates of world government see that you cannot have world government with imperialism or world government with racial discrimination. When they grasp the necessity to include all mankind in their schemes of world government, their strength rests upon this developing idea in history.

But, going a little beyond Whitehead, I think that we see that there is another idea now working in history. Or perhaps it is a new emphasis, a new accent, upon the old idea. This is the idea of universal human responsibility. The idea is not yet expressed in any great series of documents and ethical statements, as is the idea of universal human freedom and dignity. I think that the idea is nevertheless apparent. It begins to be seen that all men are brothers not merely in rights but in common responsibilities. It is not enough to accord freedom to move about, to find a living, to all men. If we are to continue to live together on this planet, then we must all share responsibility to making the common arrangements that will enable us to live together. Willkie saw this when he came back from his trip around the world and said in substance that all of us, everywhere, must plan the peace for all of us everywhere. Some aspects of this new sense of world-wide responsibility appear when Walter Reuther or James Warburg or Stringfellow Barr advocates a world-wide economic-development program, to be administered, not by the United States, but by the United Nations or some other agency of common human responsibility. It is seen that each of us is, indeed, his brother's keeper.

In the case of those who in the United States see this necessary idea of universal common human responsibility, there is encountered the paradoxical difficulty: the very fact that the people of the United States have most of the wealth of the world and so the most of material aid to contribute is an obstacle to realizing universality in the responsibility. For it is not universal responsibility if the United States feeds the rest of the world, on its own decision. I think the idea again will in the long run remake the material facts. As the idea becomes clearer, so will the effort to raise the level of material existence in other countries go forward; and as these material conditions become less unequal, so will the sense and the practice of responsibility become more nearly universal. Meanwhile we are shut out from the world community by our very wealth.

The emphasis upon universal responsibility for positive action to make tolerable conditions for human living for us all, everywhere, has been caught and exploited by present-day Communism. The strength of the Communist movement lies in large part in its dependence upon this great developing idea in history. Communism says that all the people must work together to help all the people. I have seen in northern China how this aspect of Communism, this appeal to all men to work together to make life good for all men, inspired Chinese peasants and professors and turned them to the new regime then coming into power. But it seems that Russian Communism will accept such positive action only under its own direction and according to its own plan of action. Its sense of universal common responsibility is not really all-inclusive, except on its own terms. Under Communism the effort toward the realization of common responsibility is devoid of experimental creativity; it abandons all the fructifying effect of dissent, criticism, free experiment. And the opposite face of the great idea in history, the conception of universal human dignity, is denied abundantly and terribly in Russian practice.

On the other hand, in our own country, the idea of universal human responsibility is hardly seen and when seen is reluctantly grasped. We tend to see in the realization of such an idea in political or economic institution only tyranny. We have not seen yet that this world has now become so crowded and so closed that there remains for us a choice between dangers of tyranny. To set up universal institutions to take positive action for us all is to risk tyranny. But, on the other hand, not to do so, by leaving the world in desperate anarchy and much of it in desperate material need, is to risk that tyranny which war imposes on us all and hunger and sickness on most of us.

The movers for world government, though they may not know it, and though they may fear it if they do see it, have founded an effort toward practical action on the combined strength of the idea of universal freedom and the idea of universal human responsibility. They actually propose to the problem of war an institutional solution which rests upon justice. Moreover, the justice upon which their movement rests is not simply freedom from things. It is duty to things. It requires that all men, through their representatives, sit down together to plan durable peace by planning a just society. Thus their movement is strong where Russian Communism is weak, and it is strong where the American impulse toward universal practical action is hesitant.

The dependence of the movement for world government upon these two ideas in combination, universal human freedom and universal common responsibility, is the reason why the movement is so revolutionary and why the movement has power in the face of almost every unfavorable immediate circumstance. The movement is like the meeting of two straight lines drawn at an angle. Institution and great idea come together in one future event.

If you know the workers for world government, you will know that I am not saying what all of them, or most of them, would be saying about their own movement. Many of them do not accept what seem to me to be the inevitable consequences and implications of their effort. Some of the workers for world government think of world government as hardly more than police power in international hands. To them it is just a bigger policeman that will keep the boys from throwing bombs. Others who work for world government hesitate at interfering with colonialism or retain a confidence that the world's economy can make a good life for everybody if merely American business is allowed to expand. They do not yet see that universal common responsibility is universal effort to make not only peace but a tolerable life for everybody. What they are advocating is so bold and constructive in its necessary nature when fully understood that workers for world government can hardly bring themselves to say or to see what it is. It is not remarkable that they tend to present it as the cheapest and smallest package of social change that a prosperous American community might be hoped to look upon kindly. But it seems to me that there is no limited world government in the sense of a government limited to preserving the status quo. The people of the world do not want the status quo. The great ideas moving in history, of universal human dignity and universal common responsibility, demand that the status quo be changed. That is why the movement for world government is both revolutionary and strong.

You have perhaps hoped that I would say whether I think world government can be attained—assuming it to be desirable—before there is a great war. But how should I be able to say? A social scientist is not a forecaster of the chance of events that admittedly hang in precarious balance. Perhaps we shall have war this year. Perhaps we shall avoid it entirely. Perhaps, with or without war, world empire—Russian or American—will come. Perhaps, with war, anarchy will be intensified and civilization stricken down. There are many possible outcomes.

My assertion is simply as to the power of the movement for world government because of the reality, as forces in history, of the great ecumenical ideas. There are some who say that to contemplate the possibility of federal world government soon is to judge by wishes and not by facts; the facts, they say, call for war and world empire by conquest. But I say that such persons fail to see other facts, also essential to full understanding. Political and military power are tremendous facts. But so are the great creative ideas in history. The proponents of world federalism have the one set of facts against them. But the other set are for them. Whether the time of realization be short or long, they have conceived through human reason a possible institution which would carry out the great creative ideas in history. The workers for world government have against them all of power politics and all the anarchy of national rivalry. They have with them only the major trends of history. It is from a fact that they draw their strength, a fact that has been stated by the thinker whom I have quoted many times in this hour, namely, that in the long run civilization is the victory of persuasion over force.

THE DANGEROUS DUTY OF
THE UNIVERSITY

On its sixtieth birthday, we salute the University of Chicago in pride, in hope, in a spirit of perpetual rededication. May it survive, deserving survival. May it strive always to enlighten, knowing it will always be misunderstood. May it fall neither into complaisance nor into popularity. May it ever put creativity above conformity and intellectual courage above security. In the eternal questioning that is its productive life may it often include a re-examination of its own nature and purposes. May it be forever discontented that its discontent lead to new excellence.

As we all know, the University of Chicago has been more than once officially investigated with a view to the discovery on its campus of subversive activities or professors and is widely and persistingly regarded as dangerously radical. Only the other day I was assured by a taxi driver that this university is the place where "those Reds" are to be found, and I do not know what the newspapers say about us today as I have not read them. I do know that when General MacArthur passed this way recently, certain members of his police escort, recognizing some youths standing out of line as students in our college, quite naturally ordered them back as "you so-and-so Reds." It cannot be denied that there is a considerable opinion outside the university which sees it as a place of dangerous ideas and dangerous men.

No investigation of the university has turned up any Communist teachers because there are none, and indeed a great free university is not a place where a reasonable man would expect to find them because the life of such a university is freedom of thought and expression which is just what communism cannot practice or tolerate. That the reputation of the university as dangerously radical is quite opposite to the fact leaves the discrepancy between fact and reputation something to be explained.

I put forward the view that this reputation for dangerous radicalism is an evidence that the university is doing its duty. I suggest that it shows that the university is engaged in defending the very liberties which its detractors believe it to be endangering. I would go so far as to say that if the university were not from time to time accused of dangerous thoughts its professors could not then be doing their duty to think. It is good that university people make some other people a little uneasy because that uneasiness is a sign of their activity in the public service.

Perhaps the most important service which a great free university per-

An address delivered July 1, 1951, on the occasion of the sixtieth anniversary of the founding of the University of Chicago and reproduced with permission from *School and Society,* LXXIV (September 15, 1951), 161–65.

forms is one which goes largely unappreciated even by the professors and students who are performing it. This service is the contribution the university makes to strengthening certain values of the common life. This is just an instance of a kind of public service which each beneficial group of specialists can and does perform, each in its own way. I should like to make this point clear in its general form before I come back to professors and to the particular service they do.

Every specialized activity for the good of others involves the practice of the virtues that are necessary for that activity. Each group of specialists emphasizes for the people as a whole the virtues needed to carry out the functions of that group. The soldier makes us all a little more resolute in the face of danger because he is more commonly resolute in the face of danger than are people generally, that being a necessity of his calling. The lawyer encourages us all to respect reasoned argument and the guidance of consistency and precedent. The very division of labor among us brings about a sort of specialization also in the practice of the virtues and so in the preservation and development of some part of the values of the community as a whole. Ideals are maintained as they are expressed in activities. Their realization occurs in the fulfilment of the different roles which fall to us according to what each is called upon to do. Values are not equally held or equally realized in the conduct of all our people. The values of the common life are preserved and carried forward in a sort of symphony of the interests and callings.

In a university the virtues necessarily emphasized are those we sometimes call "intellectual." They are the probities of the mind. What are they? The use of reason and special knowledge in reaching understanding and in deciding how to act. The unswerving faith that truth may be approached by the exchange of idea and the test of fact. An exaltation of the importance, both as means and as an end in itself, of freedom of thought and speech. A willingness to listen to the man with an idea opposed to one's own. A disposition to attribute reasonableness to the other fellow.

Now I do not suppose that these qualities of excellence are to be found in the teachers and research workers of a university in greater degree than they are found among other kinds of people for the reason that teachers and research workers are nearer divine grace or because they are more naturally endowed with good qualities than are other people. Indeed, to be candid, I remark that I have not found professors more than usually kind or generous or humanely disposed. With regard to these qualities I think I would at least as soon trust myself to carpenters or to taxi drivers. But professors do have in notable degree the intellectual virtues, and that is because they just cannot do their work without them. I will not go so far as to say that professors exhibit the intellectual virtues as fully in their campus affairs or their community affairs as they do in their libraries and laboratories. But I can at least assert that, in the conduct of their research, in the carrying on of academic discussion and investigation, they do, because they must, to notable degree exhibit devotion to freedom of inquiry, the use of reason, and the test of special knowledge. I think also that there is some carry-over of these qualities into the less professional part of the professor's life, and I certainly think that there ought to be some carry-over, or the professor is not doing all of his duty.

Now these virtues of the mind are values of the general community. These goods are part of "the American way." As a people we are strongly in favor of reasonableness rather than force. We have faith in persuasion resulting from open competition of ideas. We have embodied freedom of speech and thought in one of our most solemn and ruling documents: the First Amendment of the Bill of Rights. We use with approval that quotation as to the obligation to defend to the death the right of another to say that with which I disagree. Of all freedoms we are proudest of the freedom of the mind. And it is in the university, above all places, where this freedom is most consistently exercised. Freedom of discussion, the appeal to the evidence of fact and the persuasion of reason, the deliberate effort to listen to unconventional ideas or heterodox theories—these are the ambient of the university. So it is especially in the university that this important part of the common values is cultivated and preserved from tyranny, from cowardice, and from ignorance. The professor, because his virtue derives from his work, is constantly maintaining and defending the freedom of thought, the reliance upon reason and special knowledge, in which we all believe.

But we—all the people—do not merely believe in freedom of thought and the intellectual virtues. We also fear them. It is another part of our nature that we are uncomfortable in the presence of the unconventional idea, the viewpoint or hypothesis that shocks our settled attitudes. Even to discuss certain matters is felt at least as unpleasant and not uncommonly as subversive. These tender subjects change somewhat with the times, of course: once it was the truth of theological dogma, then it was the animal origins of man, later it was sex, and now it is the benefits of American business enterprise or the views and theories of Karl Marx. In a university, in the course of the development of knowledge, any and all subjects may be examined, and any intellectually significant viewpoint or idea receives study and fair consideration. Therefore things are said and thought and proposed in the universities which people outside of them are not themselves in the habit of saying and thinking, and a great deal more that is not said and thought in the university is believed to be said and thought there. The fears of people create that mythical radical with the mortarboard cap and the maniacal expression that we see in the cartoons. So it comes about that in the very course of defending by its exercise the freedom of thought which stands high in the values of the whole community, the university comes to be regarded by some part of that community as a hotbed of dangerous radicalism, a hiding place of pernicious Communists.

When I referred a few minutes ago to the values of the common life as realized in a sort of symphony of the interests and callings, I over-emphasized, considerably, the harmoniousness of affairs. The effort toward ethical excellence sometimes appears more like a fight than a symphony. The interests and the callings are as much opposed to each other as they are complementary to each other. The definition and re-definition of the common values is an argument, a dialectic, a struggle of competing and conflicting impulses. "Behavior," writes Gunnar Myrdal in the more stately language of social science, "is conceived of as being typically the outcome of a moral compromise of heterogeneous valuations." As we carry on our common life we make choices, reach decisions, pass laws, utter judgments, condemn or applaud statesmen, soldiers, or other people; and in these acts we oppose or reconcile valuations that are in conflict with one another. If one group sees its local values in serious conflict with a wider value, that group may move away toward greater disharmony: Governor Talmadge may threaten to close the schools of Georgia rather than admit Negroes. Or, on the other hand, the decision of the Supreme Court requiring Texas to admit a Negro to its law school may be accepted in Texas as a reconciliation of local practice with the more general value of equality and democracy. So, too, the impulse that is widely felt to keep thought free and invite the reasonable discussion of all issues is at times in conflict with the impulse to protect ourselves from enemies, both real and imagined. Within any one individual both impulses, both values, will be represented at the same time: for freedom, and for security. How much freedom will I give up, just at this time and in this connection, to bring myself how much more security? How much immediate security am I willing to forego in the conviction that to preserve even a dangerous freedom is in the long run also to assure my security? These are the issues that we all must decide, constantly, if often half blindly and confused by ignorance and passion.

The reconciliation of the values of freedom and security is a perennial effort, an endless problem. It recurs in countless forms. Recently it appeared again in the decision of the Supreme Court sustaining the conviction of the eleven Communists. The issue there was whether the constitutional protection of the right of free speech made invalid a law punishing a conspiracy to teach the overthrow of the government by force. On the one hand was the admitted necessity to protect the country from destruction. On the other was the admitted necessity to keep speech free. The eleven Communists were convicted on evidence showing that they associated to teach others those doctrines as to forceful revolution which appear in the writings of Marx and Lenin. There was, I believe, no evidence that the defendants taught anybody how to throw a bomb or to set fire to a building. They were convicted of a collaborative effort to advocate the general doctrine of revolutionary communism. Which value, security or freedom of speech, should prevail? Four justices decided for security: they held that it might constitutionally be made criminal to conspire to advocate revolutionary communism. Two justices held for freedom of speech: they took the view that an effort by a group to teach a doctrine, though a doctrine of revolution by force, where no particular acts of violence were shown to be threatened, was protected by the First Amendment: "Congress shall make no law . . . abridging the freedom of speech." The eleven Communists will be punished. But some people will continue to doubt the wisdom of the decision. Some will wonder if the danger created by the teaching of these men was really so clear and present as to justify that they be silenced. Perhaps, if motives could be searched out and made known, we would see that these men were really convicted not for what they taught but because there was a feeling that they might blow up a bridge or betray a military secret to Stalin, or because we feel safer just now with the power to jail Communists. And some of us are likely to feel concern because of another abridgment of freedom of speech.

The concern with the preservation of freedom of speech, thought, and discussion is likely to be strong in a university, for the reason that I have already tried to give. I do not say that the professors at the University of Chicago think the majority decision in the case of the eleven Communists was the wrong decision, because I do not at all know how lies opinion on our campus as to this question. I do say that whenever freedom of discussion or of speech or of inquiry is in danger in this country at large, university people are more likely than is the average man to do something toward protecting that freedom. This I think is natural. This I think is right. University people so depend upon these freedoms, so use them in their work, that the importance of this value is ever strongly felt by them. Is it not a good thing for the whole community that when most of it, perhaps because of fear, is disposed to put security above freedom, that part of the community that cares deeply about this kind of freedom should urge its preservation? Is it not right that the men and women who more than ordinarily understand freedom of speech and thought because they work with it daily should say their say on the subject at a time when the country must make some difficult choice between values, some difficult reconciliation between freedom and security?

If the university people do take public positions in defense of these freedoms, they are likely to be criticized for taking them. If professors argue that the minority opinion in the case of the Communists should have been the majority opinion, it will be said that the professors are defending communism. If professors join in a movement to oppose the Broyles Bill at Springfield or to repeal the federal McCarran Act which, among other things, punishes having almost any connection with certain listed organizations, then it will be said that we have another evidence that the university is subversive and ought to be investigated. But these are risks that professors should run. If professors did not speak out on these issues, they would fail just where they are needed. And furthermore, if they failed to speak out, they would be cowards. For professors are more secure than are most men. It is very hard to fire a professor. Because this is so, the obligation on the professor is heavy: he must discharge his responsibility to contribute special knowledge and informed opinion to public discussion with exceptional fidelity to truth and without self-seeking, and he must not fear to do so when the occasion demands it.

The present occasion does demand it. We are in danger and we know it. But we are not always clear as to where the danger lies. The enemy is both inside ourselves and outside the community, and it is always easier to see the enemy outside. There is a tyranny in Russia, and this tyranny threatens us. In response we tend to turn, only a little and yet significantly, toward tyranny. We do not always see that we have to defend our freedom both against Stalinists and against ourselves. We do not clearly note how much of freedom we have already foregone, how much of tolerance and generosity of spirit we have given up in taking measures to protect ourselves from militant communism. But we have foregone a good deal. What is the situation of freedom and fairness today? We have seen the reputations of loyal and useful citizens destroyed by irresponsible accusations made against them. We have suffered the embarrassment of watching our immigration authorities detain or keep out of the country excellent persons for the reason that they once had some nominal and perhaps inescapable connection with a totalitarian organization. We have seen a spreading demand for loyalty oaths from good persons whose patriotism could only be made a degree less confident, less devoted, by a futile and humiliating exaction. We have watched a great sister university suffer serious damage from one such exaction. We have written into our laws authorization to administrative officers to compel organizations to register as Communist organizations and severely penalizing persons belonging to or giving money to organizations put on this list. We have authorized the institution of concentration camps in case of war or insurrection and the summary arrest and imprisonment of persons believed—on what ground of rumor is not said—to conspire to commit sabotage. And daily we are investigated by officers of a government that does not tell us of what dubious acts, of what hint of disloyalty, we are charged. Frequently we are asked by some investigating agent to tell something, with the door closed, about the loyalty or disloyalty of some friend or acquaintance. In hidden ways, in a secrecy that should be abhorrent to our traditions, your friends and mine are found unworthy of employment in the government or are denied the right to travel abroad. Clearly the danger from within is growing. The nature of the danger was recently put by George F. Kennan in the following words: It is a danger "that something may occur in our own minds and souls which will make us no longer like the persons by whose efforts this Republic was founded and held together, but rather like the representatives of that very power we are trying to combat: intolerant, secretive, suspicious, cruel and terrified of internal dissension because we have lost our own belief in ourselves and in the power of our ideals."[1]

If this should happen, if this spirit should become the way of the rule of the land, then we should have lost our struggle without losing it to Stalin's communism. Then we should become as our enemies outside. Then the universities could no longer exist. Then it would not be communism, but the free mind, that would go underground. In that case, against a tyranny ruling us, the university could and should be truly subversive.

To strive that this will not happen, that this spirit shall not prevail, is a constant duty of the university. It is the public aspect of its private task. We are still free to perform the task. The effort to define and to realize our values in which we all take part is still an effort conducted for the most part in a generous spirit and with an open mind. The conflict is controlled by the desire to compose a symphony. The struggle is still reasonable and fair, a struggle of competing viewpoint and opinion. University people greatly help to keep it so. Therefore the worth of a university lies not only in the extensions of knowledge which it achieves but also in the example and leadership it offers as to freedom of thought.

[1] G. F. Kennan, "Where We Stand on Communism," *New York Times,* May 27, 1951.

The university is not to be deterred from speaking out for freedom of this kind by the fact that it will be misunderstood and criticized. If the university continues to do its duty, some people will continue to regard it as dangerous. When people begin to find thought dangerous, they will suppose universities to be dangerous, and then the duty of the university includes the obligation to incur the charge that it is dangerous. If professors remain willing to take part in reasonable discussion of public issues, if they continue to speak and act in defense of the freedom of the mind, if they go on studying and considering every reasonable idea and position, they will be attacked in the press and investigated in the legislature. Some of them will have to spend quite a little time explaining why they supported this cause or joined that movement or made that speech. The president or chancellor of the university will be in hot water. But that is where, from time to time, he ought to be. A president or chancellor who does not spend a considerable part of his time in hot water is not worth his salt. He must defend the freedom of the country by defending the freedom of his professors, and he must use his leadership to encourage his professors to rise to their responsibilities to truth and freedom. His water will be heated for him both within the university and outside it.

The reputation of this university for dangerous radicalism is falsely but honorably earned. It is unfortunate that the university is wrongly suspected. It would be worse if it were not suspected at all. For if everything that university people did were acceptable to all influential segments of public opinion, the university would be failing its duty. Where the mind is free, the mind is troubled. The university, though misunderstood, should be just a little troublesome. The remedy for misunderstanding is more effort at understanding. This is the prime effort of the university, not pleasing people. We do not preserve our liberties by pleasing people. A wholly pleasing university cannot be great and free. The University of Chicago, as it begins its sixty-first year, is still both.

THE DIFFICULT DUTY OF SPEECH

The civil rights are also duties; they must be exercised to be enjoyed. The greatest threat to them is the unwillingness of the people to exercise them. Often, and especially in times like these, to do so is an effort, even a peril.

This is particularly true of freedom of speech. If one does not feel a strong desire to speak and does not speak, the world seems to wag

Reproduced with permission from the *Quarterly Journal of Speech*, XXXIX (1953), 6–14.

along much as it did before and one's comfort is not disturbed. The pressures that inhibit expression of opinion and creation of novel ideas are subtle, and the arguments against speaking in a time of stress are plausible. The question is asked: Why stir up trouble? And: Do you want to make difficulties for your hard-pressed country by raising that issue? And again: Are you trying to be a martyr? All these arguments may have merit, and it is not easy to be sure when they are justly persuasive in making a man hold his tongue and when they are not.

Yet no real freedom of speech exists unless men speak frankly whatever they honestly believe is important to say. For freedom of speech is speech in fact freely exercised. It is people talking and writing and creating fresh ideas and discussing old ones. It is a climate of inquiry and experiment and invention. It is especially a listening to what the other man says. It is people talking, not merely people who are not prevented from doing so.

In this sense freedom of speech is both a means to good ends and an end in itself. People need it to reach just decisions in which many participate, and they need it because the creation and exchange of ideas is a good in itself, like music or human sympathy. Speech and writing should be of all kinds, as Professor W. E. Hocking has said in his book *Freedom of the Press:* grave and gay, spontaneous and deliberate, logical and poetic, playful and intensely serious. Freedom of speech is realized when men say whatever comes to them to say, whether it be a sonnet, a criticism of a public officer, a scientific hypothesis, a vote dropped in the ballot box, a protest against a miscarriage of justice or a bad bill in Congress.

I think I understand that I have a duty to make my contribution to this flow of ideas, impressions, reported experiences and arguments, and all kinds of verbal creations and influences. I think, too, that I understand, again following Hocking, that this duty-and-right of speech is subject to conditions and limitations. It is conditioned upon honesty. The liar has no right to speak; to lie is to abuse the right and to fail in the duty. Also the right is conditioned upon a certain measure of good will. The malicious speaker abuses the right and fails his duty. Thus, when we judge the utterance of a senator, the issue is the extent to which he really believes what he says and the extent to which he says what he says in order to harm someone rather than to make clear an issue. If he speaks maliciously and out of no deep genuine conviction, he has abused his right, and we cannot use his utterances to convince us as to the truth of what he says. A man who tries to get the police into trouble by shouting that there are pickpockets in the crowd when he does not have the proof he pretends to have is not to be trusted; if later a pickpocket is found in the crowd the shouter is not therefore justified. Nor can the shouter justify a claim that he has been exercising his right to speak; rather he has perverted it.

Yet the conclusion does not follow that restraining lying or malicious speech is wise. To be sure that speech is a deliberate and malicious lie is so difficult that suffering such speech is better than repressing it. To restrain the liar by law may so intimidate the honest man that he too is afraid to speak. But when, as today, much speech is intemperate and malicious, the duty of each man is increased to utter informed and responsible speech. The duty of speech becomes a heavier burden.

The right of speech is enjoyed by everyone, and the duty of speech falls upon everyone. But right and duty are proportionate to each man's power to speak. He who has more to say has greater obligation to say it, as well as greater pleasure in the exercise of his power. Moreover, a man's power to speak is not final, God-given. It too depends in part on each man's will. No matter how ignorant, how held down by the immediate tasks of life, each man has some opportunity, and in this country a good deal of opportunity, to increase his power to speak by reading and thinking and talking with his neighbors.

As a professor, I reflect upon the special case of the professor. His training and experience have fitted him to speak exceptionally well upon at least one subject: his own. Moreover, the inference is reasonable that the mental habits of science and scholarship are peculiarly adapted to the formation and utterance of responsible opinion. The deliberate exchange of ideas toward the truth is the everyday business of the professor. He may exercise these habits of the rational mind upon political and social questions as well as upon astronomy or philosophy. The duty of the professor to speak is more exacting than that imposed upon the man who is not trained as the professor is trained. By virtue of the role which he performs in society as a specialized seeker for truth and a trainer of developing minds, his obligation to speak freely and disinterestedly, and especially to speak out of special knowledge, is a heavier duty than most men bear. If the professor fails in speaking, his failure is the greater.

On the other hand, the professor is subject to special difficulties and special temptations in discharging his share of the duty.

The professor is in a privileged position with regard to his audience. When the Commission on the Freedom of the Press was discussing these questions, Mr. Hocking remarked that to make speech free and listening compulsory would hardly do, although that would be the speaker's dream. Mr. Hutchins replied that this is doubtless why men become professors. Mr. Hutchins was thinking of the young people who more or less dutifully troop to attend lectures. The professor has a sort of captive audience. The best situation for freedom of speech is the soap box in Hyde Park; the speaker is quite free to speak, but whether or not he has an audience depends entirely on whether he can attract one. A professor, talking to younger and dependent people who perhaps come to something called a required course, is privileged as compared with the speaker in Hyde Park. As a result, some tendency may exist for the professor to assert his views without meeting an adequate and informed criticism, in the classroom. But so long as there are many universities and many kinds of speakers in any one university, this danger is not serious.

A difficulty also lies in distinguishing clearly that speech by a professor which carries special weight because it is spoken on a subject in which the professor is especially informed and that speech by the professor on other subjects. In this respect at least two mistaken positions seem to arise. The statement is advanced—even by some professors—that the professor should express himself only on subjects of his special competence and not at all on other topics. Then the professor would not speak on public issues except as they extend into his teaching. On the other matters he would be silent. But to adopt this position is to deny the professor the rights of the common citizen, which he continues to be while being also a professor, and to deny to the society the value of that voice on that issue. On the other hand, not only the professor but also other people sometimes accord to the opinions of the physicist on matters of politics and finance a high degree of importance because the speaker knows about physics. This is an opposite confusion. In the light of this double difficulty, the duty of the professor would seem to be to make plain when he speaks from special knowledge and when he speaks only out of common knowledge; but this distinction is not always easy to draw.

There is also the difficulty in discharging the duty of speech which arises out of the ambiguities of academic tenure. Academic tenure is a degree of protection accorded the professor against being fired for doing his duty: to advance free inquiry toward truth. But sometimes academic freedom is invoked to protect a professor who is not advancing the search for truth but is merely holding on to his job. Academic freedom then becomes tenure by the unfit. The man whom the American Legion or the offended member of the Board tries to fire is in some cases not much of a teacher and nearly nothing of a research worker. On the other hand, those who wish to get a good professor fired will not always disclose their real reasons for doing so but will hide the reasons behind the stringency of the budget, if he does not have tenure; or if he does, they will be unable, perhaps, to find him the laboratory assistant he needs. Academic tenure therefore does not always protect the freedom of inquiry that should be protected, and sometimes something unworthy of protection is protected in its name. Moreover, these matters of defense of academic freedom of inquiry take up a good deal of time, and occasionally professors seem to be so busy defending themselves—which they must do also on behalf of society as a whole—that they do not have time to take their proper parts in the give and take of idea and opinion in the formation of national decisions.

Fourth among the special difficulties which the professor meets in discharging his duty to speak is the fact that often he is torn between the feeling that he ought to spend his time and energies on research and teaching and the feeling that he ought to do something about what is going on in Congress, crime in his local community, or the terrible danger of war. A man has just so much to give, and perhaps a professor serves best by being just a professor. But if he fails to speak and act as any good citizen would, does he not fail as a citizen?

These difficulties of the professor in discharging his duty to speak call for no special tears. They are the kind of difficulties which are encountered, in some form, by any men living in a complicated society, and they are encountered even when the times are not so very bad. More important are the problems of duty of speech that are created or enlarged by the special circumstances of our times.

What has happened to society in the past decade which makes discharging the duty of speech especially hard and at the same time makes it more than ever before urgently necessary?

The rapidity with which we have come to hate and fear communism is hardly realized. A colleague of mine, clearing out a desk, found two magazines. One was a copy of *Life* in which the leading article presented portraits and biographic notes of leading Soviet scientists, praising them highly, including Lysenko, the Marxian geneticist. That number of *Life* is less than ten years old. The other magazine was a Communist quarterly, so titled and self-declared. It looked much like the *Yale Review*. It, too, was less than ten years old. Of the contributors to that particular issue, all but a few have either recanted or gone to jail.

I think Stalinist communism is indeed bad and dangerous. I am convinced that it is an evil, cruel, and dehumanizing tyranny. The important point here is that with our growing fear of communism has come an intensely partisan spirit that makes reasonable and fair discussion difficult. Today every man must be a partisan; it is forced upon him. A partisan joins a party and accepts its decisions and actions as his decisions. In intense partisanship these decisions are put beyond criticism; reason is stilled; the ultimate partisan "thinks with his blood" as the Nazis put it. Today one is pushed to be a partisan by the suspicion directed against any act or utterance associated with the partisans of the opposite party. If Owen Lattimore advocated a policy something like what Russia was advocating for probably quite other reasons, then Owen Lattimore is said to be working for communism. Because the Communists have used the word *peace* for their own bad purposes, the honest man who now speaks for peace seems to be speaking for communism. Because the Communists exploit our country's failure to realize equality as between the races, a man who has spoken in favor of racial equality becomes suspect. There are coming to be just two kinds of partisans: Communists and people who are against communism. The man who considers each issue on its merits has no place in this alignment; a man is no longer asked to contribute his own reasoned opinion; he is pushed to declare himself: Are you for us or are you against us? The proved partisanship of the Communist who has recanted becomes a sterling virtue. Those who were once Communists now attack communism with just what is today approved: passion and the least possible critical judgment. Such ex-Communists are wanted, but the independent mind is not wanted. It is positively distrusted.

These are some of the changing circumstances which make difficult fulfillment of our duty of speech. The service the professor professionally renders is critical and independent judgment. The increased partisanship of the day makes it very difficult for him to perform this service. If he questions the McCarran Act, he attracts unfavorable attention; if he discusses philosophical Marxism, he is "teaching communism."

The matter is not so simple that a mere adherence to principle will tell a man what in these circumstances he ought to do. One cannot simply resolve: I will say what I think on every issue and let the consequences fall as they may. If a man does that today, he may find that the consequences are to impair seriously his special usefulness to society.

Not long ago I received one of those many letters calling upon me to join in a public statement approving an important piece of impending national legislation. I agreed with the statement I was asked to sign; the matter was one on which I had some competence. But, to assure myself that I was not misunderstanding the matter, I telephoned a colleague who had, I knew, also received the communication. I asked him what he thought of the statement he was asked to sign. He said he was well informed on the matter and agreed with the statement. I asked him if he was going to sign it. He replied that he was not. And the reason? Some of the names appearing on the letter were associated with organizations or activities suspected or charged with indirect Commu-

nist connections, and, said my colleague, if he should sign the statement, with which he agreed, he might also be tainted with this association and then could no longer be useful as an occasional adviser in the
State Department and elsewhere.

The fact is that my colleague was right—right, in that if he did sign
too many such letters he would lose his usefulness as a contributor "at
high levels" to the formation of national policy. He just would not be
asked any more.

What was my colleague's duty? Should he remain silent when asked to
join others in making a public statement as to whether the pending bill
should become a law? Then the nation would lose the force of his
especially informed opinion on that issue. Or should he add his name
to those making the public statement and run the risk that the mere
association of his name with the names of others perhaps already under
suspicion in the office of the FBI or the attorney-general would remove
him from other counsels held in the national interest? Perhaps he found
the time to compose his own letter expressing his views on that issue.

More and more men hesitate to expose their names in connection
with public issues or with the names of other men. The emerging result
is that the people who sign letters of protest, or who publicly oppose
legislation to bring about what is called nowadays "security," are fewer
than they were and are the same people, over and over again; probably
not much attention is now paid to them. They are simply the people
who sign letters of protest.

More and more the issue upon which I am asked to speak or on
which I feel that I ought to speak, is one on which those who associate
themselves with me in speaking are in fact partisans, not critical thinkers, or are people who are wrongly supposed to be Communist partisans.
If I speak in their company my speech will be disbelieved or discounted
simply because I am in the company of such real or supposed partisans.
Shall I then refrain from speaking? But if I refrain, then only partisans
will speak, or only those will speak who have been falsely condemned
as partisans and whose opinions no longer count. Perhaps the cause on
which I am asked to speak is just—the man should be defended, the
bill that threatens liberties be defeated—and if I fail to speak I have
left a just cause to the defense of those who use the just cause for their
own bad ends or to those who have become unjustly ruled out of public
confidence. Shall we make ourselves useless by submitting to the consequences of this form of guilt by association?

Partisanship and guilt by association make difficult the discharge of
our duty of speech. But other difficulties have become recently acute.
We are no longer sure that to express certain opinions is within the law,

and even worse, a man may now be a criminal because he belongs to an organization that has certain purposes—advancing revolutionary communism. He may be convicted of crime without any evidence that he did anything to bring about such a revolution. Apparently it is not necessary even to show that the accused knew the purpose of the organization was revolutionary communism; that knowledge may be imputed to him from the fact of his membership.

The convictions of Communists under the Smith Act is the point at issue. In the decision of the Supreme Court in June, 1951, the majority of the court apparently adopted the views that had previously been expressed by Mr. Justice Hand in his opinion in the same case when it came to the Circuit Court of Appeals. Taken together with Hand's opinion, the effect of the decision in the case of the eleven New York Communists limits the protection given free speech by the First and Fourteenth Amendments in two important respects. In the first place, the "clear and present danger" rule apparently is now so interpreted that the world-wide menace of communism is sufficient justification for jailing one who advocates revolutionary communism, even without a showing that what the accused said about revolutionary communism was having any direct effect on public safety. Moreover, the rule that a man accused of crime must be given a clear idea of the crime of which he is being accused has been widened or loosened. The Smith Act is vague as to what teaching revolutionary communism means. The Supreme Court in effect held that the general seriousness of the present situation is a sufficient ground for dispensing with the requirement of certainty imposed by the Supreme Court in other cases.

The general drift of this and other decisions of the Court is to make it possible for Congress or a state legislature to pass, in spite of the Bill of Rights and the Fourteenth Amendment, laws that either make expressions of certain opinions criminal, or that have as inevitable consequence coercing people into silence on certain important matters.

In March of this year the Court upheld the constitutionality of the New York State law which provides for the disqualification and removal of teachers in public schools who are "subversives" or who belong to "subversive" organizations, such determination to be made by the school board. This apparently authorizes an administrative board to determine who and what is subversive, and as it is unpredictable what opinions will be held by such a board to be subversive, the effect of the law can hardly be otherwise than to make teachers afraid to speak freely. Mr. Justice Douglas, dissenting, simply stated that the law inevitably turns the school system into a spying project. In a recent deportation case, the Court upheld the constitutionality of those sections of the Smith

Act which allow the United States to deport an alien because of membership in the Communist party even if the membership ended before the act was passed. I find it difficult to escape from the alternative interpretations placed upon this majority decision by the two dissenting Justices (Douglas and Black): either a person once a Communist is forever tainted, or else punishment by banishment may be imposed for what an alien once thought. Neither interpretation can be squared with the fundamental conceptions of human liberty which Americans long ago adopted. In the Carlson case, the Court approved the right to jail certain aliens without bail pending the determination of their deportability and in effect removed from this special class of persons the protection of the Eighth Amendment prohibiting excessive bail. Apparently the Supreme Court thinks that the Eighth Amendment prohibits a judge from demanding a bail of ten million dollars but does not prohibit a judge from denying bail entirely, at least in certain cases.

What this comes down to is that the Supreme Court, in view of the world-wide threat from Stalinist communism, now qualifies in important respects the protection of civil liberties, especially free speech. The narrow result is to make Communists and people who have political ideas like those of Communists criminals or possible criminals. The more important and widespread result is to make everybody, and especially a good many teachers, afraid to speak freely.

The rise of the partisan spirit with ascription of guilt by association and the growing uncertainty as to whether one can keep one's job—or perhaps even stay out of jail—by reason of opinions one may express or associations one may make contribute to what seems to me an increasing acceptance of a certain loss of liberty and creativeness in America. Some thoughtful people have expressed the opinion that Americans have never been so ready to defend their liberties as they are now. My own impressions are different. It seems to me that a good many fairly serious restrictions upon our liberties have come about and that on the whole Americans regard them as necessary for their security or accept them without thinking much about them at all.

I think of such changing circumstances as the following: the many states that now require oaths of certain classes of people; the attempts to purify textbooks; the banning of books and magazines from public shelves; the endless investigations as to loyalty (I am told of a questionnaire which asked men considered for appointment: "Did you ever receive any mail from any of the following twenty-eight organizations?"); the endless questioning as to security; the man with the federal credentials who seeks you alone in your office and asks if you have anything unfavorable to tell him about some friend of yours; the passports denied;

the loyalty hearings of employees or of scholars seeking to do research or to travel—usually polite, but on charges not clearly presented and without opportunity to meet these charges fully; the growing silence of administrative government; the authority given to civilian agencies to classify information as secret and not disclose it to the public; the increasing use in public correspondence and official announcement of that phrase, with its unpleasant connotations in other countries, *in the public interest*—this grant has been terminated, this man discharged, this information denied, all "in the public interest"; the scholars and scientists not given the visas which would allow them to come to this country to join in academic discussion with their American colleagues with a result that European scholars have come to think of some sort of unpleasant curtain lying also to the west of them.

Is it not true that the effect is not so much to stimulate our people with a new vigor in exercising and defending freedom of speech but rather to dull the habit of protest and the courage of inquiry? Do we not on the whole either accept these changes as necessary to security or let them come about hardly realizing that they have happened? I do not see that the American mind is now unusually courageous and creative. In recent months the National Opinion Research Center has found that more and more people show reluctance to answer the questions that are asked them when the opinion-taker comes to their doors. More people must be asked, and it is harder to get answers from those who do make replies. The reluctance is greater in the cities than in the country and is especially evident when questions are asked about international affairs. A colleague, who is concerned with the planning of research in the sciences and with the selection of research projects and workers at the national level, is convinced that more and more students and more mature scientists are disposed to undertake only the "safe" problems. By this he means not merely that scientists do not like to risk the impediment of formal security regulations but also that scientific research workers have, in his judgment, become reluctant to undertake the study of any problem that is so imaginative as to be risky of result and of general approval.

The man who is no partisan and thinks that the exercise of independent judgment is useful and delightful is hard-pushed. Much of what he says is misused by reason of its associations with partisan positions, and many times he does not say what he thinks because what he says may be misused, may injure an innocent person wrongly identified with communism, or may be taken by Communists for their own purposes. Probably no simple plan will solve these difficulties. An uncompromising position compromises. No, better content oneself with clarity, honesty, and prudence. A list of simple resolutions might help. I do not offer the following as suitable for other men; each must solve his own problem. But, talking to myself, I set down the following seven-point plan for conducting myself, with regard to freedom and duty of speech under present conditions. These are only seven admonitions—me, talking to myself:

1. *You don't have to join up.* Short of torture and the destruction of the mind, you can't be forced to partisanship. You don't have to become only an anti-Stalinist or only an anti-McCarthyist. You are free to say that you think that Stalinist communism is a cruel and mind-destroying tyranny, a menacing totalitarianism, and also to say that in America there is great danger to liberty from the mindless suppression of all dissenting opinion which we see in the work of McCarthy and McCarran. As Governor Adlai Stevenson remarked recently in the very different context of a meeting of Democratic politicians: "Who wins is less important than what wins—what ideas, what concept of the world tomorrow, what qualities of perceptible leadership and courage." You are free to try to make good ideas win, not partisans.

2. *Your special task is to keep reasonable talk going.* Keep the element of fair discussion alive in the eternal struggle. Life is a fight, but it is humanized in so far as people talk things over reasonably. This is where you come in: you were trained for reasonable discussion. So practice it, not only with your students, but wherever you are. You can't make things worse that way, and you may make them better. Make it plain you are ready and eager to talk anything over reasonably with anybody—yes, Russians and Senator McCarthy included. The assumption that the other fellow has something human and rational about him is absolutely necessary.

3. (For myself as a professor.) *Your job is not to be an intellectual but to be intelligent.* If you have special knowledge, put it to work; but special knowledge does not excuse you from the necessity to think for yourself if you can manage it. The charge upon you is, in Lionel Trilling's words, "to take your chance of being wrong or inadequate, to look at things simply and directly, having in mind only the intention of finding out what they really are, not the prestige of the great intellectual act of looking at them."

4. *You make mistakes too.* Just like everybody else. And like everybody else you took time to learn how bad is Stalinist Russia. Once, for example, you said in public that the Soviet policy toward cultural minorities was admirable. That was many years ago and before you or other people had learned what the Soviets were doing to cultural minorities. Admit such mistakes. If you didn't ever make a mistake, how could you learn anything? People will try to frighten you into reconstructing your own past to fit the suspicions of today, but don't try so to reconstruct it. You have learned, like other people; say so.

5. *Freedom of speech depends upon you talking reasonably: so talk.*

This will make trouble for you and make other people find you troublesome, but the mind that is never troubled is not free. Freedom is a lot of bother. When you are sure that the McCarran Act ought to be repealed, say so. When you are convinced that hunting for treason in a school textbook is silly, make your reasonable argument to that effect. The men who make a stand at a line that they have thoughtfully drawn and who argue, but do not shoot, from that position defend freedom effectively. The California professors who lost their jobs resisting the oath really did defend freedom.

6. *But you can't be an expert on everything.* Concentrate your efforts on matters you really know about. Don't join every movement of protest and don't sign every letter. Come to understand the issues involved in a few cases and keep at just those issues. Your resources of influence and special knowledge are limited; use them prudently.

7. *Freedom of speech is a joy in itself; enjoy it.* Liberty is best defended when it is loved. To defend freedom of speech merely as one's own private right is selfish and meager; to exercise it merely as a duty is pretentious and tiresome. Freedom is fun; have the fun. Freedom of speech is not formal dialectic; it is not mental chess; it is not bargaining in a market-place of ideas. It rests upon faith in human improvability, and it flourishes where men take delight in one another.

This, I say to myself, I may attempt, though we do not know the fate of freedom in our future. It is the way of an inquiring mind, as contrasted with the way of the True Believer (as Eric Hoffer has recently described him)—that he is never sure of his success and always doubtful of his program. He is only sure that freedom is both means and ends, that an inquiring and creative mind in any man is a good to enjoy and to defend. He knows that such minds have never been numerous and are always in danger. And knowing this, he does the little he can, praying only for a little room to turn around in, and a heart without bitterness.

DOES AMERICA NEED A HEARING AID?

We Americans have long been known as a talkative people. While the strong silent man is one recognized type among us, visitors find most of us very ready with our tongues. Mrs. Trollope wrote in 1828 that "Americans love talking," and she recorded some of the abundant talk that she heard—and did not admire. A little later Alexis de Tocqueville characterized us as "garrulous" and reported that the American "speaks to you as

Reproduced with permission from *The Saturday Review*, XXXVI (September 26, 1953), 11–45.

if he were addressing a meeting." The French observer was also impressed with the fact that what the American talked about was often himself. He recognized that those Americans were proud, with reason, of their achievement in building a new and democratic nation. It was our patriotism that Tocqueville found garrulous. He found us unsatiable of praise and ever willing to tell strangers of the superiority of the American way of life.

Has this perhaps become a national habit? Do we still talk a great deal, and often, about our own virtues? Today we have an immense governmental enterprise officially named the International Information and Education Activities, and popularly known as the "Voice of America." Transmitters on land and sea girdle the globe and "the stentorian voice of free men must be heard." We are still talking about ourselves and about what's good about us. We know it is important that people understand us; it is plain that the Soviet Union constantly lies about us; and it is desirable that other people see the good about us that can give them reason to like and to help us. So we help them to see the good about us by telling them about it. We "sell" the American way.

I do not condemn our attempt to tell other people how good we are. There are great good things about us of which we should honestly speak. I think it is necessary to talk to other people and human to want to talk about one's self so as to appear in a good light. When others lie about us we must meet the lies.

But I do think that our talking is insufficiently balanced by listening. I do not think that we listen enough to what other people are trying to say to us about themselves, and I do not think we listen enough to the sound of what we say in the ears of him to whom we say it. We are guided chiefly in deciding what to say by the conceptions we have of what those others ought to like about us if they were just like us. And they aren't. They are different in respects to which we are inattentive. Just because we think great combines moving over vast fields of wheat are proofs of what great fellows we are, we took it for granted that Chinese and Middle Eastern peasants would look at pictures of these combines and admire us. By just listening for a moment to the sound of our voices in their ears instead of in our own we could find out that the combines, the tiled bathrooms, and the skyscrapers in most cases make those peasants feel more remote from us and more suspicious of us than they were before.

Talking is good, and it is necessary to make clear what we truly are. But mutual security depends on mutual understanding, and for understanding you have to have a conversation. A conversation is not two people talking loudly at each other, and certainly it is not one person with a megaphone. It is first one person listening while the other talks, and then that one talking while the other listens. In the Big Room where all peoples meet much of the talk is just the loudest voices shouting what they mistakenly imagine the others might find impressive to hear.

Would it be untactful to suggest that America needs a hearing aid? We have done something to raise our voice; can we do something to improve our listening? Something to improve it is being done in what is called "monitoring" Russian and other foreign broadcasts and in that technique of the expert called "content analysis." Something has also been done to understand better in just what respects Russians, Frenchmen, and Chinese are different from us in recent studies of national character. Something has also been done by the Fund for Adult Education's "Voices of Europe" radio series, which gives the general American public the chance to listen to Europeans who would otherwise be inaudible. I suppose that in so far as the sciences concerned with human behavior have anything to contribute to the improvement of America's listening to other people they are doing it. But today I am thinking of the art of listening to other peoples as anyone may practice it. Good talking is an art; good listening is obviously even rarer, and it is rarer because as an art it is more subtle and difficult. But, as it is something that Americans need seriously to cultivate for their own safety, it is worth considering if there are ways to cultivate it.

How shall we listen to the voices of the other personalities that stand about us in the Big Room? We may conceive of each nation, each people, as if it were a single person. There is a Frenchman there, and an Iranian, a German, and a Mexican, and there is this half-hidden Russian who talks only through a curtain and in a strange shouting language of his own. Of course each of these is really a multitude of voices (except perhaps the Russian); each is a myriad voice coming to us from real individuals of many sorts speaking through books, travel, newspapers, and personal contact. The differences among individuals I for the moment ignore, because it is also true that in general ways each nation, each people, has a character of its own; each taken as a whole is saying something that stands for all the separate individuals that make it up; we can learn to listen to the nation as if it were one person. Now our attention is on one of these talkers in the Big Room; for the moment we cease our own talking to listen to him; what do we listen for?

I suggest that we learn to listen for three things: National Character, Mood, and Human Nature.

The national character is the way that a people tends to be, pretty steadily, over long periods of time. It might also be called the collective personality or the group heritage or perhaps just the persisting peculiarities that make the people distinguishable from their neighbors. This is, among other things, the particular arrangement of human qualities, the unique and flavor-full constellation of qualities, the emphases and shadings of the universal human that make a Frenchman or a Chinese and not an American or an Italian.

It is a good thing that these differences exist, for they make the world a more interesting and enriching place. The differences between one man or woman and another, and the differences between one culture or national character and another, are sources of delight and stimulations to originality and creativeness. One of the terrible things about what is going on now in Russia is the subordination of the individual differences to one monstrous mask of the state, one set of opinions and attitudes to be worn by all. Once it seemed that the differences among ethnic groups in Russia were to be preserved under the Soviets, but now it appears that these too are to go in favor of the state-made mask. The pressure of the state, or the pressure of public opinion, is an evil in any country when it moves to suppress individual and ethnic differences. It is an evil when, as now in our present condition of tension, it appears in America. The variety of opinions in the United States and the variety of cultural heritages are sources of strength; under the name of Americanism to make Americans afraid to express these differences would do a great injury to ourselves.

The expression of a people's culture, its national character, might be the only thing we needed to listen for if all the world were a place where nothing much happened. The world of isolated primitive peoples is that kind of world. To understand the cultures of such people is all that is needed in comprehending how they are different from us. But the world in which modern peoples live is, of course, changing all the time, and it is changing very abruptly for people you and I need to understand: Asiatics, Africans, Middle Easterners, Latin-Americans. It is probably true that no previous human generation ever experienced such a great transformation of viewpoint as by that generation of Chinese, Indonesians, East Indians, and Middle Easterners who *now* assume political leadership.

Each of these people has a culture, a national character, a persisting traditional way of life that, in spite of changes, still influences the way the individual thinks and acts. But each has something else. We are to listen for this something else. I have called it Mood. The word at least suggests part of what I mean: the short-run feeling-tone of a people. Just as to understand our friend we need to come to know not only his lifelong character but also the particular mood that he is in at the moment, so too in understanding the Japanese, the Iraqi, the French we are to attend also to the mood of each. He may be hopeful or despondent, insecure or confident, calmly complacent or extraordinarily sensitive. What he is in these respects today may not be the same as he will be at some later time.

The word "mood" does not suggest all that lies in this second level of a people's nature. This second thing about a people is the response they make to a marked turn in their fortunes. It is their temporary set, or "stance," we might say, toward circumstance, fate, and other peoples than themselves. In a village of Mexican Indian peasants that I was studying I saw the idea of progress, preached by modernizing reformers from the city, take hold upon the imagination of a plodding, tradition-bound people. In a very short time the whole mood and set of the people changed. They became confident, forward-seeking, disposed to welcome almost any reform that was approved by the city-bred prophets of progress. Their culture remained for the most part the same, but their mood and set was radically altered. And a little later, when in the same enthusiastic mood they were hard at work building a masonry structure for their new school, the edifice collapsed, killing and injuring some of the workers, their mood changed again, for a time, to one of doubt and even despair. We Americans ought to understand moods, for our people as a whole have passed through a succession of quite notable moods, as we have encountered wars, depressions, isolation, and exposure. Just at present, for obvious reasons, our mood is characterized by a heightening of tension and anxiety. One of the resemblances between peoples—indeed one of the bonds between them—lies not in common culture but in similar mood. The East Indian feels close to the Middle Easterner in part because he has a similar mood and set; his stance toward Russia, the United States, imperialism, and independence is similar; they are brothers in mood.

In listening to the expressive utterances of other peoples, we are to attune ourselves to a blending of meaningful sounds. National character and mood are not distinct; the one is affected by the other. The Nigerian and the Arab today share the sensitive mood of national pride and resentment of any domination that I have just tried to describe. But Nigerian and Arab express this mood in different ways, each according to his national character; in understanding the Arab's mood we have to attend to the familial and tribal loyalties, and competitiveness, the conceptions of obligation to guests and friends, the fierceness of revenge and the nobility of forgiveness. In fully understanding the same mood in Nigeria we need to understand the different culture and national character of the Nigerian.

The tuned blending of national character and mood is itself blended with a third element in what these peoples say to us about themselves. We are to listen also to this third element. It is human nature, the qualities that all men share with one another. This is ever present, rarely explicitly distinguished, and necessarily assumed. We cannot talk with other people at all understandingly, but for the fact that in some things they are like us and like everyone else. The Arab is sensitive about some things that do not seem to us a matter for sensitiveness, but we are both sensitive about something. We do not go to such care as did the old-fashioned Chinese to protect himself from a public failure or rebuke, but we, too, lose face if we are shown wrong or foolish before those whose respect we crave.

Pride, shame, enjoyment of the company of those who are near and dear, delight in children, and laughter, a certain satisfaction in one's work well done, anger in the face of an injustice—however justice may be conceived—these and a multitude of other elements of human nature are very widely and generally distributed among the peoples of the world. We have always our own expression of human nature with which to understand another's different expression of it. While today some of us reassert the traditional American emphasis on self-reliance, striving to keep the control of our affairs in our own hands and out of the control of either powerful business or bureaucratic government, we can use this human impulse of ours to understand the mood of those Asiatics and Middle Easterners who want to keep the control of their affairs in their own lands —and out of ours. Their situation has at least this additional cause for calling up the human disposition to run one's own life: we to them are foreigners, and, as part of Western industrial civilization, conquerors.

Human nature is the medium through which communication is ever possible, in spite of curtains of steel and shouting radio transmitters. It is hard to hear human nature in the official iron throat of Russia. But it is there. If we were today in Russia we would find people like ourselves, in spite of the menace about them and the imposed uniformity of opinion. They can still talk to us out of the common human, given the chance. While we strain our ears for some accent from the iron throat that speaks for all humanity, we can exercise our familiarity with the Russia that was as human as other peoples. Two Russians wrote as no other writers ever wrote of that which in men is most universal, most richly and compellingly universal to mankind: one wrote of the humanity that is uppermost, and the other of the humanity that is undermost. The Russia of Tolstoi and Dostoevski cannot be extinct, and we can, by reading of that Russia and by exercising our own most generous and compassionate human side, keep ourselves prepared to talk again with it some day.

The only hearing aid we need is a practiced sensitiveness in recognizing in what other peoples say the contributions to the whole of national character, mood, and human nature. By reading of and talking with peoples of other lands we can come to hear what they say as one would turn a knob on a cabinet so as to emphasize upper or lower tonal registers. The same utterance speaks to us of what is pretty steadily true of the speaker, by virtue of his accumulated tradition. It speaks also of the state of mind and feeling in which recent events have put him—in which we, perhaps, have put him. It speaks also of his nature as a man, like us, asking that the same fundamental satisfactions be his that we, in our different way, also require.

Our exercises in practiced listening are not yet done. We are to cultivate another and more complicated kind of hearing. If we are to change the simultaneous shouting and babbling in the Big Room into something closer to a conversation, a give-and-take in which our words reach their audiences with the effects we desire, then we need to listen to something about which I have as yet said little. This is the sound of what we say in the ears of him to whom we say it. The mechanical analogy is now radar. We need a developed capacity to catch the meaning in what we say as our hearer catches that meaning. Our talk-waves are to bounce back to us from those other people; by listening to what has happened to them in bouncing back we learn how we are understood or misunderstood and why.

The opportunity to use this psychic radar is provided when foreigners come to our country, for then our whole way of life beats upon their receptive organs, and the reaction in the foreigners may be greatly illuminating to us, did we take pains to listen for it. As it is, when a group of South American students or Siamese technicians come here our first impulse is to talk hard to them about ourselves. As "indoctrination" is a bad word, we call it "orientation." I have taken part in such programs of orientation. The visitors are whirled through factories, laboratories, and talks by Americans about America. It does not often occur to us that maybe the visitors would like to do a little talking themselves. If we stop talking long enough to listen to them we may find that they can tell us a good deal about ourselves and about the way we seem to them. At one such gathering of Formosan technical specialists arrived only a few days in America, I, with difficulty, persuaded the American leader of the orientation program to leave a few minutes for questions to be asked by the Formosans. There was time for two questions. One Formosan asked: "Flying from California here to Chicago this Sunday we noticed that around the cities your wide roads were crowded with your big automobiles. There were so many automobiles that none of them was moving at all fast. Where were all those people going, and why, in this efficient country, were they going so slowly?" The second Formosan said: "This morning we were taken for a drive through a part of your city in which Negroes are living. We noticed that the houses and living spaces of these people were very poor in comparison with other parts of the city we saw. Why do you not have a Marshall Plan for the American Negro?" Answering these questions, I found a vigorous exercise in understanding.

When we talk to the foreigner who remains in his own land we need someone on hand when he hears what we say to report how it sounds to him. So often, being in a hurry and pretty confident about our own efforts, we just talk. Sometimes much of the talk is wasted. I remember that in those years just before and during the war when we were striving to gain and keep the good will of the Latin-Americans, we made a great show to them of our industrial and military power and our technical skill. Afterward I was told that what really appealed to the Latin-Americans was the sculptor Jo Davidson, the Yale Glee Club, and the Radio City Rockettes. It is a recurrent mistake of ours to suppose that flexing our muscles makes people love us. Yet there are frequent hints of this truth in the daily newspapers. I read of a Nigerian native who told Senator Wiley recently that all the propaganda about America's high standard of living just made the Nigerians fear and dislike America, and of a Pakistani official on the northwestern frontier who made the same point for his people, adding that what we ought to send to the northwestern frontier was our poetry. The people there would admire that. Mr. Graham Peck, in his book, "Two Kinds of Time," reports how our propaganda efforts sounded to the Chinese during the war there. The Office of War Information sent out words and pictures to "put over the idea that our way of life was absolutely best." Constant boasting about our high standard of living contrived a picture of an America where every family lived in "a ten-room, colonial style, suburban home, where all chores were done by electricity, nobody ever got sick or into debt, roofs never leaked and clothes never wore out." Mr. Peck found that this material was ineffective; he tried not to use it. On the other hand, the man back in Washington, who had no radar and probably needed a hearing aid, suppressed in a hand-out the sentence, "The new American army is revolutionary in that its soldiers are taught what they are fighting for." The sentence seemed to him alarming. And when, in spite of the efforts in Washington to prevent the story of General Patton and the face-slapping from reaching China, it did, the effect was notably to improve the opinion the Chinese held of Americans. Did not this event show that Americans were, after all, very democratic? Actually, in America, a general could get into trouble for slapping a soldier.

If we listen to another people we help to ease the pain of that people's mood. If your friend is worried you do not help him by talking to him constantly. You listen to him; then he feels better. It even helps if, without listening, you merely fall silent to give him a chance to relieve himself by talking to you. So it is with these peoples of the middle third of the world whose moods are now so painful to them and dangerous to us.

Finally, the improvement of the art of carrying on the little conversations is an exercise that meets and combines with the more organized discipline of the "great conversation." Great books and plain and sensible conversation together maintain the company of the free mind. Together they can enlarge that company, taking in more and more people, even while the Russians strive to restrict it. Freedom of speech is not just speaking; it is speaking honestly and as one thinks. Also, it is listening. No one is really free to use speech effectively unless other people listen, and no one has earned the freedom to talk to a listening audience unless he listens when another talks. The perception of both difference and likeness is a necessary basis for a conversation between two individuals or between two nations. To talk as free men each must in effect say: "You have a different view from mine, but we are both reasonable and human creatures, and I should like to know what your view is." That this ideal is not usually realized in life makes its influence on us no less. We know how great is the distinction between allegiance won blindly and that won understandingly. In a political campaign a vote won by an emotional appeal is only a vote won. A vote won by a reasonable argument understood and accepted is also a mind grown stronger. Our country, in peril in the Big Room, needs all the strength that reason can give to our powers of understanding. To indulge hateful passion for political advantage is to drive ourselves downward toward that dark reliance on force which today is Russia's. At home and abroad to talk and then to listen, to listen with the help of reason and then reasonably to talk, is to strengthen us just where we can be so much stronger than the Soviets. It is to build the community of free minds, "the civilization of the dialogue."

THE GENIUS OF THE UNIVERSITY

For most of the same span of years my life and that of my university have run along together, and it occurs to me to say one thing about any man's life and that of any university. For the most part both are busy doing what there is to do and not what their own better natures would have them do. In human being and in institution there is a natural bent, a power of right growth, that is hard to discover in life as it is lived. If, however, an observer stands off a little way from the growing thing, he

An address delivered October 17, 1956, at the University of Oregon, Eugene, Oregon, and reproduced with permission from *Old Oregon*, XXXVI (December–January, 1956–57).

may perceive the outline of direction and symmetry, as he sees a vine grow in all directions and yet grow upward. This outline is the bent of the thing, its essential right nature.

You and I, who have been so close to a university that we have been parts of it, know that we have lived the life that is peculiarly appropriate to a university, as a special kind of thing, only once in a while. Much of what we have been doing might as well have been done elsewhere, at a club, perhaps, or at home, or somewhere down at the corner with the boys. Much of it was pleasant, a good deal of it was necessary, and only a small part was downright bad, but it did little to make stand forth the direction and symmetry of our own essential natures or that of our university. I could join you in personal admissions that would support what I have just said, but from now on I leave the man and talk only of the university.

The ordering of life, in a university as in anything else, is most immediately a matter of just keeping things running. We are all housekeepers. Housekeeping is a universal preoccupation, an unavoidable distraction. It is no wonder that we have dignified it with a Greek name and made a science of it. In the case of the university, it is the professor as well as the comptroller and the registrar who is busy keeping house. He records grades, tries to get placed on reserve the books for his classes, and argues with his colleagues as to required courses or permitted sequences. It sometimes seems as if the realistic organization chart of a university would show all the arts and sciences depending from the Department of Buildings and Grounds, the office of student records, or the investment committee of the Board of Trustees. Students too keep house, in the sense that they must eat, sleep, and more or less dress, and must manage the routines of study.

I have felt this inversion most strongly when our faculty representatives have come together to discuss university affairs. The talk is often about how the house is to be kept. I think of arguments as to the competing claims of faculty groups for pieces of the pie of the student's working time, of talk about faculty housing, and of long reports on a choice of plans for retirement allowances. Yet there was a period in the history of my university, to which I can look back, when at such meetings there was occasional talk about education. I can still recall the exhilaration of such unusual moments. There was aroused a joyful surge in the breast; one felt something grow within, something essential and true. It was exciting, hopeful.

Together with housekeeping, other ways of passing the time deflect the university's natural bent. The activities on and around our campuses are so varied and mixed that I am sure I mention only some of them when I name play and recreation, academic politics—a very serious matter—perhaps some participation in civic affairs, and the usual private and domestic life. It is so long since I have myself seen at close range that great sector of the powers and the passions of a large university that begins with spring practice and ends with a bowl game or, perhaps, a penalty from the Conference Board, that I dare not speak of it here. I believe that it exists, and has more than a little to do with the confusion of the natural bent. All these things take our time and our strength, lead us in a variety of directions of enjoyment or disappointment, and make a university as difficult to characterize in single terms as the shows now playing in New York or the people of the United States.

And yet a university *is* one kind of thing, or would be, if it grew rightly. Before it grows at all its true outlines may best be seen—with the mind's eye. When Paul Henry Newman spoke so eloquently of the idea of a university, the one he came to found in Dublin was not really in existence. So he could see it as it should be, "a place to which a thousand schools make contributions; in which the intellect may safely range and speculate, sure to find its equal in some antagonist activity, and its judge in the tribunal of truth." And he continued: "It is a place where inquiry is pushed forward, and discoveries verified and perfected, and rashness rendered innocuous, and error exposed, by the collision of mind with mind, and knowledge with knowledge."

There you have it. A university in fact and not merely in name is a place where people meet to expose knowledge and ideas to the test of other people's knowledge and ideas. Words Newman uses are speculation, error, rashness. In a university the mind is encouraged to take reasonable chances, to ask questions that are difficult and far-reaching and perhaps a little outrageous; and this is done safely in a true university because it is a place of critical examination of all significant ideas and pieces of knowledge, because the others who have joined in the concourse of minds will test and judge what is put forward.

Newman writes also of the passion that goes along with the thinking and the reasonable discussion. He speaks of the professor as a missionary and a preacher, not meaning that he promotes religious or other doctrine, but that the works of the mind are conceived in devotion and even love, and one who sees some part of truth that others may not have seen pours it forth, as Newman says, "with the zeal of enthusiasm." The zeal is the moving engine of the exploring intelligence. It is governed by the communications with others. And it is restrained by the humility and habit of doubt that are part of the discipline and tradition of universities. The missionary of the mind's adventures puts forth ideas and conclusions in enthusiasm, but, if he serves truly, he welcomes the tests and checks that come upon him in the meeting place of knowledge.

To say, as we often do, that the university is engaged in education, scholarship, and research is to say what is true but incomplete. What has to be added is this: A university is carrying on a special kind of life, the life of the mind. This life is intellectual and passionate. Its exercise takes place in a community arranged for that purpose. Its participants are provided with opportunities not found elsewhere to carry on such a life. In so far as they take part in it, they make the assertion that such a life is important. They say, in effect, that the life of the mind is a part of the good life for anybody, in the university or out of it. The education and the learning are the business of the university; they are its ways of doing things that are needed by all the people. But by doing these things those of the university community do something that is a good in itself and so keep that kind of good alive and possible for other people too. The people of the university carry on their conversations and their investigations for two reasons: that the knowledge gained may be put to use, and also that the life of the mind may flourish, as one among many of the great goods that are good for their own sake—like music, prayer, and the joy of living. The life of the mind is work, and it is delight. It is men and women, young and old, coming together in an activity human and angelic.

Fine words. But are they true? Does this really take place in a university? How can it be said that it is true, when all the other things that I have mentioned, the housekeeping and the distractions, the lesser pleasures and the small tasks, make up so much of what goes on? The main business of the university, the teaching and the advance of scholarship, by no means takes place always in a spirit of joyful adventure. Much of what is necessary to research is a mere repetition of small tasks. Much teaching has become only routine. I am sure that in the classroom and in the workroom a great deal goes on that is perfunctory, tedious, and wasteful.

And yet I am here to say that the mind's adventures *are* pursued in a university. I say that it does happen that there young people and older people exchange with one another their insights and discoveries in the library or the laboratory in a spirit of delight in the effort, of commitment to the endless search. I have seen it happen. I have taken a small part. I recognize the moments or the hours in which the life of the mind is lived. Sometimes they happen as the student listens to the occasionally effective professor. The professor is talking about something that he feels deeply to be important and on which his intelligence is working. To the student he communicates the importance, the indications of the means whereby the new understanding may be reached or confirmed, and the sense of a struggle to cross a frontier. Maybe the student cannot yet fully join in the effort, but he sees that one can join and that the effort is a good thing in itself; and the frontier beckons to him. He has entered, though silently, into the life of the mind. Sometimes these luminous hours occur as the student too makes his contribution, talking to the professor and to the other students. He can himself frame the words, point out the facts, suggest the difficulties and the doubts. The conversations of intelligence are widened and refreshed. The young go oftener astray, perhaps, as they struggle toward the frontier, but, on the other hand, they are bolder; they will ask questions that the more experienced man has forgotten; they will propose an apparent irrelevance that suddenly turns out to be a challenge. A collection of professors without students could continue scholarship and research, but the rot of routine would become a greater danger than it is with the participation of students. And, further, in this account of the moments in the life of the mind, I have seen them occur as one professor listens, really listens, to another. I think this is relatively rare, but when it does occur, it is splendid. I have seen a half a dozen professors from different departments and with different specialties talking, seriously, with one another about a thoughtful question which all of them found important and to which each found his special knowledge relevant. A good university is not a collection of private offices. It is a meeting place, a coming together of many kinds of seekers and searchers.

In these moments or hours the inquiring bent of man's nature, disciplined by reason and learning, moves forward, upward. It then seems to me that some important part of the human spirit has found its voice. It is as if an indwelling being had announced itself. Before the word "genius" came to be applied to anyone with conspicuous talent, it had reference to such a being: the tutelary god or attendant spirit presiding over one's destiny in life, a personification of the characteristic inclination of man, institution, or people. If the Roman people recognized their genius, so, with as good reason, may the university. Pagan and Christian have had this conception of a presiding and guiding inner being: guardian angel, *daimon, genius.* I am talking of the genius of the university.

When its influence is felt, the life of the mind is lived. This life is a kind of communion. It is intercourse, intellectual and, in its own way, spiritual. The communion may be with a mind recorded in a book, with the observations and the thoughts of Charles Darwin or Henry Adams. It may be the communion of the face to face, in classroom or laboratory. I have spoken of the mind's efforts, of the sense of importance, of the feeling that one or several together can make clearer what is confused or may push knowledge beyond the line of doubt and difficulty where now it stands. I add that in this effort, at its most intense and best, the self is lost. In this respect—I hope that the comparison will not seem strained—

the life of the mind is like love. One is forgetful of one's selfish interests; one merges with that toward which one strains: the understanding, the truth. But in the works of this particular genius, belonging to the inner life of the university, that toward which one moves is not singular but universal. I think it was Michael Polanyi who described the propositions of science as made "on behalf of everybody." The propositions of all scholarship and learning, scientific or humanistic, are made on behalf of everybody. They are offered for all to accept, if they will, or to take so that better propositions can be made, again on behalf of everybody. In the work we do with colleagues and students I feel this movement toward selfless communion. Teaching and talk may begin at that level where one is aware of Brown's tendency to overgeneralize, of Smith's argumentativeness, and of, perhaps, one's own disposition to talk too much. But if the discussion advances, these things are forgotten; student and professor, as selves, begin to disappear as the question clarifies and the search gets keener. All the minds that now participate are upon the question, the idea, the impact of fact on theory. The genius presides.

In trying to describe the manifestations of this presiding spirit of the true university, I talk about something that is not much talked about. It is not the aspect of the university that "makes the newspapers," or that to which its proud alumni or the parents of its students commonly refer. When the President invites a gift of money, he is more likely to mention the need for a building or to suggest the possibility of finding a cure for some disease through research than to say that his university should be helped to keep going, for the sake of all of us, an important kind of life, a habit of truth-seeking, a choice among values. Moreover, it might be thought unseemly for him to do so should it occur to him. A man does not talk easily and naturally about his own personal genius, and I suppose it is hard for those who speak for a university to speak of its inner and better nature. Maybe I am unseemly in trying to talk about it now.

I make the attempt because I think this genius is a good genius, and because I think that its presence is to be recognized and welcomed. Its appearances are to be encouraged and its influences gratefully received. I do not make any claim to special superiority in academic people. The university is only one among many institutions each of which strengthens some component of the good life. The judges do not talk much of how their work makes all of us more firm in maintaining the rule of law, justice, and equity; they are mostly busy hearing and deciding cases. But in hearing and deciding cases they exemplify and make stronger, in any who are by them influenced, the great principle of the rule of law. The doctors show us, more firmly and exactingly than do other people, the obligations to guard life and health. The Marines are tougher than most of us can be, and the extra fortitude they show in danger helps us all to show some of that quality. So too the craftsman strengthens the responsibilities of workmanship, and the artist the power and value of the creative imagination. Each who does well the kind of work that is his not only gets that work done but, in the doing of it well, makes firmer, for us all, that virtue which his kind of work demands. So it is with those whose business and happy fortune it is to carry on in a community the search for truth and the extension of learning. They make discoveries and they learn new things, and these achievements are good because they are useful. Also good is the activity itself by which the learning is reached and the truth approximated. It is good because this life of the mind, like making things well and like judging cases justly, is a right manifestation of human powers and delights. It is strengthened by its exercise. When theoretical research in the sciences is supported by argument, it is usually said that many unpredictable practical applications are likely to come from research that appears purely theoretical. This is a good reason for carrying it on, but there is another reason equally good. It is that theoretical inquiry, in scientific and in humanistic fields alike, is a good thing in itself, one of the important themes in the human symphony. It too calls out virtues: clarity, intellectual rigor, respect for the facts, humility before the advance of truth, freedom of thought, and boldness in the search for understanding. When I hear the suggestion that research in the physical sciences be checked or limited because we may destroy ourselves with its fruits, I am troubled, because I feel that such restraint upon the inquiring mind is the wrong way to protect us from ourselves. It is wrong because the search for further understanding, of all the universe and everything in it, is a desirable part of the human spirit. To prevent the mind from exercising this essential nature of mankind would be to deny the human genius.

In great universities the genius is encouraged. In others it is denied. How shall we tell the one from the other? We may look to those formal signs of distinction in science and scholarship: the listings in *American Men of Science*, the memberships in academies and societies, the prize awards. But these are only signs, and they do not always point accurately to that community of scholars in which the life of the mind is really carried on. For one thing, achievements by professors, as individuals, do not always prove the presence of those exchanges among professors and students wherein the genius rises to full power. Some universities are collections of men working alone. Others are such men guiding and stimulating one another. For another, the genius is at work, not only in specialized research and scholarship, but also in the teaching of young students, and there are few formal signs of success in undergraduate instruction.

One must experience the difference between the teaching where the genius presides and that where it does not. The movement toward selfless struggle to understand, the difficulty and delight of the effort shared, appear in one classroom and not in another, though what happens in both is recorded identically in the books of the registrar and in the salary checks of the teachers. Yet if one happens to enter the one, it is as though the air were charged with electrical excitement, while in the other there are only the hiss of the radiator and the low buzz of sleeping minds.

It is difficult for academic people to recognize, for their own lives and purposes, the work of their genius, and if it is improper and uncomfortable to talk about it if they do recognize it, how much harder it is for the rest of our American people to see what really that genius is and to comprehend what obscure and yet immense good may be going on in the true university when the genius is encouraged to prevail! I do not have to remind you that the two communities, academic and lay, do not always understand each other. University people are regarded by some people as futile or as dangerous. In recent times of unusual uncertainty and peril, the misunderstanding between academic people and other people has, in some places, taken on the aspect of a small cold war. We all know of the questioning of professors with regard to their political attachments or opinions, of jobs threatened or lost as a result of such challenges from outside the university, of legislative investigations of universities, and of attempts to reassure the general community as to the university by the requirement of that dubious symbol, the oath.

In these events it is not easy to separate the suspicions as to the loyalty of some one academic person from the more general distrust that some people entertain as to any community that sets itself up to think and to question. And this is just what a true university is set up to do. In carrying on its proper duty and function, the university arouses suspicion. The position of the professor is comparable with that of the soldier or the judge. A soldier may be criticized by other people for exposing others to risks so as to develop fortitude—risks that the civilian thinks unnecessarily great. Even our highest judicial officer is today criticized for doing his duty in developing our law within the unfolding principles of our Constitution. But it may be that the misunderstanding of the intellectual, especially of that man of the mind who is employed in one of the universities, is an even greater misunderstanding.

If the misunderstanding is real and serious, I should think that the first responsibility to do what can be done to remove it lies with the academic person. It is his business to clarify, to communicate. He is in a better position to see the differences in interest and viewpoint between the citizen outside the university and himself, because it is his habit and his task to

look objectively at things and to present their nature for the understanding
of everyone. People who study and who think should be able, if anyone
is, to understand, for one thing, that current fearfulness of people about
war and communism exaggerates whatever tendency they have to distrust
people whose job it is to think and question. The man who travels where
thieves are about is fearful of his honest companion. And the man of the
university can probably see more clearly than the troubled citizen outside
of it that the misunderstanding in part arises from the fact that town and
gown have different questions in mind. If the professor talks about Karl
Marx, his question may be: What did Marx mean? Or: What became of
Marx's views in the light of later events? If the professor studies the Fifth
Amendment, he may ask: What rights of the citizen did its framers seek
to protect? But the man outside of the university, who feels himself
threatened by war and by Russia, may be asking of the professor quite
different questions, such as: Is he teaching my child to follow the Marx-
ists? Or: Is he soft on communism? Moreover, there are unhappily those
fellow citizens whose real questions about what goes on in universities
are indeed ignoble. These men are really asking, privately, if I attack this
outspoken professor or that research associate who pleaded the Fifth
Amendment, will it get me a headline or a vote? But these men too may
be understood. Of course I would deny a false charge. But it is even
more important to make plain what the professor's job is to show that he
is put where he is to pursue truth by questioning and searching, for the
good of everybody. The best reply to charges and misunderstanding is to
be but what one can best be and to make it known that that is what one
is. For the university this is to live the life of the mind when it can be
lived and to show it forth, in word and deed, making known to others the
nature of its goodness.

As I state these bases for the misunderstanding of the university—mis-
apprehension of its intellectual functions; a certain lack of sympathy in
this country for the life of the mind; the confusion of examination of an
idea with its endorsement and propagation—they seem to me insufficient
to explain all the distrust directed toward the university. There are deeper
troubles. I should like to try to state one of these. The questioning and
considering which is so much of the business of the university leads to
the raising of a *kind* of question which other people do not easily raise.
Most people in most places, when they at all ask questions of general interest, ask questions as to how something can be done. How are schools
or roads to be financed? How is industrial production to be maintained
or increased? How is this threat of war to be averted? Our talk and our
newspaper comment are filled with "how-questions." It is natural and
necessary that "how-questions" be the kind of question usually asked.

They have to be answered if we are to live at all or to live with enough freedom to let us think of other matters. The practical and activist bent of American life has given them a special prominence in our country. An East Indian or a Latin-American is likely to think us too much concerned with these how-questions, even while he is eagerly learning from us the technical answers to many of them.

There are, however, questions other than how-questions. There are very many "what-questions." These are questions as to the nature of things. They ask, "What is this that I look upon?" The questions are asked because one wants to understand, whether or not one may do something that needs to be done with the knowledge. These questions are the ones mainly asked in science and scholarship. Other people ask them, too, but less systematically and persistingly. And now I come to those of the "what-questions" which are also "why-questions." These are the questions as to why any of the things we do, or might do, should be done at all. They are the questions as to final ends. They may be asked in small words, but they are very large questions indeed. They include the following: Who am I? Why am I here? What is the meaning of human existence? What is the nature of the good life? These questions are distinguishable from the how-questions in that the answers to those questions depend upon the answers one gives to the why-questions, so that, for example, the question as to how to increase production seems to stand aside and wait as soon as one asks why production should be increased at all, and pursues the reply given back to the point at which some choice of ultimate goods, some conception of the meaning of life, is stated. They differ also in that the why-questions are questions that are the same for all men. Not the answers—of these there are innumerable. But all men confront these same questions, and they have been asked for thousands of years. In the communities of primitive men, answers are given in the myths, the ceremonies, and the teachings of the young by the old. In civilized societies they have also been the central questions of reflective people, and the struggles with these questions are recorded in the books that we recognize as great.

I think that one of the sources of the certain uneasiness that is felt about the university arises from the fact that these why-questions are considered more often, and more characteristically, in universities than they are considered in factories, offices, and homes. Much of the thinking in universities, too, takes up how-questions; this I recognize. But I think it is also true that the why-questions get considerable attention. From time to time, ever and again, in classroom and in study, the marshaling of facts to bear on idea and of ideas to bring order in the facts, and the clash of mind with mind moves away from questions as to how to do things to questions as to why things should be done at all. The university is a philosophical kind of place in its central tendency, not in that many men there are professional philosophers, but in that it is philosophical to ask the largest and most fundamental questions.

I think it makes some people uneasy when the why-questions are asked. It makes especially uneasy those whose own habits of mind are with how-questions and those who feel insecure when that which they take for granted is held up for examination. The living of life requires that on the whole the ends of life be taken for granted, so we can get on with other things. To raise these questions is to lift the stones of the pavement on which we work. The university *is* subversive, not, of course, in the special sense of trying to overthrow our government, but in the simple sense that in fulfilling its special duty it turns the stones over to look on the other side. It is the human genius never to forget that the why-questions are the ultimate questions and to try, from time to time, to answer them. Here the genius of the university serves the very heart of our common human nature: our essential, questioning spirit.

I will say again how I think of the duty and the goodness of the university. Ours is not a society in which the underlying morality, to which all more or less adhere, is expected to be maintained equally, each man being as brave, as carefully just, as persistingly questioning and truth-seeking, as every other man. Courage, justice, and the freedom of the mind are common virtues, yes. But we have special occupations and special institutions in which these virtues get special attention, where certain of them are more highly in connection with some task necessary to our society—the armed forces, the law courts, the universities. The man outside of any of these activities and institutions will not understand, as he will not fully share, the standards of performance, the special dedication to the particular appropriate part of the common morality, of these various specialists and special institutions. It follows that as the judge and the soldier must expect occasionally to be criticized, so too must the man of the university. The criticism, in each case, will come about as a consequence of the doing of just that which the criticized is put there to do. I will put the matter in another way. If a university is never criticized for being just a little dangerous, it is no university.

We must all take these consequences or fail to do what we are here to do. It seems impossible to avoid reference, in this connection, to that hackneyed advice that Polonius gave. If the university is true to itself, it cannot be false, though it be called false by others. Falsity arises when the university pretends to be something other than it is. In an effort to please those who expect that a university be something other than it is, something to which they are probably more used, I have seen a prospectus, addressed to high school graduates and parents, that made a college course look like a four-year visit to Sun Valley or Coral Gables. The pleasantness of life at many a university is not its essential nature; it is, at most, a secondary feature. If too much goes to pleasantness, the genius of the university will be, I think, at least a little thwarted. A university that represents itself as just like other agreeable places to spend time either is no university or is deceitful. A true university cannot reflect the total society in its tastes and interests. It has made a somewhat different emphasis in choosing among the many goods open to man. On behalf of one university I heard it declared that its administrators were seeking to bring to it "well-rounded students." I am not sure I know when a student is well rounded, but if the word means that the student desired is to be like the average American, then I say that it is the nature of students, like other people in universities, on the whole, to become not well-rounded. If he is perfectly round when he comes into a university, he will not be so when he comes out. In his composite nature the academic person is just a little elliptical. The bent of growth pulls him in the direction of the life of the mind. This student may not be pulled that way at all, and that professor may long ago have resigned all attempt to live such a life, but the university of which I am proud is that one in which the glorious and helpful ellipticallity exists and is made known. The possibility of realizing its genius is open to every university as to every man. Before our failures I am humble; before our successes, such as they are, I am even more humble. For whatever sector of the good life is ours to maintain, the opportunity to do so is a gift granted, a blessed boon.

PART V

THE GOOD LIFE

DESIGNS FOR LIVING

This is the first time I ever delivered a convocation address, as, I assume, it is the first time you ever had a convocation address delivered at you. Therefore you and I should soon become friends, for little can stand between people who set out together on a new experience, especially when the outcome is uncertain. In half an hour this will be a situation that can never again cause us the apprehensions of novelty; we shall all be veterans, with one more milestone behind us.

I reflect for a moment on the fact that while a convocation address may have novelty for you and me, it has none for mankind in general. The giving of such addresses is a custom going back to remote antiquity. I suppose its roots lie in such practices as are still to be found among some of the primitive peoples upon occasions when the young men and women are initiated into the tribe or are passed from one age-grade to another. On these occasions it is customary for the old men of the tribe to address the young on solemn subjects. In many cases they reveal tribal lore to the initiates, in the form of sacred traditions or myths, and in some cases they exhibit to the young people sacred objects which have theretofore been kept hidden from them. In Australia, for example, the sacred object is a painted board, symbolizing and validating the relation of the novice to his supernatural ancestor. In some places the older generation solemnizes the situation for the younger in a more vigorous manner. If this occasion today were taking place as it takes place among certain peoples, I would have to come down among you and knock out your upper front teeth.

Tradition has, however, only imperfectly impressed itself upon this moment. I realize that it is only anticipated that I celebrate this rite of transition with words that will express some wisdom I have gained in the twenty years since I became an alumnus of this school and, supposedly, went out into the world. At once I am in difficulty; for although I was formally graduated, I never actually left school. It was in 1910 that I first entered a branch of the great educational institution of which this high school is also a part, and, with the exception of brief intervals, I have continued to attend the institution in one way or another ever since. I represent a case of school-attendance in its more chronic form. You may observe how the habit settles itself upon me. It is like pipe-

An address delivered June, 1935, at the University High School Convocation, Chicago.

smoking or hypochondria; after a while the subject comes to enjoy his addiction.

In truth my case is not so bad as that. I have had a special experience out of which I would speak to you. As one of those whose job it is to study the primitive peoples, I have from time to time left the campus to go and stay in Indian communities in Mexico or in Central America. From these extended visits and from studies that others have made of tribal and peasant peoples, I have learned something about that form of living which does not involve cities, or books, and which must have characterized all the people on earth at a time not so remote. The contrast between the primitive way of life and our own has been made very real to me by this alternation of residence and attention between the isolated village of Indians and the excitement and complexity of Chicago. On a recent Friday I was climbing the narrow, rocky streets of such a village on the mountainous shores of Lake Atitlan in Guatemala; and on the following Friday I was urging certain changes in the curriculum of the social sciences before a faculty committee at the University. The going was easier on the former occasion than on the latter.

My experience, both direct and indirect, with the tribal and peasant peoples leads me to look at our own way of living, that we call civilization, against a background of comparison with the ways of living of these many others. I would claim a somewhat special vantage point from which to consider contemporary Western man, as the artist is supposed to get a fresh view of the sunset by looking at it through his legs. The ways of life of the primitive peoples exhibit an extraordinary variety in their details of custom, but they tend to be alike in certain respects in which they differ from the way of life that is yours and mine. Considered in comparison with the primitive peoples, civilization would appear to be unique, a social oddity, as the white skin and light eyes of the northern European are a biological eccentricity in view of the overwhelming numerical predominance of darkly pigmented races.

The point I would emphasize about the primitive peoples is this: Their ways of life tend to be describable wholes in which the parts fit one into another. There is a congruency, a balance, a close interdependence of institution and belief. The ways of life constitute a system, with a character, a style, that is special to that people and that fits them and the environment where they live as a face comes to fit the personality that wears it. Such people live in relatively small groups, and, having little contact with other peoples and much contact with one another, ideas get shaken down, so to speak, into a pattern for life. The customs form an organization. The sowing or the hunting tends to be closely involved with prayer or with magic; the rituals express the wishes and the fears of the people; and the myths that are told dramatize these wishes and interpret the rituals.

The pattern is ready at hand for each baby that is born into the group. What the child is to do while he is a child, and what he is to do and think and strive for as he grows to maturity and advances to old age, are determined for him by this pattern. He does not have to reflect about it very much. Generally speaking, there is but one way at hand in which to act and to think, and the people about him are taking that way. And that way, I repeat, is not to be compared to a list of instructions, but to a costume, uniform for that group and adequate for the needs it faces, which the individual assumes, without the need to fashion it. Or, to change the figure, it is a plan of existence, defining the goals toward which the individual moves. It is a plan which none has planned; a scheme without a schemer. Into that unpremeditated plan fit the many acts of life. The plan says what is worth living for; and the acts of life, from birth to death, are consistent with the declaration implicit in the plan. Therefore the notions of right conduct seem to spring from the inner being of the individual, who feels them to be right without having to argue himself into that state of mind. The Maya Indians of the older generation in villages where I have stayed have a word, *taman*, which has within it all the connotations of right conduct. To define this word fully is to reveal the life-plan of their group. In this case, I will add, the plan is no longer intact, because missionaries from the United States have come into these villages and have greatly confused life for the natives.

I will borrow a phrase from Noel Coward, put it to a use very different from his, and call the life-plan of such an isolated group its "design for living." All along the margins of the modern world, wherever groups of people live by oral tradition off by themselves, are to be found designs for living. Even in these days when many of these designs are torn or even destroyed by the trader, the missionary, the school teacher, and the moving picture, there are enough of them left to keep many people like me busy studying them. Although these designs for living differ much one from another, in so far as the group remains isolated each is complete within itself, ready to provide the child with his chart for life.

This then is the respect in which I assert that the situation of modern Western man is different from that of other peoples of the world; he is not provided with a ready-made design for living. I find a design for living present, characteristically, at least, among the tribal and the peasant peoples. I believe it existed in the old civilizations of the East. It seems to me not quite so evident a feature of the life of the proletariat of the great cities of history, and it seems least characteristic of the people I see about me in this century and in this country. As an ethnologist set to describe the way of life of the people of Chicago, I would be baffled at the outset by the great heterogeneity of attitude and sentiment; and even if my task were limited to describing the mode of the people of Hyde Park, or of some class of people in Hyde Park, I am sure it would be a distortion of the fact should I attempt to describe it in terms of a design for living. There is no well worked out system of beliefs and practices, fitting one into another, into which each and every individual moves without much stress or effortful choice, as tends to be true in the case of the primitive peoples. In our case the pieces for a design for living never leave the cutting table; constantly they are being chopped up again and fitted into new combinations, which soon dissolve into others. We observe the difficulties of the immigrant who must make an adjustment to a new social environment. In a sense we are all of us in modern cities perpetual immigrants, forever moving into new environments, as rapid social changes take place. Side by side live people whose views on good conduct differ as much as do those of two widely separated primitive tribes—how differently is a vote or a policeman looked upon in this neighborhood as compared with the way in which it is looked upon in certain west side areas! It is true that we take over from our neighbors and our elders a great stock of notions: some of us are born to be Democrats, or Baptists, or bohemians. But we are always being jostled by people who are other things, and we are always being called upon to gaze inward and backward at ourselves and admit that we got that way by accident and that to hold such views is not based on reason, but on convention and habit. You may be a Babbitt, but somebody will make fun of you for it, just as someone will then come along and take a superior attitude toward your detractor for being so naïve as to expose Babbittry. Therefore no true design for living ever emerges, and life is a matter of catch-as-catch-can and every man for himself.

Under these conditions things are not left alone long enough to become sacred, or to remain so. As an elder of the tribe called upon at this initiation rite to produce the sacred objects that the tribe treasures, I am not at all sure what these sacred objects are. Among the many changes and influences that beset us we have come to consider everything objectively, to challenge and to examine, so that all halos are dimmed.

The very business of teaching and of learning what is deliberately taught, in which you and I are engaged, is an evidence that we have no clear design for living, because there is much difference of opinion as to what should be taught. The question of what is to be taught to your successors in the high schools of the country is today a matter of great controversy, some holding out for something that is called the Wisdom of

Our Fathers, which has probably ceased to be, while others argue for something called the New Collectivism, which has probably never been at all. Whatever may be said adversely of primitive life, at least it involves no professional educators and no deans.

This then is the observation I would make on the world in which you and I live: In contrast to the situation in which the native African, the primitive Indian, or the old-time Oriental found himself, to us is presented no well-defined design for living.

With this observation one can either come to a full stop, or one can raise that most dangerous of all questions, What of it? Due perhaps to the novelty of the situation in which I am, I find myself somewhat out of control and will raise the question and briefly answer it.

The question is in a fashion answered by those writers of our times who express the sense of littleness and loneliness, of insecurity and of longing in a cosmos that is perhaps chaos. All modern sensitive people know the mood which was Matthew Arnold's on Dover Beach. Many of us have felt ourselves alone as on that darkling plain where ignorant armies clash by night and have yearned for an ordered imperative to set all parts of existence into a pattern. There are people, if not ourselves, for whom living has design. Read Ruth Bunzel's account of the world of the Zuñi Indians, as it appears in the forty-seventh annual report of the Bureau of American Ethnology, and catch a glimpse into an ordered and harmonious cosmos, clear as blown glass and meaningful as a work of art. About our own world our introspective writers are apt to feel differently. Conrad Aiken has put it into his thousands of lines, and others have said it in less.

> This is the world: there is no more than this.
> The unseen and portentous prelude, shaking
> The trivial act from the terrific action,
> Speak: and the ghosts of change, past and to come,
> Throng the brief word. The maelstrom has us all.

It does seem to matter, if when you want a design, they give you a maelstrom.

I, for one, do not like the idea of designless living, and one reason I do not is that I do not like the people who live that way. There are plenty of them all about us; we see them in the streets and we hear them on the radio. One may meet them in the novels of Vina Delmar and in some of the wry, wise stories of Ring Lardner. Having no design for living, they get along without and live by mere habits and the shrewd current skills and zests that fill the stomach and the hours. Their imperatives arise out of nothing deeper than the widespread appetites of human nature and are defined by little more than the popular interests of the moment. They collect briefly in the eddies of fashion and fad, and of the ancient cultures in the deeps below them they know nothing. A sort of social plankton, they are interesting to observe and study. But they are also like purple cows; I would rather see than be one.

If, then, a design for living is wanted, where shall it be found? We cannot find it in a social pattern that age and isolation have woven for us to take and to wear, without questions, as can the Zuñi Indians. For there is no such pattern ready. Can we make one then? Can we rebuild this civilization in which we live and fashion a new system of moral imperatives to control us all? I do not know if we can; I do not believe we can; but I am sure that I for one would not if I could. I would not live in such a world as that in which live the Indian and the Melanesian. Too precious are our intellectual liberty, our freedom to question, to challenge, to experiment, and to study so as to control. Life among those simple people with whom I have stayed is often restful, but it is often dull. Few of us, in exchange for a ready-made design for living, would give up science and a free and bold intellectual life. Our world may be in flux, but we are free to think what we like about it and to study it. Our problems may be great, but we are free to invent solutions for them if we can. The intelligence that is ours has been built out of the accumulated experience of the literate generations; I would keep it and the chance to put it to good use, even though in the end it prove inadequate for the complexities of life; and I would not be tempted by the security of a ready-built mind.

We know something of what it would mean should we attempt to impose a uniform design for living upon a modern nation from some of the nationalistic experiments now in progress in Europe. At least one of them is a sort of reversion to tribal life, even to the myth as to common ancestry. The experiment involves the enforcement of a sort of artificial isolation with elimination of free discussion, and the advent of tyranny to the precious republic of the mind. When, today, in our own country, pressure is put upon us to restrain the freedom to study, to discuss and to deal with life around us in all its political and economic forms, we rightly resist that pressure, for on that freedom depends democracy and the integrity of our civilized intelligence.

No, society is not going to provide us again with a fixed design for living, and I would not want it to do so if it could. There is nothing that can or should provide each man of us with a design for living, but that man himself. You may build yourself such a design in terms of which to live your life, or you may go without. Nowadays life does not hand you a program; it throws you on to the middle of a stage where a great number of people are trying to write a great number of plays all at once. You have, however, a good intelligence and both a right and a duty to use it. If you want to look at the old scenarios, most of them are in the library, and there are plenty of people in schools and universities who will talk them over with you. It seems to me better to try to write one's own play —to know in terms of what unities of action and good conduct one will say one's brief lines—than to abandon oneself to the vagaries of those who live without design.

Even if I were wise I could not tell you in what shape your design should be cut. It is the essence of the situation that it has to be worked out for oneself. For my own part I like the old-fashioned virtues; they wear well. There is plenty of good material in what good men have written and lived. It is certainly easier to make the design if the task is shared with those who are most intimate with one. Fortunate is the family whose grown children are its alumni association.

You see now the outcome of inexperience. I started out expecting to deliver my first convocation address, and I find I have delivered my first sermon. Even as a sermon, the thing has not quite come off, for a preacher tells his hearers what they ought to do, while the best I have managed is to suggest that it is better to do something than to do nothing. I have no sureness that a man may make his own design for living. I only assert that life is worth making the attempt and that without making it, it is worth little.

THE WISDOM OF HUCKLEBERRY FINN

When Mr. Seyfert asked me to make this talk, he told me to aim half way between the parents and their children, thus assuring me a perfect miss. But on second thought it seems to me that Mr. Seyfert probably understood that it is not expected that a graduation address hit any target. From his much greater experience with these things he has learned that we have graduation addresses not because there are people who need to hear them but because there are people who need to give them. A graduation address is an arrow shot into the air by someone who has a frustrated desire to shoot. If the speaker finds that his arrow is after all no arrow but a song or a sermon and that it has lodged in some friendly heart, he has a better fortune than he should expect. That he has spoken his piece should be enough.

Graduation addresses are given, on the whole, by people who have im-

An address delivered June 16, 1950, at the University of Chicago Laboratory School Commencement, Chicago.

pulses to deliver sermons and no other approved opportunity to do so. You will have noticed that our graduation speakers are usually drawn from one or both of two classes of mankind: fathers and teachers. Now these are just the two kinds of people who have every temptation to deliver a sermon and no authorized pulpit from which to do so. Fathers and teachers are people who are constantly provoked into telling other people —younger and dependent people—what they ought to do. They feel like delivering sermons, but they find themselves awkwardly in places where sermons are inappropriate. A sermon belongs in church, not in school or at the breakfast table. So fathers and teachers are frustrated people. I am sure you have noticed an occasional father who pushes aside the morning cup of coffee to begin something in the homiletic manner. At that moment he feels the table is a pulpit and the napkin a surplice. But his audience just sees father getting a little tense. And that teacher or college professor who has the nervous habit of straightening his tie as he lectures: it is really his impulse to turn his collar around the other way.

It is because of these facts that we have addresses at graduation exercises. In the case of our own school the opportunity to relieve this pent-up impulse by means of such an address is particularly good, because so many of the fathers are also teachers. Of course if the speaker is in addition really the minister of a church, like Mr. Pennington, we may hear a graduation address unembittered by the gall of frustration, and then we have a very exceptional and fortunate circumstance. But more often the school audience hears a parental or pedagogical amateur sermon and, understanding wherefrom it springs, listens forgivingly.

My own text this morning is from the thirty-first chapter of *The Adventures of Huckleberry Finn.* Huck Finn is sitting on the raft, trying to think out what he should do now that he knows that Jim has been locked up by people who will return him to his owner in the North. As he ponders over what he has been doing—helping a slave to run away from his owner—his conscience hurts him worse and worse. "The more I studied about this," he says, "the more my conscience went to grinding me, and the more wicked and more low-down and ornery I got to feeling." It occurs to him that the capture of Jim is the plain hand of Providence showing Huck what a wicked thing he has been doing: "stealing a poor woman's nigger that hadn't never done me no harm." He tries to pray, but the words won't come, and he judges this is because he isn't really giving up this sin of stealing a slave. So then he sits down and writes a letter to Miss Watson telling her that her slave is at the Phelps place near Pikesville. At once Huck feels "good and washed clean of sin." He knows, he thinks he knows, that at last he has done what is right. He feels sure that now he can pray.

But he doesn't pray. It is harder to pray now than it was before. Thoughts come into his mind that dry up this flood of imitation virtue as he attempts to enjoy it. He thinks of the days and the nights that he and Jim have spent together; he thinks of Jim's gratitude to him and of the confidence that Jim has placed in him. As he thinks these thoughts his eyes fall on the letter he has written telling Miss Watson where she can find her slave. And instantly Huck knows he is making a decision, basic, profound, eternal. He studies a minute, "sort of" holding his breath and saying, "All right, then, I'll go to hell," tears up the letter. Thereafter he gives the problem of right conduct no more thought but proceeds joyously to steal Jim out of slavery.

When I think of this episode, of Huck alone on the raft trying to figure out what he ought to do, I have a feeling that Socrates must have been hovering somewhere near by. I can almost hear Socrates' little whistle of admiration. Socrates was wont to hear a voice murmuring in his ears; and this voice expressed the result of thinking that Socrates did and assured him that no matter what the opinion of the world, he, Socrates, knew what was right. Huck, too, turned inward to hear the voices that spoke to him from out the struggle of his arguments and the conflicts and impulses. Huck and Socrates alike examine the problems of the good.

But in the case of Huck there was that before which even Socrates might bow in admiration. For Huck followed the inner voice that told him where goodness lay while he thought he disobeyed it. What Huck mistook for conscience was merely the approval of a slave-holding society. What Huck thought was sin was the sense of justice and the virtue of loyalty to a friend arising from his heart against and in spite of the public opinion that would condemn him as a slave-runner and against the law that ordered him to return the slave. Socrates, wise and clear, could make the reasoning that he did as to his own duty to remain to drink the hemlock consistent with the *daimon* that spoke to him within his soul. Huck thought he did wrong while he knew he did right. That sentence sounds odd, but let it stand: it says what should be said. When Huck found himself saying, "All right then, I'll go to hell," the words sounded terrible only if imagined as spoken in the conventional context of the talk and the preaching of the slave-holding community where Huck had been raised. The overtones of these words, as they fell upon the inner ear of Huck's private and incontrovertible sense of decency, were joyous and confident. It was only after he had said them that Huck really felt free and clean and able to act. Huck's inner voice spoke to him when not even Huck knew it had spoken.

The wisdom of Huckleberry Finn lay not simply in the fact that he did what we think he ought to have done: he helped his friend to freedom.

We like Huck for that, of course. And we like him for doing right without righteousness: it never occurred to Huck to think well of himself, and this for the odd reason that he thought he had done wrong. Huck knew that problems of conduct are immensely difficult, and he wasn't one to set himself up to tell people the answers. He wrestled with the conflict between what everybody expected him to do in the name of duty and obedience to law on the one hand and his own private convictions on the other, and when the latter prevailed, justly and mysteriously, he did not stop to applaud himself. Like the girl in "Oklahoma," but in reverse, Huck had won his wrestling match, but he had an awful feeling that he'd lost.

The thing about Huck's conduct that most impresses me is that he wrestled. What seems to me significant, especially today, is that he examined a problem of conduct and made a decision as to what was right, for him. He confronted the commands of public opinion, of all the people with whom he had worked and played, and in the end resisted them because his own convictions as to loyalty and humanity were deeper and stronger. And this he did alone, in circumstances where no one watched him to praise or blame him, where he could as easily or more easily have done the other thing. The search for excellence within the soul: nothing, Huck knew, is more compelling. He examined the choice he had to make and knew it was an important choice because goodness and badness are important. He did not tell himself that it did not matter because all morality is relative or because life is futile anyhow. He did not dispose of the matter by simply doing what people around him would expect him to do. And he made his choice by looking at the thing he did in the end do and the thing that he might have done and considered them in terms of the good or the bad that he could see in them for himself, in the light of his own feelings about doing such things.

Huck did have the advantage of a chance to reflect alone on a raft in the Mississippi River. He might not have wrestled to such good purpose if he had had to do it in a room filled with people of his own age and experience and with the radio turned on. Huck was fortunate in a chance to think it over alone. It is not a common happiness today. And he was generally fortunate in that his days and nights were without that noise in the ears which today assails us from a multitude of billboards, loud speakers, headlines and twelve by eighteen non-reflecting, non-flicker, non-stop television screens. He did not even have to meet the daily obligations of an integrated curriculum or to give his mind to a pressing series of well constructed learning experiences. The search for excellence requires that we talk and listen in the company of others. It also requires that we think alone.

Of course it is not easy to think alone. The difficulties that come in the way of the search for excellence are various; what makes it hard in one generation of men may be different from what makes it hard in another. In Huck's time, and in earlier times, it was the authority of the past that made it hard. In these times it is the authority of the present. Then it was grandpa's stiff-necked rule and religion that was the obstacle. Now it is the unrelenting pressure of the current and popular. We exchange one tyranny for another. I remember when the principal problem of young people lay in three words: life with father. That was Huck's problem: do you remember old man Finn? Today the struggle with father goes on, of course, and to many it may seem to be still the only problem. But I compare the struggle as it went on in my world, in Huck's world, with the struggle in the world today. And I seem to see that although that battle is not yet won, it is at least progressing favorably. I even seem to detect a faint old-fashioned air coming over the teachings of Dr. Freud. The difficulties of the young are now not only with father and the rule of the past but with that new dictator, that capricious and often cynical ruler that goes by many names. In the large community of the young and the old together this ruler is known as public opinion, or sometimes simply as popularity or even as success. In the technical talk of the sociological trade it is called the peer group.

Life with the peer group has an air of freedom about it that life with father does not. So many similar people are having such good times together. So many people are playing the same recordings to one another in the same sort of living rooms. Nobody feels the iron hand beneath the velvet glove. Yet it is there. In some circles today it is practically impossible to openly admire the music of Tchaikovsky. In part this is because in the peer group everyone is so busy saying things about the music that everybody else is also saying about it that nobody can listen to the music. On a raft in the Mississippi if there were music one might listen to the music. Happy and wise those young people who, in silence and shadow, make their living room into a raft on the Mississippi and who listen, but listen, to the music that then turns out, perhaps, to be Mozart's music!

Life with the peer group in Hyde Park or Woodlawn is life under a ruler that rules for no clear purpose and to no good end. The rule is whimsical and unconstitutional. The old tyrant was unbending and often harsh; but at least he cared about goodness and stuck to his view of it. The new tyrant seems often not to care about excellence at all, and under his rule there is no private and persisting search for it. There is only a gathering of people echoing from one to another the words of the many and the tastes of the vulgar.

The pronouncements of this ruler seem not to issue from any throne. They are uttered as if they were not edicts, but as if they were self-evi-

dent propositions, and they come from everybody's mouth. In tone they
are casual, in effect they are disarming, in the end they are the real opium
of the people. They are received, and yet it is hardly noticed that they are
received. They take many forms, but whatever the form there is one message, one mandate: Abandon the search for excellence. One says, some
fault can be found with everything; therefore praise nothing. Another
says: I hear that in such-and-such a Pacific island the natives occasionally ate their children; one man's morals are as good as another's. A third
says: Life is short and the new fashion in wars will destroy most of us;
turn the radio up a little louder.

You too will go to Ludlow Fair and leave your necktie God knows
where. It will be great fun and I hope you don't miss it. That fellow from
Shropshire apparently did little else, and probably that is why he took a
narrow view of excellence. Ale is indeed the stuff to drink for fellows
whom it hurts to think, but that limits the search for excellence to the difference between the products of two breweries. If goodness is chiefly that
point of view of the world as it is not which is provided by the bottom of
a pewter pot, then one may manage to live for a time but only, shall we
say, in straitened circumstances. "Mithridates, he died old." But it is
not reported that he died happy. Whereas look at the fun Huck had! After
he had wrestled with Apollyon and emerged with a victory he didn't even
recognize, the fun he had stealing Jim out of slavery! Huck took a larger
view of excellence and had a larger and more interesting time. I must
admit that Huck took a pretty dim view of conscience. But this was because he thought conscience was something painful, like a toothache.
Perhaps it is not conscience that is wanted but simply the joy of the private search for excellence. If you can sit on a raft, and if Jim and other
good people are there to help you talk together and to think alone, then
maybe that joy speaks up from within, as if it were music, "like the sound
of a flute in the ears of a mystic." And then perhaps goodness comes, on
the raft in the living room, out of the darkness, and the outer music and
the inner music are one harmony. I hope so.

THE TRUE FUNCTION OF THE NURSE

Albert Schweitzer tells us that he decided to become a medical doctor
in Equatorial Africa so that he might work without having to talk. He felt
that he had talked enough as a theological teacher and preacher, and he
wanted to put his religion of love into practice. Apparently he is today

Reprinted by permission from the *Modern Hospital,* 83, No. 3 (September, 1954),
57–88. © The Modern Hospital Publishing Co., Inc., 1954.

content at his jungle station in Lambaréné, and I do not suppose he misses the audiences to which he used to preach. The organ is there on which he may express himself, and the rest is serving by doing.

Every profession offers the satisfaction of direct action. Each tells us that while talk is good, action is better. A profession is a permanent assignment to some sector of human need. To enter one of them is to commit yourself to a responsible position in some long series of troubles and crises. When the cry goes up, you will be there.

ACTS THROUGH LEARNING

In the case of the learned professions, the satisfactions of action are gained without loss of the intellectual interests. The law, the ministry, the various medical and healing professions brace and delight the mind with complex and specialized knowledge. The professional person acts through learning that the layman does not have. To act well he must understand why he acts, and the acquisition and development of this understanding is a good in itself. It is a good closely bound with the satisfactions of action. The mind and the hand join in a common discipline.

Furthermore, in the true professions, these satisfactions at once of the mind and of the hand are realized only in the course of a certain kind of personal relationship peculiarly compounded. This is the relation between the professional and the man or woman whom he helps. It is a relationship mixed of helper and helpless, knower and ignorant, trusted and trusting. The special knowledge could be terribly abused; therefore it must never be; and every true profession expresses and enforces in code of ethics or Hippocratic oath the important and exacting obligations of responsibility to client or patient. There are holders of special knowledge—those who know how to repair our television sets, for instance—whose relationship to those they help is unprofessionalized. The special knowledge is there, and the dependence is there, but not the same basis for trust that the knowledge will be used altruistically. A true professional is a trustee for some part of the accumulations of science and learning. He acts always in a fiduciary relationship to the ultimate beneficiary.

What I have just said about the professions is familiar enough. Perhaps I say something less familiar when I now assert that some professions are more humane than others. In the sense in which I use the word "humane," the ministry is a humane profession; indeed, it is a profession dependent on its own humanity as much as on its theology. But electrical engineering is not humane at all. We might begin to wonder if medicine is a humane profession.

It will be at once understood that I do not use the word "humane" in a sense as restricted as its use in the title of the "humane society": as referring to one exhibiting compassion toward children and animals. I mean here by "humane" to refer to all the feelings and inclinations proper to man. A humane relationship, in this sense, is a relationship between two people each of whom accords to the other all the feelings and inclinations proper to man. An inhumane relationship is one between a man and a thing, or, of course, also that between a thing and a thing. If a man treats another man only in part as a human being, and in some part as a thing, the relationship is in that latter part inhumane. In so far as the attention of the professional is upon a thing, or upon some fragment of the whole human being separated from the rest and so become a thing, the professional is not humane. In so far as the object on which the professional centrally acts is the human being, as a whole, the professional is humane. These professionals are so situated that they apply their special knowledge to man or woman while taking account of the feelings and inclinations proper to man or woman.

WHAT MAKES HUMANENESS

The circumstances that make for more or less humaneness in the professions lie partly in the knowledge and practice of the profession and partly in the social and personal conditions of professional work. A bridge-building engineer knows people have to ride over his bridge, but his mind is mostly on the bridge, not on the people. The beauty of his bridge comes out of his mechanical problem and his materials and he may achieve a successful bridge without thinking much about the whole nature of man. Architects I know differ greatly among themselves as to their humaneness. Some build houses as if to compel people to adjust to "machines for living." Others create houses so beautiful and so unlivable that it is as if they believed that people went through life solely in a condition of esthetic contemplation. And still others design their houses with attention to the whole man: a being who wants not only beauty but closet space, furniture that children can climb over, and an opportunity to be pretty messy once in a while.

If every architect lived in a neighborhood composed of families living in the houses he had designed, architecture would be a more humane profession than it is. The general practitioner of the law or of medicine in a small community has to assume responsibility for so many kinds of human interests and difficulties that he is necessarily a humane man. It is bigness, remoteness and specialization that dehumanize. The professional who gets only tax cases or thyroid glands has some difficulty in attending to all the feelings and inclinations proper to a human being. I worked once for a law firm which specialized in legal validation of special assessment proceedings. A special assessment is a kind of tax laid on the property adjoining a street to be improved by a paving or a sewer. I came to be something of an expert in the legal description of sewer manhole covers. It was not a humane occupation.

I am taking the liberty of making these remarks to nurses because the impulse to do so is rooted far back in poignant personal experiences in sickbeds and hospitals. There have been times when I have wished that the profession of medicine had given fuller development to its humane nature. Rolling down the hall toward the elevator that leads upward to the flat table and the tanks of ether and oxygen, I have sought in vain for a fully humane understanding of my situation. No one, I have thought, cares about me; they all care about my appendix. No doubt they will do a good job with my appendix; no appendix in the world will be better dealt with; but in the meantime what happens to me? At such moments I have felt myself less than human. I seemed to be only an adjunct to a clinical chart, a reservoir of bioptic samples.

A modern hospital is a wonderful thing, but it takes human beings apart in more than the obvious sense. It dissects the whole man into clinical specializations; it puts an organ in this department and a function in that laboratory. The human being at the center is dissolved, denied, ignored.

But not quite. Human beings have a wonderful toughness, and manage to stay together in difficult circumstances. If the doctor is the right kind of doctor, and the patient does not hesitate to lay claims on the whole interest of his physician, a good deal of humanity can take place between the enameled walls and within the tight, swift schedule of things to be done to things.

One does not, however, see much of doctors in hospitals—patients don't. That marginal being, the intern, is less rare; his face shown around the door on Tuesday may be remembered as almost familiar when seen again on Friday. But the male beings of this odd world around the patient are for the most part functionaries and not persons. They do not light long enough to become persons. And when their interest does appear, it is absorbingly with some special segment of the anatomy that each of us patients carries around with him apparently for the benefit of hospitals.

In this situation contact with the human race is chiefly maintained through that other and far more important person. She is, indeed, a person in a real sense. She looks at us, almost often, as if we had sentiments and inclinations worthy of mankind. With her our humanity is safe. She will listen to the remarks we make to raise our spirits; she may even laugh at our enfeebled witticisms. She will check the spiritual dissection which is the subtler part of the suffering of the sick.

This female person of the hospital stands between my failing humanity and the tendency of the medical profession to become inhumane. Sometimes I have felt that she and I entered into a sort of mute conspiracy to preserve the essential nature of man. If, seizing a moment when the clinical chart has been placed within my range of vision, I read something written there, she is not so shocked at this breach of taboo as she sometimes appears. Her professional learning struggles with her common humanity. I know, when I ask her a question about my condition, that she answers with that cheerful evasiveness which is her instructed duty, but I know that she knows that this is all pretty much humbug. She has not really forgotten that I am an adult and a rational being. She talks this childish nonsense to me because those beings who rule above her have it so. She does her duty in these matters, but she humanizes that duty. And she will find time to talk to me in the language that people talk, not the language of instructed functionaries. Her simple naturalness will do as much for me as scalpel or belladonna. Her words to me will recompose my nature, will make me again a person. I salute her.

TALK WITH A STRANGER

One day last month as I sat on an old bench near my house on the outskirts of Chicago, a stranger appeared and sat down beside me.

"Do you mind if I join you?" he asked. "There is some information I want very much to get. But perhaps I interrupt your thoughts?"

I told him that my thoughts were at the moment not much—I had been trying to think of an address I was to give to some college students.

He asked me what I would say to them.

"Give them good advice," I replied. "That is the usual thing to do."

"About what?" He seemed really interested.

"I don't quite know," was my answer, "but the usual thing is to tell them about the importance of the free mind and the privilege they enjoy in getting an education. And that sort of thing. You know—exhort them and commend them and encourage them."

"If you can advise them," said the stranger, "perhaps you can advise me."

I remembered that he had said he wanted information. My first thought had been that he would ask me about what kind of dog food I bought for my dog—you know, market research—or that perhaps he was making

Reproduced with permission from the Center for the Study of Democratic Institutions, the Fund for the Republic, Inc., published paper, 1958.

a political canvass of our neighborhood. But his first question showed me that these guesses were very wrong.

"I wish you would explain to me about this war that I hear is going on—the war that is now cold and might get hot. Are you people at war with each other?"

That didn't seem to me the way to put it. I started to explain. "The Russians want to conquer everybody, by propaganda if they can and by force if they have to. So they make monstrous weapons that threaten us and that force us to make monstrous weapons to threaten them. We have some bombs big enough to kill millions of people that we carry around in airplanes in case the Russians begin to drop bombs on us. For the Russians have bombs just as big, and now they are learning how to shoot them over to us with rockets or maybe pretty soon from spaceships circling overhead. So of course there is a kind of war—two sides all ready to shoot at each other."

He didn't say anything for a while. He seemed to be thinking. Then he said, "Tell me, do you yourself know anything about war?"

"Well, yes." I tried to sound modest. "I had some personal connection with a war in 1917 and I saw something of another one in the 1940's."

"And this cold war you speak of," he continued, "when it becomes hot, when the monster bombs are dropped, will it be like those old wars you knew?"

At once I understood that it would be quite different. But I found it hard to get out the words that would describe the new thing we were calling war. I thought of the sober estimates of scientific advisors to our President that if the bombs are set off, whether by design or by accident, about sixty million Americans would be killed, our greater cities would be reduced to ruin, and the survivors—in whatever appalling chaos they might find themselves—as well as their children and children's children would be poisoned and distorted to an extent impossible to predict. I thought of this and knew that the provincial little massacre I witnessed on the Aisne River in 1917 was something else again. I thought, but I could say little.

"No, it would be a new kind of experience," I said.

"Then," said the stranger, "it should have a different name. Not 'war.' 'Mutual suicide,' perhaps. Or maybe I should put it down that you people are getting ready for your own partial extermination. Is that it?"

I felt I was becoming confused. And a little annoyed with my visitor. I didn't like the way he kept saying "you people." What did he mean by "you people"? I asked him that in so many words.

"Oh," he said, "you people—you, and Khrushchev, and the young college people you are going to talk to, and John Foster Dulles, and the boys down at the corner in Brooklyn, and those fishermen drawing up their nets on the Malabar coast."

He did talk in a strange way. Where had he come from? I tried to get our conversation back into easier paths.

"Do *you* come from India?" I asked.

"No," he said, "no. I come from farther away than that."

He sat silent, and I tried to get a good look at him. But although he sat close to me on the bench, I could not see him well because the sun was setting just behind him. It was he who took up the conversation.

"I suppose you people want to go on living?"

I said that most of us did.

"Then," he said, "I suppose you people are doing what you can to prevent this thing that you call a war but would not be a war but a kind of suicide?"

"We are doing what we can," I replied. "In this country we are spending more money for missiles and maybe we can get the Europeans to put our missiles on their land nearer to the Russians and maybe we can build spaceships before the Russians do and so get the drop on them that way. We have been working pretty hard to make our weapons as big as or bigger than the Russians' weapons. You know we were the first to kill people with atomic bombs and we were the first to make bombs one thousand times bigger than the little ones that killed only about seventy-five thousand people apiece in Japan. We had to make the very big bombs because if we hadn't the Russians would have made them first and then we wouldn't have had security. Neither side wants to start a war when it is clear that the starter would be destroyed also. Of course it is true that the Russians made the very big bombs too and now they are going after space and the moon and we have to go after these things too. Two-thirds of the national budget for next year will be used for military purposes of one kind or another. So we *are* trying to prevent it from happening."

He made a gesture of interruption. "You go too fast," he said. "I can't quite follow. You say you Americans are doing these things for security? And you Russians are doing these things too?"

You Russians! He addressed *me* as "you Russians"! I took him up. "I can't speak for the Russians," I said. "We can't trust the Russians."

"Why not?" he asked. "Don't they want to live too? And can't you trust their common interest with you in continuing to live? It seems to me quite a basis for getting together on some arrangement not to shoot at each other. Two men with firebrands in a room of explosives share one very immediate common interest. But there is something else in what you just said that puzzles me. I think you told me that you went ahead with making more monstrous weapons in order to have security. Tell me, now that you have the thousand-times-bigger bombs, do you feel more secure?"

My impatience had subsided, and, besides, I saw that he had a point or two. I tried to answer his question honestly.

"No," I said, "I don't really feel more secure now than before we had the hydrogen bomb. For at least two reasons. The destruction that could be done now is very much greater—all civilization could be blown to bits. And also, so many countries are getting the weapons and their management is getting so difficult and complicated that the decisions whether or not to fire a missile or drop a bomb must be left to many different people—base commanders, airplane pilots, and so on—so that the chance that the first big explosion might occur through a misunderstanding or a rash act grows greater and greater. We might more and more easily have a catastrophe by a sort of inevitable accident. No, I don't feel more secure."

He was thoughtful. Then he spoke again. "I shouldn't express an opinion. But I can say I am confused. You seem to be telling me that you are working hard to prevent this mutual suicide by making bigger and bigger weapons to shoot at each other, and that the more you make, the more likely they will go off of themselves. It is like piling more and more explosives into this room with the two waving firebrands. It seems a strange way to seek security."

Again there was a silence. Then he asked me if I thought that the young college people would continue to choose the same way to security when they took over matters. I told him that I could not predict as to that.

"They might find some other way," he said. "They might call the thing that you are trying to prevent not war but mutual destruction. They might become less bellicose about that struggle that is now going on between some of you and others of you. They might talk less about how each wants to destroy the other and fears to be destroyed by the other and talk more with each other about your common interests—in keeping alive, in keeping down the cost of threatening each other. They might even move some of the explosives out of the room—what difference would that make to mutual security if each can destroy the other several times over with the explosives that are left? They might even stamp out the firebrands and walk away from the explosives.

"These young people don't *have* to do just what you have been doing," he continued. "They will do better. They are more experienced than you."

"*Less* experienced, I think you mean," said I.

"No, I mean more experienced. They start knowing not only what you know but also what you did—which is more than you knew when you started. So they are a more experienced people than you. And I suppose I am at liberty to believe that you people learn by experience? That you do things better as you go along?"

"Yes," said I. "That is progress. Progress is something we all believe in. Or maybe used to believe in. There seem to be doubts now about progress. Progress, it appears, is not going forward step by step, or leap by leap, to the better and better. It seems to me like going ahead and backward at one and the same time, by the same effort of movement. Or like—"

"Like what?" he asked.

"Like a strange dream in which one opens door after door down a corridor with a light at the end of it only to find that each door opened makes the light brighter and the darkness darker. There is more light all the time: the antibiotics and the good music that comes out of my loudspeaker and the old slums torn down. And there is also more darkness: people living longer to suffer from other diseases, and many wasted hours in front of the TV, and the new slums growing up around the overcrowded cities. Progress seems to me very untrustworthy. She can't just be believed in. She has somehow to be managed."

"You are becoming eloquent," he said. "If I may say so without offense, eloquence is like progress—bright and shining, but untrustworthy. Let us try again to understand the problem of how to go forward without going backward, to let new light shine undarkened. May I ask how you people are doing with space control?"

"Not much—yet," I said. "We have put some satellites into orbit and our President proposed that space be controlled internationally—an interplanetary police force, some day—"

He interrupted. "You misunderstand me. I referred not to interplanetary space—which by the way seems to me a very poor place to be—but to space right here on your own planet, where you people live. How are you people doing with respect to control of your own terrestrial space?"

I remembered a piece I had been reading by Paul H. Sears about how badly we had been doing, and I recalled some facts about occupation of terrestrial space. So I began at once to provide the stranger with information about the topic he had just raised.

"The population of our planet is increasing at a rate of about forty million a year. By 1987, when college students of today are putting their children through college, at the present rate of growth there will be about six and a half billion people. The world will then be more than twice as crowded as it is now. China will have a population of five billion people in a hundred years if the present rate of growth continues. Indeed, stranger, if your wish was to get to know us, you have come at a favorable time, for about twenty per cent of all the people who ever lived are alive now. But more important than this great number of us is the fact that the rate of increase overcomes much of the advantages we think we give ourselves by modern medicine and technology. The Egyptians are probably poorer than ever because there are so many more of them. Most of the increase that India has achieved by better technology and planning is no real increase at all because medicine and hygiene have caused the number of people who eat the food to increase as rapidly as the food has."

"You do indeed go forward backward toward a darkened light," said he. "However," he continued, "you don't look so badly off right around here—on this American patch of your terrestrial space."

"We are very proud, we Americans, of our standard of living. I will give you another statistic. It is estimated that with present technology this planet of ours could support, with the standard of living enjoyed by Americans, less than one-third of the people who are now on it. So some of us are doing pretty well. And we shall probably do better. Gunnar Myrdal says that on this earth the rich nations are getting richer. Of course he also says that the poor ones are getting poorer."

"That does not sound like a very desirable arrangement," went on the stranger. "It must cause some hard feelings. And I suppose you people who are Americans do pretty well by making and consuming things? Don't you ever use up any of the things you need for getting along better?"

I had still another statistic for him. "The people of my nation, with about seven per cent of the world's population, are now absorbing about sixty per cent of the world's minerals—mostly irreplaceable. We are indeed great consumers. We consume raw materials, use up water so it sometimes has to be rationed in cities, pollute air and rivers with waste products, and almost take pride in the piles of junked automobiles. It all goes to make the American standard of living the highest on earth. Now that I understand that it is the control of terrestrial space in which you are interested, I can say that we overrun it rather than control it."

He was silent and thoughtful. "What is that great wall of earth over there?" he suddenly asked. I followed the line of his gaze.

"That is a superhighway under construction. It will get more people around places faster."

"It certainly overruns space," he remarked. This time I did not say what was on my mind—that industry and highways take out of agricultural use about a million acres of American land yearly, and Sears's prediction that the agricultural surpluses that are now so troublesome will be only a memory twenty years from now. Instead I said that Chicago was growing very fast and needed better transportation.

"You are indeed an odd people," he said. "In your efforts to get security from war you make yourselves more and more insecure; in your efforts to get a good life, you rather mess up much of the life you are busy improving. This is indeed a darkened light."

The sun had set now and the twilight made that wall of earth loom larger against the amber sky. My mind, perhaps tired by the effort to explain how things are on this earth, relaxed into reminiscence, into dreamy consideration of times past. I said something like this to the stranger.

"Where that superhighway runs, there used to be a cornfield. In June the unfolding leaves made a neat, fresh carpet there—nine acres of it. In August one walked slowly between the rows of stalks, taller than one's head. When we went into the corn on very hot nights and stood still and listened, we used to tell ourselves that we heard the corn growing. And over there farther, there was a piece of aboriginal prairie that had never been broken by the plow. Only native plants grew there, prairie dock and tickseed, downy phlox and bluegrass. And up there where there are so many houses, the oaks stood very old and tall, and I used to find yellow adder's tongue growing beneath some of them.

"Do you know what I miss? I am thinking just now, although the season of the year is not appropriate, that I miss very much the sound of the whetstone on the scythe—a good, clean sound. Oh, and many other things I miss—the voice of the bobwhite, the flight of the red-headed woodpecker as he flashed along the dirt road to fling himself like a painted dart against a telephone pole. And I miss the fields filled with shooting stars. And the clang and rattle of the windmill when the vanes swung around in a shift of breeze, and the puddles of water at the well where the wasps came in summer.

"Excuse me," I said. "This must bore you. Older people tend to look back on things that are gone and were good to them. If now you were talking to a young person, he would not have on his mind these changes that are losses to me. It is a great and necessary thing about young people that they look forward with a confidence unshaken by such regrets. It is a good thing that some things are unremembered as the generations pass. Really you should be talking to the young people. Why don't you go to some college town and talk to young people?"

He told me that he might do just that. I could see that indeed he was growing tired of me. Neither of us spoke for a time and in the

growing dusk I thought I could see him looking through the pages of
a notebook.

"Young people," he said. "I do have some notes on the topic. I have
been looking into some of the authorities you have on young people,
at least young people who are Americans. The matter has been investigated by *The Nation,* David Riesman, William Whyte, Alan Har-
rington, and others. I have here a summary of the results of research
on this subject. Yes, here it is: 'American young people are uncom-
mitted and other-directed; they have no heroes and few illusions; they
seek security and togetherness; they want only to find places in the
slots of employment and safe advancement; after comfortable years in
college they become organization men and succumb slowly to creeping
contentment.'"

His words stirred me to a disagreement, even resentment, that I
could not at once express. Was this true of our young people? I wanted
to argue the matter with him but could not find the words. But my
resentment was growing. Somehow I felt that the view of us people
that he was developing was incomplete. He saw us, but in a queer,
unnatural light, a light from firebrands and neon signs. It was true,
and yet it was not true. Or not all the truth, and my resentment was
directed also at myself, for had I not been telling him things, true
things yet not all the truth, about us? Somehow I had responded to
him in such a way as to help him to form this true yet not quite true
view of us. I wanted to turn upon him, to make *him* say something,
make some observations that I could contradict. He had risen and I
saw he was about to leave me.

"Stranger," I said, "before you go won't you tell me what your impressions are, on the whole, thinking over what you know about us,
all of us here?"

When he did speak his words were only one more question. "How
do *you* know all these things you have been telling me, about war and
space control and the multiplication of people and so on?"

"I read things," I said, "and then we have many studies of these
matters. And commissions and reports and committees and conferences."

"I see," he said. "You have commissions and reports and conferences.
Tell me, did you ever have a conference on the good life?"

"On what?"

"On the good life. On what a good life would be for all you people.
Just in case you stamp out the firebrands and go on living with yourselves. A conference as to what would be a good life, for everybody,
given the limitations of earth and space and the nature, whatever it is,
of all of you."

"It seems a large subject. And not too definite. How would such a conference be organized?"

"I think I could make some suggestions," said the stranger. "I could propose a tentative agenda. The topics could be formulated for group discussion in the form of a list of questions. Like this:

ITEM ONE: Do you want more and more people existing together somehow or do you want not quite so many people living well?

ITEM TWO: What is growth?—is it getting bigger or getting better?

ITEM THREE: What is a good standard of living, more things to consume or better things to appreciate and discriminate? This third item on the agenda would require much subdivision and consideration of particular subtopics. You could appoint a subcommittee for each subtopic, you know. For example, Subtopic 37, Production and Consumption, Subsubtopic 49, division b, 3: Do you want to buy the car of tomorrow today only to find that tomorrow it is already the car of yesterday and you are expected to buy another? And so on. Oh, it could be quite an agenda.

ITEM FOUR: What is the right relation of man to the cosmos? Again, a subtopic: Which is the better use of the moon: to hit it with a rocket or just to look at it?

ITEM FIVE: Where are the frontiers of human enterprise? That item could be put in different ways, for example: should people build and pioneer always outward or sometimes inward?

He must have seen that I still looked puzzled. So he tried again. "Item Five could be put more concretely," he said. "Like this: To take risks, make adventures, create and add to human life, is it necessary to climb a mountain or build a spaceship, or could one also adventure and create within a limited world? Find new good things within the limits of earth-space, production, and consumption? Exercise restraints to free one's self for the making of new things for enjoyment, improved experience, wiser and finer judgments? Where is freedom? In always doing more and more or in doing fewer things to do them better? That, of course, amounts to asking if the very abundance of material goods may not result in a loss of freedom."

I was trying to take this in. "It would certainly be a difficult conference to organize," I said. "And it would make some people very uneasy. It seems to ask questions that are somehow, where I live, not quite the sort of question to ask. And so different from what is discussed at the conferences that I do go to! Those conferences are concerned with how to do things. Your conference would be concerned with why one should do them at all. And with what is good to do and why."

"Just so," he said. "And now I say goodbye. It has been nice knowing you people. You *are* odd, and, from what I have seen of you, pretty mixed up. But I wish you well. Goodbye."

He was gone, and I have not seen him since. But what he said is much in my mind. It troubles me a good deal. Somehow the conversation was unsatisfactory. I didn't like being asked so many questions. And such questions! As an anthropologist, I am used to being the one who asks the questions; I find out about other people. With this stranger I felt that somehow I had caught hold of the wrong end of the stick. And I felt that I had held up my end badly. I hadn't said things about us that he ought to know, if he really wanted to understand us. Ever since he went away my mind has been full of what is called "staircase wit"—those clever or right things you didn't say and wish you had as you go down the stairway jamming your hat on your head and getting angrier and angrier with yourself.

I had told him truly things that indeed show that mankind is confused. I could not deny that we are in a terrible predicament. It had to be admitted that we waste our substance and threaten ourselves with a perhaps ultimate destruction. It is so that at least locally, here in America, we are inclined to trust too much in technology to get us out of trouble, pretty complacent about ourselves, and unwilling to look the human tragedy in the face. So much of the worst about us he had got out of me with his unexpected questions. If you come to us, just like that, from somewhere outside of our human affairs, we do appear a mixed-up lot of people leading a totteringly precarious existence, and doing much that is both stupid and base. And yet that is not all that is true and important about us. What had I failed to say?

As I turned it over in my mind and struggled to understand my dissatisfaction with the interview, one clarifying thought came to me. So far as I could tell, the stranger had found out nothing about our past. He had asked about us now, what we were doing now, what we are like now. Can a stranger come really to understand a man by asking some questions about his present situation only? I might meet a man at a moment of crisis, when his affairs were confused and his very existence endangered; learning this about him I might conclude: This is a hopeless incompetent on his way to immediate destruction through his own folly. But, if I had the story of his life, if I saw how he had acted in other crises, if I came to know not only his present predicament but his character, I might change my judgment of him and his prospects; I might come to see that in spite of his current mistakes he had managed to deal with earlier difficulties and, perhaps, had shown that he did indeed learn by experience; that he had been growing, adding to his capacities, making some judgments more wisely than he had been able to at an earlier stage in his career. So, I thought, it was with this interviewing stranger: he showed no knowledge of the human career; he gave no indication that he had looked into the story of the collective human life from the days of the cave man to today. I just wished I had kept him with me long enough to take him to a performance of Thornton Wilder's play, *The Skin of Our Teeth.*

I began to say to myself some of the things I should have said to him. A phrase came into my mind, a phrase used by Albert Camus when he replied not long ago to some questions put to him by another French novelist. The phrase was, "the spirit matures." Yes, it does. Our human career is growing up. Though our follies continue and our dangers increase, it is also true that if not century by century then millenium by millenium we grow more and more worth saving. We learn to put some bad things behind us and we make new good things that we could not make before. Slavery and legal torture are no longer respectable. We learn to write books, and good books! The cave man could not give us the Platonic dialogues. Once there was no Bach, no Tolstoi, and no Einstein, and then, after the spirit had further matured, there were these men. That stranger, coming to us at one moment, could not know these things.

Yes, I went on saying to myself and as it were to him: On the whole we people are busy making a living, keeping house, and avoiding boredom. We might seem to be so many ants, living and dying one after another in an eternal, changeless anthill. But it is not so. Over and beyond the eating and the sleeping, the mere living and dying one after another, the spirit adds, invents, creates what is better than what was before. Other words spoken by Camus came to me and I imagined myself saying them to the stranger. It was plain that he had thought us a pretty poor lot. But I wished that I had spoken as Camus spoke; then I would have caused him, I thought, to pay "homage to the miserable, magnificent life we live."

How badly I had replied, or how I had not replied at all, to his remarks about the young people of America! He had been led to form a judgment that they are complacent seekers of a mean society. I thought of the replies I should have made. I should have doubted that this is the full truth about them. There are so many of them, and among the many are some, I might have said, who will take the risks of being truly themselves, who will speak and act for the common good though it be to their own injury. There have always been such, and there will be such again. I should also have said that the people of a generation change, become something different from what they were, as they grow older and as the terrible demands of the human predicament press upon them. The young people of today will be a different kind of people. Now we are all in a condition of shock from abrupt realization of the human predicament. But these young people of today will later have borne with the shock and will have found the strength to deal with the predicament.

And then I should have recognized my own limited, parochial mind in responding, with silent resentment, to his succinct report on American youth. American young people so described are not all of us. We people are composed of many kinds, and each kind has its virtues and its weaknesses. If Americans are complacent and shelter themselves with an unconsidered optimism, others of us are basely cynical, and still others of us are more resolute in confronting tragedy. If, in my own country, there is an aversion from or denial of suffering, some others of us have seen the necessary part of suffering in the maturing of the human spirit. Dostoevski wrote it, and it is heard in the great music of Beethoven. We are many, of many kinds, and though today each kind tends to think of itself and for itself, one may venture to recognize a growing tendency, as yet small, for the different strains of the common humanity to affect one another, and perhaps one day to develop a mankind whose best men and women speak not for just one kind of us, here in America, or somewhere else, but for all of us.

And then I had responded badly to the stranger's easy lumping of all mankind into one kind of thing. I had resented his calling me "you Russians." I should not have resented it; I should have thought about how I can and do speak also for Russians, and yet cannot and do not always speak for them. I am one with them because they and I are human, because we live and love and work and laugh and feel tender or unhappy as do all men. They and I share this earth and whatever annexes to it come about in outer space; and we share the responsibility of making it a decent place to live for us all. Further, Americans are like Russians in particular respects in which others—say the people of India or the South Sea Islanders—are not like Russians or Americans. We both like to make big things; both look for material results and probably make too much of technology; both have a class of managers to run most of their affairs. In these respects we join in a common effort to give the growth of mankind a bias, a bent toward one side that may not, in the very long judgment of human kind, prove to be a wise deflection.

On the other hand, we who are Americans are different from the

Russians in ways that place upon us special responsibilities, that give us, in these respects, the larger share of power and duty to extricate us all from the predicament. We mean this difference when we say that we are free, and they are not. We are a people all of whom have some power and responsibility to think and speak and act as to what ought to be changed, as to what measures to take, as to what new lines of effort to pursue to avoid the mutual suicide and to work upon the good life. The Russians today, the common, ordinary, on-the-street Russians, cannot stand up and say, "This we do is wrong. The right lies there." But we, in America, can. In this we *are* different; here I can speak only for a Russian who is silenced and perhaps waiting; but we in America have made a society in which differences and dissensions are the very stuff of public life. Every one of us can, if he will, speak, strive, persuade, decry, and insist. So, though we on this earth are, in the stranger's words, "we people," we are a diversity within our unity, and to each kind falls the responsibility to make strong, to put to work for all on earth the virtue and the power special to his own kind.

I thought I might have said these things and then I thought of the immediate peril to us all, the threat, the still-increasing threat, of an ultimate destruction. In answering his questions about that peril, I had told the truth; I could not, in the second thoughts, imagine myself denying that peril. I had to admit that the growth of the human spirit might, by destruction, come to an end. It could end in nuclear violence; it could end in abasement to a nihilism of values, a tyranny of doctrine, police power, or material things. What a fragile thing is human spirit! So threatened are we that a stranger might well conclude his investigations of us with a judgment that we are neither able to save ourselves nor worth saving.

And again I found my mind imagining that he had not spoken with me but with some stronger and wiser one of us. I thought once more of the words of Camus: "We suffocate and we survive; we think we will die of grief and life triumphs. . . . Anyway, we have no choice . . . wherever we are and to the best of our abilities we must do what has to be done so that everyone can live together once again." "The very fact that atomic warfare would make the future meaningless gives us back our freedom of action." These things he said. And he said, "We have nothing to lose—except everything. So let's go forward. . . . If we fail, it will be better to have taken our stand at the side of those who want to live rather than with those who destroy."

What words! As I remembered them, I wanted to recall the stranger so that he could hear them. Those words were spoken from the maturing human spirit. It will speak, like that, from this one or that, no matter how great the peril. We are indeed an odd people, but odd in ways that I fear the stranger did not fully understand. We are a thrust upward amid dangers and darknesses of our own making. We have no promise from the universe that we shall survive. We live for the growing of the human spirit, and in spite of all, we strive toward that growth, up to the last moment of possibility.

APPENDIX

WRITINGS OF ROBERT REDFIELD
RELEVANT TO THE SOCIAL USES OF SOCIAL
SCIENCE BUT NOT INCLUDED IN THE TEXT

PUBLISHED WRITINGS

1934 "Training in the Social Sciences under a Divisional Organization," *Association of American Universities, Journal of Proceedings and Addresses,* pp. 107–16.

1936 "What Is an Education?" (a pamphlet, now unavailable), Chicago Parents' Association of the University of Chicago Laboratory School.

1943 "The Japanese-Americans," in *American Society in Wartime,* Charles R. Walgreen Foundation Lectures, ed. W. F. Ogburn. University of Chicago Press.

"What We Do Know about Race," *Scientific Monthly,* LVIII, 193–201.

1944 "The Ethnological Problem," in *New Perspectives on Peace,* Charles R. Walgreen Foundation Lectures, ed. George B. de Huszar. University of Chicago Press.

"La raza y la naturaleza human y social," *Revista mexicana de sociologia,* VI, 163–71.

1945 "Social Science in the Atomic Age," *Journal of General Education,* I, 120–24.

1946 "Consequences of Atomic Energy," *Phi Delta Kappan,* XXVII, 221–24.

1947 "The Price of Peace," *Common Cause,* I, 1–2.

1949 "The Chinese in a World Community," *Common Cause,* II, 389–90.

"Ideological Differences and World Order," *Common Cause,* III, 158–61.

"Visit to China," *University of Chicago Magazine,* XLII, 9.

1951 "Joad's *Decadence*" (an extensive book review), *Measure,* II, 343–50.

"It's a Human Problem," *Journeys behind the News* (radio scripts), XIII (1950–51). Social Science Foundation of the University of Denver.

1952 "Internal Security in America," *World Frontiers,* I, 12–19.

"The Frontier of Underdeveloped Areas," in *Frontiers for Freedom,* ed. R. Gordon Hoxie. The University of Denver Press.

1953 "Escuchar a los pueblos del mundo," *La Torre,* I, No. 3. Translation of address given at Occidental College, October 24 (a slightly different version of "Does America Need a Hearing Aid?").

1958   "The Two-Edged Sword" (a commentary on the symposium, "Man's Progress Today," which was published in the London *Observer*, and in which Arnold Toynbee, C. P. Snow, and John Zachary Young participated), Chicago *Sun-Times*, December 7.

UNIVERSITY OF CHICAGO ROUND TABLE RADIO DISCUSSIONS IN WHICH ROBERT REDFIELD PARTICIPATED*

1943   "Minorities." Discussion No. 262 with Ralph McGill and Avery O. Craven.
"Is the Good Neighbor Policy Here To Stay?" Discussion No. 268 with Percy Bidwell and Eric Johnston.

1944   "Peace as a World Race Problem." Discussion No. 335 with Louis Adamic, Ernest Colwell, and Harley MacNair.
"The Crisis of Our Time." Discussion No. 353 with William Hocking, Robert Hutchins, and Reinhold Niebuhr.

1945   "Death and Resurrection in the Life of Nations." Discussion No. 367 with William Hocking, Charles Merriam, and Reinhold Niebuhr.
"Peace and the Atom Bomb." Discussion No. 399 with Reuben G. Gustavson and Robert Hutchins.
"The State of the Nation." Discussion No. 406 with Reinhold Niebuhr, William Hocking, and Thorfin Hogness.

1946   "The Little Man in a Big Society, What Can He Do?" Discussion No. 417 with Saul Alinsky and Louis Wirth.
"Mexico, the Next Six Years." Discussion No. 455 with Ramón Beteta and Alejandro Carillo.

1947   "Equality and Educational Opportunity." Discussion No. 486 with George Stoddard and Louis Wirth.
"UNESCO and Freedom of the Mind." Discussion No. 503 with Jaime Torres Bodet, Reuben G. Gustavson, and Julian S. Huxley.
"The Latin-American View of the Good Life." Discussion No. 504 with Daniel Cosio Villegas and Alfonso Reyes.
"Prospects for the Scientific Study of Human Relations." Discussion No. 510 with James B. Conant and George Stoddard.

1949   "Mankind in a Revolutionary Age." Discussion No. 606 with Prime Minister Jawaharlal Nehru.

1950   "What's Past Is Prologue." Discussion No. 615 with Richard P. McKeon and Louis Wirth.
"Pattern for Peace." Discussion No. 645 with Mordecai Johnson, Trygve Lie, and Clarence Pickett.

1951   "The Integrity of the University." Discussion No. 708 with James B. Conant, Lawrence A. Kimpton, and J. E. Wallace Sterling.

1952   "The Study of Man and the State of the World." Discussion No. 742 with Daryll Forde and Alfred Kroeber.
"Academic Freedom in America and Britain." Discussion No. 743 with S. G. Raybould, Bertrand Russell, George Shuster, and Alan Simpson; Robert McKenzie, moderator.

* Transcripts of the *University of Chicago Round Table Radio Program* were published as pamphlets, Nos. 1–896 (1938–55) by the University of Chicago.

"An Arab's View of Point IV." Discussions Nos. 749 and 750 with Ali Othman.

1953 "Propaganda and Psychological Warfare." Discussion No. 781, including "Listening to the World's Peoples" (a slightly different form of "Does America Need a Hearing Aid?").

RADIO DISCUSSION

1949 "The Mind of Primitive Man." *Invitation to Learning* with W. Lloyd Warner and Leon Duprée.

UNPUBLISHED PAPERS AND ADDRESSES

1941 "How Shall the City Attempt Philosophy?" Convocation address at the University of Chicago, August.

1942 "Race Is What We Make It."

1943 "Jews, Christians, and Professors." Talk given at the Conference of Christians and Jews, January 18.

"The Education of the Will." Convocation address at Elmhurst College, May 30.

1944 "Area Programs in Education and Research." Talk directed to anthropologists, April 27.

"Are All Men Created Equal?" A short piece asked for but turned down by the *Negro Digest.*

1945 "Should Research at Universities and Colleges Be Supported by Federal Funds?" Ten minutes devoted to the question of the support of the social sciences at the Sigma Xi Panel Discussion, December 6.

1948 "The Community of Scholars." Speech at the Annual University of Chicago Board of Trustees Dinner, May 12.

1950 An introduction to a talk by S. L. Washburn at the dinner for the Citizens' Board, Autumn.

1951 "Government by Just Not Telling." The frustrations of corresponding with the State Department on the matter of a Chinese professor in danger of deportation, May through July.

1952 "Remarks Made at the Retirement Tea for Miss Olga Adams." The University Laboratory Schools, June.

"The Commands of Reason." Address delivered at Occidental College, October 22. Partly published as "Internal Security in America."

"The Pressure To Conform." Convocation address at Occidental College, October 23.

1953 "The Defense of Academic Freedom." Address delivered at the Illinois Institute of Technology, May 23.